Ersatz in the Confederacy

SOUTHERN CLASSICS SERIES
John G. Sproat, General Editor

Ersatz

in the

Confederacy

Shortages and Substitutes on the Southern Homefront

by MARY ELIZABETH MASSEY

with a new introduction by Barbara L. Bellows

UNIVERSITY OF SOUTH CAROLINA PRESS
Published in cooperation with the Institute for Southern Studies
and the South Caroliniana Society of the
University of South Carolina

Published in Columbia, South Carolina, by the
University of South Carolina Press in cooperation with the
Institute for Southern Studies and the South Caroliniana Society
First edition 1952
First paperback edition 1993

Manufactured in the United States of America

00   99   6   5   4   3

Library of Congress Cataloging-in-Publication Data
Massey, Mary Elizabeth.
    Ersatz in the Confederacy : shortages and substitutes on the
southern homefront / by Mary Elizabeth Massey, with a new
introduction by Barbara L. Bellows.
        p.   cm.
    Originally published: Columbia : University of South Carolina
Press, 1952.
    Includes bibliographical references and index.
    ISBN 0–87249–877–8 (pbk.)
    1. Confederate States of America—Economic conditions.
    2. Substitute products.   I. Title.
HC105.65.M3   1993
338′.02—dc20
                                            92-23314

CONTENTS

GENERAL EDITOR'S PREFACE

The Southern Classics Series returns to general circulation books of importance dealing with the history and culture of the American South. Under the sponsorship of the Institute for Southern Studies and the South Caroliniana Society of the University of South Carolina, the series is advised by a board of distinguished scholars, whose members suggest titles and editors of individual volumes to the general editor and help to establish priorities in publication.

Chronological age alone does not determine a title's designation as a Southern Classic. The criteria include, as well, significance in contributing to a broad understanding of the region, timeliness in relation to events and moments of peculiar interest to the American South, usefulness in the classroom, and suitability for inclusion in personal and institutional collections on the region.

* * *

On one level, a factual description of the "make do" homefront economy of the wartime South, Mary Elizabeth Massey's *Ersatz in the Confederacy* suggests as well a plausible answer to the intriguing question of why the South lost the Civil War. Massey gave her book an awkward title; but, as Barbara Bellows observes in the introduction to this new edition, her research was prodigious, her reasoning meticulous, and her contribution to southern history significant and lasting.

Bellows also provides readers of this Southern Classic with a perceptive and poignant commentary on the difficulties "pioneer" women historians like Massey encountered in having their work—and themselves—taken seriously by their male colleagues in the profession.

John G. Sproat
General Editor, *Southern Classics Series*

INTRODUCTION

Rich in detail, thoroughly researched, and deeply empathetic, Mary Elizabeth Massey's *Ersatz in the Confederacy* tells the story of southern ingenuity during the Civil War. Her broad-ranging study of the homefront chronicles the trials of civilians struggling to overcome wartime shortages of such basic commodities as food, clothing, and medicines. She gives her readers a penetrating insight into the impact of "total war" upon individuals by vividly demonstrating the ways that this conflict touched every life in the South.

Massey makes it clear that the Civil War exacerbated, but did not cause, the economic weaknesses that pushed the South's leaders to choose between guns and butter. The region's historic antipathy toward commerce, resistance to industrialization, and addiction to cotton as a cash crop all forced overdependence upon external markets. Domestic production languished because of the southern tendency to import everything from the food they ate to the books they read. Stubborn agrarians had vaingloriously ignored for more than a decade the warnings of southern Cassandras, such as editor James D. B. DeBow and manufacturer William Gregg, who urged diversification and self-sufficiency. So when the war came, the last-minute flurry of factory building and establishment of retail stores ultimately proved futile in the face of the South's ravenous wartime demand for goods, the ever-advancing Federal forces, and ineffective methods of distribution. With civilian needs deemed secondary to those of the military, the Confederate government conscripted domestically made products for the use of its soldiers. The army also laid first claim to food crops that had been painstakingly produced with scarce seed, little fertilizer, and much-mended tools. The Federal blockade of Confederate ports grew more efficient with each passing year. Hoarding and speculation pushed the price of food beyond the ability of most southerners with their worthless dollars. "The Confederacy," as Massey explains, "was always hungry."[1]

The Confederate government's inability to relieve the gnawing deprivation of its citizens more surely led to its demise than did defeat on the battlefield. Massey contends that the southern cause was not lost at Gettysburg or in any other military engagement, but rather when dressed rats hung alone in Richmond butcher shops and the term *Confederate* came to mean something bogus and second-rate.

Southern civilization, as most had understood it, seemed to be slipping away despite the desperate efforts of women to preserve tradition in the face of the most primitive conditions: sawdust substituted for soap, decorated pigs' tails and ears adorned skimpy Confederate Christmas trees, and thin cows ate their bits of grain from mahogany bureau drawers. With no ropes or nails, the Confederacy quite literally fell apart. By the time Sherman made Georgia howl, the homefront had sunk from austerity and innovation to starvation and despondency. Massey argues that the unrelenting hardship and destruction inherent in warfare combined to vanquish the southern people. They surrendered before Lee did. By Appomattox, the Army of Northern Virginia had shriveled to a fraction of its strength of even six months earlier. Every day more soldiers left the battlefront to care for their families, victims of the war at home.

The South has yet to recover from the relentless poverty visited on the region by the Civil War, poverty that, Massey concludes, has been the conflict's most enduring legacy. Written during the flush years after World War II when historians identified prosperity as the most powerful force shaping America and its "people of plenty," her work underscores the distinctive experience of southerners. Only after learning a harsh lesson about economic dependency taught by wartime shortages, did they grudgingly accede to "Americanization." As they embraced the New South ethic of industrialization and diversification of agriculture, southerners swore they would never be hungry again.

Published by the University of South Carolina Press in 1952, *Ersatz in the Confederacy* broke away from the "battles and leaders" school that had dominated historical writing about the Civil War. Massey benefited from the pioneering work of Charles Ramsdell's *Behind the Lines in the Southern Confederacy*, Ella Lonn's *Salt as a Factor in the Confederacy*, and Bell I. Wiley's *The Plain People of the Confederacy*, but hers was the first work to focus exclusively on the effects of shortages upon the civilian population. A deep feeling of respect and compassion for wartime sufferers enriches her narrative; yet *Ersatz in the Confederacy* avoids romanticizing the starving. As in her subsequent book *Refugee Life in the Confederacy*, Massey clearly outlines the hellishness of war, a vision easily imagined in the aftermath of World War II.[2]

One sign that Massey was breaking new ground with her close description of home life and shortages during the Civil War was the excruciating difficulty she had coming up with an appropriate title.

She confessed to Robert Ochs, a historian and an editor at the University of South Carolina Press, that "The title is a worry." She suggested "Ersatz in Dixie: Shortages and Substitutes on the Confederate Homefront" to him, but guessed correctly that he would not approve. William D. Workman, a Columbia radio news editor at the time, responded to a plea from the USC Press and submitted an alternative, "The Confederate Homefront," that was judged misleading for such a specialized undertaking. The inability to define her work in brief threw Massey into such despair that she even contemplated "offering a prize for a good title." Sympathetic friends and colleagues rallied to help but only contrived "equally horrible" titles, such as "Homefront Ingenuity in the Confederacy."[3]

Reflecting her desire to use history to study the common experiences that linked the Civil War generation with her own, Massey settled on the title *Ersatz in the Confederacy*. *Ersatz*, hardly a household word in our contemporary culture of consumption, was probably *the* household word during the time Massey was writing her study. Finding substitutes for butter, sugar, and other scarce commodities had occupied the entire population during World War II, but few connected this anachronistic German word with the southern cause. One bookseller puzzled over the title of the volume and confessed: "That's one general I never heard of."[4]

Technically, Massey used the term *ersatz* incorrectly. By midpoint in the war, according to her research, more people were "doing without" than "making do" with alternatives. As one reviewer pointed out, *ersatz* was an "ersatz synomyn" for shortages.[5] Although southerners, desperate to retain their "elasticity of spirit," never tired of experimenting with okra seeds or parched corn and pretending what they had was coffee, even the most imaginative could not conjure up a substitute for salt (p. 72). As the war progressed, southerners got by on endurance rather than creativity.

If the reviews that appeared in a great variety of publications ranging from the *New York Times* to India's *Pharmacy News* generally panned Massey's title as "not a happy choice," they were almost as unanimous in their praise of the themes painstakingly developed in *Ersatz in the Confederacy*. Massey's fears that her first book might be tossed "on the griddle" by critics went unrealized.[6] According to an editor at the University of South Carolina Press, having *Confederacy* in the title clearly compensated for the unfortunate *Ersatz*. The book became the "best seller" on the Press's 1952 list within a month of its publication.[7]

Some claimed another reason for the book's popularity. The *New York Times* reviewer devoted 25 percent of his copy to the now-dated pictures in *Ersatz* of a "pretty Southern girl (name not given)" modeling "ersatz" clothing and displaying Jefferson Davis's carpet slippers and other homemade articles. He heartily approved of this "innovation in a historical publication" that might encourage the public to buy serious books. Even the discussion of *Ersatz in the Confederacy* in the *American Historical Review* applauded the inclusion of "glamorous great-granddaughters of the Lost Cause" as adding to the book's "attractiveness."[8]

Since Mary Elizabeth Massey devoted her entire life to her writing and teaching, she found her success particularly gratifying. Like so many of the second generation of university-trained southern historians that came of age during the Great Depression, Massey grew up in that "faraway country" described by Louis Rubin as remote from the American cultural mainstream. Theirs was the nation's poorest region, populated by Faulker's Snopeses and ridiculed by Henry L. Mencken. Sociologist Rupert Vance was born in Massey's hometown of Morrilton, Arkansas. Yale historian C. Vann Woodward also lived there briefly during his childhood and, like Massey, attended a small Methodist college. He left for Emory University after two years, while Massey stayed on to become a social leader at Hendrix College, president of the 1937 graduating class, and, eventually, the school's first Distinguished Alumna.[9] Like Woodward and Vance, she was possessed by the need to tell the unromanticized truth about the South and its people to those who knew it only through the lens of Walker Evans or the pages of *Gone with the Wind*.

After a couple of years of high school teaching, Massey applied to the citadel of southern history, the University of North Carolina in Chapel Hill. She found she was asking for entrance into one of the nation's most exclusive men's clubs. Admissions committees routinely passed over promising women, in favor of even the most mediocre male applicants, and never even considered women for fellowships. They were considered "poor investments," given the assumption that the majority would marry and, as they should, leave the profession. Some courtly professors feared the female constitution too frail for the rigors of Ph.D.-level work. Even those who persisted and prevailed found their opportunity for advanced research blunted. During those years before southern universities built their own repositories, historians acquired manuscripts privately and shared them only through an "old boy" network.[10]

When Massey started her graduate studies in 1939, she approached Fletcher M. Green, already noted for his work with students of southern history, and told him, "I've heard you don't welcome women." The newly appointed Kenan Professor courteously replied, "It's not that we don't welcome them. It's just that we don't do anything for them." "Knowing the odds" and still undeterred, she studied with Howard K. Beale and Hugh T. Lefler and then wrote her doctoral dissertation under Green's direction. By the end of his career, Green, superb teacher as well as scholar, had been mentor to over a hundred Ph.D. students. He alone among modern historians rivaled the famous Herbert Baxter Adams of Johns Hopkins for the number and quality of students he trained. Among the contributions by former students to the still useful *festschrift* honoring Green, *Writing Southern History*, published in 1965, Mary Elizabeth Massey's historiographical essay on the Confederate homefront was the only one submitted by a woman.[11]

When Massey revised her dissertation as *Ersatz in the Confederacy*, she dedicated the volume to Green, who apparently had been supportive during her final years at Chapel Hill. Ironically, the one major shortcoming of this book as well as of her later works, the lack of critical insight into her material, is likely related to the fact that she was such a faithful student of his.

Much of the excitement that made Chapel Hill home to the premier southern university during the 1930s came from innovative work by the Southern Regionalists such as W. T. Couch, Howard Odom, Rupert Vance, and Paul Green. The History Department, however, continued to train its students in the old tradition of "unanalytical narrative." Unlike Adams, Fletcher Green never developed a unique school of historical thought. Throughout the 1940s and 1950s particularly, he insisted upon "bread and butter" monographs from his students, ground-breaking topics with the emphasis on exhaustive collection of the "facts" rather than on their interpretation.[12] Even thirty years after Massey left Chapel Hill, when she definitely had come into her own as a historian, she valued "objectivity" over theory. She clearly states her position in the preface to her exhaustive study *Bonnet Brigades*; she saw her role exclusively as an illustrator of "how the Civil War affected American women." She denied any desire to "romanticize, idealize or debunk" or "to prove or disprove the theses of any school of history."[13]

Massey broke through some barriers against women in graduate school and made lifelong friends, including Bennett Wall with whom she would later work closely in the Southern Historical Association. Actually finding employment as a teaching scholar proved a different matter. Massey served as director of Hendrix College Training School for two years after receiving her M.A. in 1940 and financed her doctoral study by teaching at Flora Macdonald Junior College in North Carolina. With increasing numbers of men going into the armed forces, Massey did finally receive a fellowship at Chapel Hill; as she later recollected, it "took a world war to bring it about."[14] Like many new Ph.D.s, Massey began her career at small schools, first at Washington College in Chesterton, Maryland, then at Winthrop College in Rock Hill, South Carolina, where she went in 1950. There she stayed, while other students of Fletcher Green went on to major research institutions. Massey served as chair of the History Department from 1960 to 1964 and was faculty representative to the Winthrop Board of Trustees in 1972. She remained, however, as did most talented and productive women historians of the time, hopelessly relegated to the large classes of small women's colleges in southern backwaters. In contrast, the "big university boys" practiced their craft aided by teams of graduate students, light teaching loads, generous grants, and well-stocked research libraries.[15] Even after three well-received books, awards for excellence in teaching, and a Guggenheim Fellowship in 1963, no university invited Massey to join its faculty.

While revising her dissertation for the University of South Carolina Press, Massey taught six days a week every regular college term and consistently won awards for her dedication to students. Each afternoon, weary from teaching her heavily subscribed courses in southern history and world civilizations, she went home and wrote late into the night. Like her female friends at similar schools, she often used every "last ounce of energy to finish an article or do a little research." To carve out more time for scholarship, Massey made an anguished decision to curtail her popular talks to local community groups, a civic activity she greatly enjoyed. Massey spent the fleeting summer vacations on hot, crowded buses traveling to the Library of Congress and remote archives throughout the Deep South. It took her ten summers after the publication of *Ersatz in the Confederacy* to complete the exhaustive research for her next book, *Refugee Life in the Confederacy*.[16] From the time she received her doctorate in 1947 until 1956 when the Southern Fellowship Fund awarded her a modest grant, she financed all her research and travel from her small teaching salary. Still, she generously contributed articles on "home management" during the Civil War free of charge to a British journal "in the name of Confederate History."[17]

Massey began to focus more sharply on the role of women in the southern past, but she did not often enjoy their company in her professional life. History remained "a man's field." Even in 1970, when the Southern Historical Association listed five thousand members, only six percent were women. But the SHA had women officers decades before the other major professional groups, and in 1972 Massey became the association's third female president.[18] Four women served with her on the large Advisory Council to the National Civil War Centennial Commission; Massey alone had scholarly credentials. The New Orleans Civil War Round Table broke with tradition when they asked her to be their first woman speaker. Massey was the only woman (and only southerner) asked to write a volume in Allen Nevins's Impact of the Civil War series. Even at Winthrop, South Carolina's state women's college at the time, men predominated in the history department. In the mid-1950s, military historian T. Harry Williams of Louisiana State University wrote his good friend Massey asking if Winthrop would consider hiring another woman in her department. He was trying to place a female graduate student he feared was unemployable "because of her size, being a very small person."[19]

Throughout her career and until her untimely death in 1975, Massey struggled under the sobriquet "lady scholar." Even when she was elected to head the Southern Historical Association not long before she died, her male associates referred to her as their "beloved president" and more often treated her with courtly manners than with equal respect. Gender conventions belittled her professional contributions even after she died. Her obituary in the *Journal of Southern History* stated that Massey had held a "unique" place in the association and was known "for her ever present sense of humor and her sensitivity to and love of people even more than her scholarly production."[20]

Massey's acceptance in professional circles had come in part from her willingness to distance herself from the so-called Woman's Lib movement that challenged America's male-dominated institutions during the 1960s. Her comment in 1970 that she "left the battles to my male colleagues" suggests more than her interest in social history. The evening she gave her presidential address to the Southern Historical Association, her predecessor, John Hope Franklin, introduced her as a pioneer in uncovering the historical role of women even before the "recent praiseworthy uprising." He applauded how far she had come without becoming "part of the feminist revolt." During that convention, Massey expressed a desire to meet with the dissatisfied women in the association to "find out what they are unhappy about and try to correct it."[21]

But although Massey already knew full well the frustrations of young professional women, she believed her own advancement had derived solely from hard work and personal merit and thus she rejected the new models of affirmative action and gender politics. As acutely as young women of the 1970s may have felt discrimination, the difference between their situation and Massey's early career was great. In her twenty-five years as a professional historian, she had observed so much improvement in women's opportunities in all aspects of southern life that she firmly believed "we are making rather rapid progress."[22]

One should not misinterpret Massey. Even though publicly she declared herself unharmed by gender distinctions, she held strong feminist convictions. Her differences with the younger generation were ones of style more than substance. Her method of self-assertion comes through most clearly in private exchanges with a female graduate student she befriended while doing research in the South Caroliniana Library. The young woman confided her exasperation at the male-dominated History Department of the university. Despite her superior academic record, the director of her master's work did not encourage her to pursue the Ph.D. and failed to give an explanation. Massey's knowing reply was that since the men had no rational reasons for standing in her way, she must "smile sweetly and push them against the wall."[23]

All her professional life, Massey had been smiling and pushing. She urged young professors to strike close alliances with open-minded men of the Association rather than alienate them. Massey had worked her way up the professional hierarchy by serving on time-consuming committees and developing strategic friendships with powerful historians. Because of her close association with the professional "establishment" (she dedicated *Bonnet Brigades* to Allan Nevins and Bell I. Wiley), insurgent women looked elsewhere for leadership. Massey believed by 1971 that "women are more apt to support men for important positions" than to support those women who did not necessarily share their views. Only after elections, she claimed, would the disgruntled complain that "women were shut out."[24]

Massey's personal experiences echoed in her historical analysis of southern women. Unlike women of the Northeast who could be understood through studies of collective activity such as temperance or abolition, nineteenth-century southern feminists, Massey believed, were more frequently individuals who broke out of the social mold and assumed responsibility for their own fortunes.[25] A southern woman might follow "specific regional conventions," she contended, and still reject society's shackles on her mind and spirit. Massey based her presidential address to the Southern Historical Association on the diary of just such a woman. In "The Making of a Feminist," she described the evolution in consciousness of Ella Gertrude Clanton Thomas, who was ill-prepared to endure the trials of war and the later humiliation of poverty brought on by her husband's financial incompetence. From 1848 to 1889, this Georgia woman passed from pampered daughter to desperate wife to emerge as temperance advocate and suffragist. Massey used the diary to argue that women's changing roles had an impact on the internal politics of the Confederacy, a theme she introduced in *Ersatz in the Confederacy*. "The southern lady, reared in the tradition of the Old South," Massey averred, "came to question its teachings and eventually to play a part in overturning many of its time-honored concepts."[26]

Massey set out to prove that slaveholding women were not coopted by their class and therefore warranted serious scholarly consideration with northern women who passed through the more traditional rites of passage. The southern lady had been dismissed by pioneers in women's studies as "an anti-intellectual, frivolous, pedestal sitting, clinging vine who has little or no interest in the world beyond her own little sphere."[27] Massey spent much of her personal and professional life trying to put that stereotype to rest.

As hesitant as she may have been to embrace social revolution in her own time, she understood the Civil War as having a revolutionary impact upon women, in the North and South. In *Bonnet Brigades*, Massey hypothesizes that the war changed women's status not because it exploded old injustices, but because it forced women "to become more active, self-reliant and resourceful," which in turn resulted in their advancement.[28] The redefinition and expansion of women's roles may, in fact, have been one of the few areas in which the Civil War brought advancement to the South. In vivid contrast to the North where the war proved a catalyst for technical innovation and social change, the conflict sent the South reeling backwards. Women scanned their grandmothers' "receipt" books for meals using only locally grown ingredients and searched their own memories for stories of how their families survived the privations of the American Revolution. Housewives studied with slaves to learn ancient herbal remedies that were part of the African legacy. The empty shops of wartime threw southern households back into the eighteenth-century model of domestic production and in doing so reconnected southern women with the power they had once held over household production.

By her focus upon the household economy as an important component of Confederate success, Massey moves women to the center stage of the war at home. Their willingness to suffer and ability to improvise made the extended war possible. Even before the war, southern society had more or less expected wives and mothers to sacrifice and suffer as part of their "religion," as Massey sardonically put it. But it also became part of their politics. When the general's wife converted her wedding dress into battle flags or skillful women fashioned palmetto leaves into Liberty Caps, they voiced support for the Cause. "Secessia," the voice of ersatz fashion in the southern press, gave southern women who had so little opportunity for formal associations with one another a sense that they were not alone. Women's shared world of deprivation cut across class lines. Although Massey does not specifically mention the food riots in Richmond and Savannah in 1863, women of all classes protested the Confederate government's inequitable system of distribution. The ever-worsening shortages undermined their support for the Confederacy that they believed broke faith with them by first taking their husbands and then letting their families suffer.[29]

Today's readers of *Ersatz in the Confederacy* undoubtedly will be struck by the uniformity of the social landscape of the Confederate world as painted by Massey. Neither the complexities of race and class in the distribution of scarce resources nor the politics of hunger are fully considered. What this book does, however, is to outline the extraordinary story of how the South was able to defy all logic by surviving for four years when many doubted it could survive more than a few months. Not only does Massey understand Confederate defeat as resulting from internal causes, but she stresses as well the role of women as actors rather than merely victims in this great national drama.

Massey deserves recognition as a founder of southern women's history. Beginning with *Ersatz in the Confederacy*, continuing with

Refugee Life in the Confederacy, and concluding with her synthesis *Bonnet Brigades*, Massey provided models for serious study of southern women. As John Hope Franklin observed, Mary Elizabeth Massey, was indeed "a social historian long before the term was appropriated for the exclusive use of persons who were learning to use the adding machine."[30] Her deeply researched narratives are humanistic and tell powerful stories. She pressed beyond the glittering memoirs of the rich and famous such as Mary Boykin Chesnut and sought to understand the contributions of the hard-working individuals who quietly wrought a revolution in feminine consciousness and condition.

When Massey began her scholarly work, Francis Butler Simkin's *The Women of the Confederacy* (1936) stood virtually alone as a book-length general study of southern women during the Civil War. Even by 1970, Massey compared the nascent state of Women's Studies to that of Confederate Studies in the 1930s before Fletcher Green set his students doing the systematic investigations of individual states that made the grand syntheses by Charles Ramsdell, David Donald, and Charles Sellers possible. At that time Massey warned against letting political demands supercede scholarly care in developing Women's Studies. Shallow surveys and general studies hastily tacked together would ultimately undermine and devalue the whole enterprise.[31]

Preliminary surveys of women in the South written in the 1970s, such as Anne Firor Scott's *The Southern Lady: From Pedestal to Politics*, ignored Massey's writings. As women's history has matured, however, scholars are rediscovering the value of her research, although they do not always agree with her conclusions. One recent study that cites Massey is Elizabeth Fox-Genovese's monumental *Within the Planatation Household: Black and White Women of the Old South*. This is the first of the great syntheses Massey hoped for, and she would be pleased that her work continues to live in the work of southern historians.

Massey's early explorations into the social history of the Confederacy helped lay the foundation for the sophisticated discipline that southern history has become. It is fitting and timely that the University of South Carolina Press should reissue *Ersatz in the Confederacy* so that this true southern classic is once again available to those interested in the history of the South and the contributions of its women.

Barbara L. Bellows

NOTES

[1]Mary Elizabeth Massey, *Ersatz in the Confederacy* (Columbia: University of South Carolina Press, 1952), 56.

[2]Mary Elizabeth Massey, *Refugee Life in the Confederacy* (Baton Rouge: Louisiana State University Press, 1964).

[3]Columbia (S.C.) *State*, June 15, 1952; Mary Elizabeth Massey to Robert Ochs, May 10, 1952, Mary Elizabeth Massey Papers, Winthrop College Archives, Rock Hill, S.C.

[4]Bell I. Wiley, *American Historical Review*, 58 (1953): 718; "Biographical Sketch: Mary Elizabeth Massey [June 1952]," Massey Papers; Houston *Post*, November 19, 1971.

[5]John K. Bettersworth, *Mississippi Valley Historical Review*, 39 (1952): 767–68.

[6]Nash K. Burger, "Making Do in Dixie," *New York Times*, November 2, 1952; *Pharmacy News* (Ludhiana, India), 64 (December 1963/January 1964): 7; Columbia (S.C.) *State*, June 15, 1952; Massey to Ralph Newman, president of the Civil War Book Club, December 12, 1955, Massey Papers.

[7]Gomez Osbourne to Massey, February 6, 1953, November 17, 1952, Massey Papers.

[8]Nash K. Burger, "Making Do in Dixie"; Bell I. Wiley, *American Historical Review*, 718.

[9]John H. Roper, *C. Vann Woodward, Southerner* (Athens: University of Georgia Press, 1987), 6, 15, 19; Houston *Post*, November 19, 1971.

[10]A. Elizabeth Taylor to Barbara L. Bellows, March 30, 1992; Roper, *C. Vann Woodward*, 77.

[11]Columbia (S.C.) *State*, December 16, 1970; Mary Elizabeth Massey, "The Confederate States of America: The Home Front," in Arthur S. Link and Rembert W. Patrick, eds., *Writing Southern History: Essays in Historiography in Honor of Fletcher M. Green* (Baton Rouge: Louisiana State University Press, 1965).

[12]Roper, *C. Vann Woodward*, 86, 180.

[13]Mary Elizabeth Massey, *Bonnet Brigades* (New York: Alfred A. Knopf, 1966), x.

[14]Columbia (S.C.) *State*, December 16, 1970; A. Elizabeth Taylor to Barbara L. Bellows, March 30, 1992.

[15]Columbia (S.C.) *State*, December 16, 1970; *Journal of Southern History*, 41 (May 1975): 292; A. Elizabeth Taylor to Massey, May 6, 1963, Massey Papers.

[16]Houston *Post*, November 19, 1971; A. Elizabeth Taylor to Massey, May 6, 1963, Massey Papers; Rock Hill (S.C.) *Herald*, December 15, 1972.

[17]Grant Proposal for "Bonnet Brigades" [1962?], Massey Papers; Massey

to Patrick C. Courtney, editor of the *New Index*, February 6, 1956, Massey Papers.

[18]See Carol K. Bleser, ed., "The Three Women Presidents of the Southern Historical Association: Ella Lonn, Kathryn Abby Hanna, and Mary Elizabeth Massey," *Southern Studies*, 13 (Summer 1981): 102–21.

[19]T. Harry Williams to Massey, [1955?], Massey Papers.

[20]John Hope Franklin, "Remarks introducing Mary Elizabeth Massey as President of the Southern Historical Society November 16, 1972" [signed typescript], Massey Papers; *Journal of Southern History*, 41 (May 1975): 292–93.

[21]Columbia (S.C.) *State*, December 16, 1970; Franklin, "Remarks," Massey Papers; Houston *Post*, November 19, 1971.

[22]Massey to Nancy N. Barker, June 20, 1972, Massey Papers.

[23]The reason, the woman later learned, was that many men had applied to the Ph.D. program and they were accommodated first. Louise Pettus to Barbara L. Bellows, November 22, 1991, March 12, 1992.

[24]Houston *Post*, November 19, 1971.

[25]Rock Hill (S.C.) *Herald*, December 15, 1972.

[26]Mary Elizabeth Massey, "The Making of a Feminist," *Journal of Southern History*, 39 (February 1973): 22.

[27]Rock Hill (S.C.) *Herald*, December 15, 1972.

[28]Massey, *Bonnet Brigades*, x.

[29]Michael B. Chesson, *Richmond After the War, 1865–1890* (Richmond: Virginia State Library, 1981), 40–44.

[30]Franklin, "Remarks," Massey Papers.

[31]Massey, "Making of a Feminist," 3.

[32]Anne Firor Scott, *The Southern Lady: From Pedestal to Politics* (Chicago: University of Chicago Press, 1970) Frederick M. Heath, "Mary Elizabeth Massey," *Southern Studies* (Summer 1981): 117; Elizabeth Fox-Genovese, *Within the Plantation Household: Black and White Women of the Old South* (Chapel Hill: University of North Carolina Press, 1989).

PREFACE TO THE FIRST EDITION

In the eighty-odd years since the Civil War many scholarly volumes have been compiled about the political and military aspects of the conflict, but comparatively little has been written about the noncombatants of the Confederacy. Various features of the Confederate homefront have, however, been studied and portrayed in recent years by scholars, notable among whom are Ella Lonn, Bell Irwin Wiley, and the late Charles M. Ramsdell, but much remains to be done if students and the general reading public are to have an understanding of what happened in the South.

It is my purpose here to undertake the study of only one problem of the Confederate homefront, that of shortages. This was an almost universal problem for those people who stayed behind the lines. Necessities as well as luxuries became scarce, and it was imperative that the southern people either do without many commodities or find substitutes for them. The constant, unrelenting search for the latter called forth a great deal of ingenuity. In attempting to portray this problem of shortages accurately I have tried to see the over-all picture; however, to catalog every scarce item and every makeshift and expedient devised by our ingenious ancestors would be an impossible task. Most of those who lived through the war years left no diaries or letters to serve as source materials for the scholar. This makes it difficult to present an accurate interpretation of life among the rank and file of the people. Although I have made use of vast amounts of published and unpublished material, I realize that many sources have not been used. I found, however, in the last years of this research that most of the material that I had neglected earlier was repetitious.

No attempt has been made in this study to deal with the military scene, other than occasional references needed to clarify and explain conditions on the homefront. Only the war years are covered, although there is in the last chapter an allusion to the days immediately following Appomattox. This is moreover a study of commodity, not manpower, shortages. Although the latter affected the quantity of goods in the Confederacy, the general subject of manpower is too extensive in its own right to receive more than indirect mention here, and no effort has been made to go into detail on the subject.

This book could never have become a reality without the assistance, encouragement, and criticism given by many friends and librarians. I wish it were possible to acknowledge all of those to whom I am so indebted, for I am deeply grateful. I would like to mention individually those who gave many hours of their time unselfishly. I owe my greatest debt of gratitude to those who assisted me during the early days of research and writing at the University of North Carolina, especially Fletcher M. Green, who gave me the benefit of his scholarship and who made suggestions which have improved and strengthened the study; Hugh T. Lefler, who read the manuscript and offered excellent suggestions; and Miss Georgia Faison, who not only rendered innumerable services in keeping with her position as reference librarian but who also had the patience and humor necessary to live with me peaceably during my days of research and writing. My colleagues at Winthrop have also given me assistance and shown amazing forbearance. Miss Dorothy Jones has helped with the proofreading, and Miss Katharine Jones has aided me in many ways, at the same time giving me necessary moral support. The history department has given me encouragement and has "listened" patiently as this study has been converted from manuscript to book.

Although not naming them individually, I want to express my appreciation to the capable staff members of the Library of Congress, the University of North Carolina Library, the University of South Caroliniana Library, the Winthrop College Library, and the Confederate Museum, all of whom rendered me special services. Louise Jones DuBose, Robert D. Ochs, and Osborne Gomez have seen this book through press and have given unstintingly of their time in so-doing. I am most appreciative of all they have done. Special appreciation is due Dorsey Jones, editor of *The Arkansas Historical Quarterly,* and D. L. Corbitt, managing editor of *The North Carolina Historical Review.* Finally, to Corinne Laney Flood Massey I wish to express my great debt of gratitude for the encouragement she gave me from the beginning of my research, and also for her suggestions regarding style and terminology. To those who have not been mentioned, I am also deeply grateful for making this book possible.

M. E. M.

Rock Hill, South Carolina

July, 1952

Ersatz in the Confederacy

I

THE PROBLEM OF SUPPLIES

NEWS FROM CHARLESTON SPREAD OVER THE CONFEDERATE STATES of America like wildfire in that eventful April, 1861. War had come! As the people heard it they displayed mixed emotions. All hopes of peaceful secession had faded. After the first stunned reaction to the news, most people assured themselves, as well as all near them, that the South would march straight to a rapid and decisive victory. After all, did not the Confederacy have that fighting spirit that develops only when a cause is right and just? Did not the Confederacy have the noblest men, the greatest soldiers of all time? Did not the Confederacy have a monopoly on the most desired product of the world, cotton? And did not this possession assure immediate recognition of the new nation by such powers as England and France? Did not the suave, dashing General Pierre Gustave Toutant Beauregard have all the qualities needed to lead his forces to an immediate and complete victory? Did not the Confederacy have boundless resources at its command? The citizens of the young nation were assured that all of these questions might be answered in the affirmative. As a result, an attitude of braggadocio developed to the point of being detrimental to the war effort. So entrenched did patriotic phrases and empty sentences become in the minds of the people in those first weeks of the war, that it took nearly two years to convince the majority otherwise. War proved to be more than parades, gilt buttons, and martial music. With all its assets, the Confederacy had liabilities, and these proved to be serious.

Among the liabilities of the Confederate States of America was their dependence on outside sources of supply for many of the essentials of life. These outside sources had been, in previous years, the North and Europe, particularly England. A lady, writing twenty years after cessation of hostilities, remembered that

3

the great fault of the Confederacy lay in its dependence on outside supply "for everything from a hair-pin to a tooth-pick, and from a cradle to a coffin."[1] Whereas the South possessed the necessary resources needed to manufacture these and other articles, it had been so busy growing cotton that most other commodities were conveniently imported.

Little had been done to make the South self-sufficient, although the region was not totally lacking in manufacturing. There were several sizable factories in the South in 1861, but they were incapable of supplying all the demands of twelve million people. Suddenly to start mass development of the resources, and at the same time to fight a war, would have been a Herculean task, impossible under the conditions. Although there had been arch-exponents of greater industrialization and self-sufficiency, they were unable to make enough progress to produce an independent South. Despite the sharp criticism of James Dunwoody Brownson DeBow, William Gregg, Daniel Pratt, and other propagandists of industry, the influence of agricultural and commercial conventions, and the constant agitation of many farsighted editors and writers, the South had not become a self-sufficient region by 1861. The repercussions from such conditions were to be felt in the war effort and the battle for the independence of the Confederacy.

Following the secession of South Carolina, the journals and newspapers in the South reviewed the economic situation for the readers. However, true to form, there was a variety of opinion expressed by the editors as to the real economic condition of the Confederacy. These editors also differed as to the urgency of the situation and the role that patriotic southerners should play. Every hue of opinion was available, and the reader could choose the one he preferred to accept. One of the early editorial warnings came in January, 1861, when the *Southern Planter,* emulating *DeBow's Review,* published an article which stressed the peril of inadequate industrialization and urged the establishment of additional industries.[2] This was followed in the summer of 1861 by the *Southern Cultivator,* which launched a series of articles entitled "Things Worthy of Attention." In these articles the Confederacy was urged to renovate its economy according to the needs of the time. Warning that there was no time for delay, this popular and widely read agricultural journal listed some of the articles of everyday use that heretofore had been imported and were no longer available. These included hay, meat, horses, butter, cheese, clothing, shoes, beverages, paper, candles, oil, kerosene, glass, rope, cordage, soap, and starch. The journal did not content itself with the mere naming of these items; it offered suggestions to remedy the situation, at the same time adding the warning that the southern people must learn to think and act for themselves. They must not be satisfied with following, but they must learn to lead. They must not continue "to imitate but originate."[3]

Some newspapers, too, joined in the campaign to build the South into a commercially independent nation. Editors variously discussed and interpreted the problem. An occasional article, during the first year of the war, not only pointed to the problem but offered a solution. For example, one paper carried a series of articles drawing the attention of the people to certain changes by which they might develop their resources and thus supply their wants. These articles included instructions for the making of such scarce items as cloth, soap, starch, and substitutes for tea and coffee.[4] Most newspaper stories written in 1861 failed to show such an understanding of the problem, however. They were too often mere hollow statements designed to bolster the courage of the southern people rather than provoke action. Thousands of words were printed about the ability of the South to overcome this dependency on outside help. An example of such wishful thinking appeared in the Charleston *Mercury* two months after the war started. The editor wrote for public consumption, "It is perfectly surprising how well we get along without Yankee notions. It is surprising how little we really needed, or should have bought their jim-crackeries. . . . We can supply every want as well as every need at home."[5] Such comments as this encouraged the public to assume a complacent attitude. When a Florida editor wrote that the South could fight a twenty year war without outside help, he contributed to the development of smug satisfaction among his readers.[6] When a Richmond editor told his readers that the shortages that were apparent early in the war were only temporary, he gave them hope instead of determination.[7] All such statements proved to be erroneous as the war continued.

At the same time that greater industrialization was being encouraged in the South, diversified agriculture was likewise stimulated. During the first spring and summer of the war the people were urged to plant more food crops and less cotton. A New Orleans paper led in the general movement in May, 1861, by telling the people that "Every foot of vacant land in Louisiana should be enclosed and planted by either individuals or neighborhoods." At the same time it warned that "southern farmers could not make too much corn and fodder if the war continues, and . . . supplies are cut off from the West."[8] While a few observers noted that such pleadings were heeded to some extent in the early months of the war and that some agricultural changes were taking place,[9] the response was generally slow. It was only in the spring of 1862 and later that the South began to forsake "King Cotton" on a large scale and turn to food crops. There were those, however, who year after year refused to give up the extensive cultivation of the white fiber, even though it meant defiance of state law. At the same time that the movement for diversified agriculture was getting under way in the Confederacy, a suggestion was made that, had it been accepted and carried through, might have regimented agricultural resources to a greater degree than was done. Some proposed that a Bureau of Agriculture be established, that it have cabinet rank and be "supplied with the requisite means to encourage agriculture in every legitimate and usual form."[10] But this worthwhile suggestion was never carried out.

One of the first moves of President Abraham Lincoln was to impose a blockade on the Confederacy, for he realized that the South must import to survive. This blockade, coupled with the dependence on outside aid, would seem sufficient to jolt even the most lethargic out of the spirit of complacency. The English traveler William Howard Russell warned that the "blockade would be severely felt. . . . Under any circumstances, the patriotic ladies and gentlemen, who are so anxious for the war, must make up their minds to suffer a little in the flesh."[11] But during those first months of the conflict, when everything was tinged with the white heat of patriotism and the rosy glow of optimism, it seemed impossible to most Southerners that three thousand miles of coastline could ever be effectively blockaded.[12] By 1862, however, the people were beginning to realize that not only could it be done, but it was being done more thoroughly with each passing month. The blockade played a major role in creating the shortages in the Confederacy.

During the first summer of the war the idea was prevalent among the citizens of the Confederacy that it would win, and the fighting would be of short duration. It was also believed that immediate recognition from foreign powers would be forthcoming. Confident of these things, the people as a whole displayed a chauvinistic attitude. They wrote and spoke with an unselfish pride. They were willing to give anything for those brave lads who defended their country's colors. The war was new to the people in the summer of '61, and no serious inconvenience yet faced them. Betty Herndon Maury, daughter of Matthew Fontaine Maury, showed this enthusiasm when she wrote in her diary that she had no new dress that summer, but she was "almost as happy as in . . . [her] best days."[13] Such minor inconveniences as appeared in the early months were thought amusing. To live at such a time was a lark. Few dared to predict as did the rebel war-clerk, John Beauchamp Jones, even in the first days of war, that troubles were ahead, and that economy should be made the rule in southern households. He warned that the gay uniforms worn by the gallant young men in the early months "would change their hue before the advent of another year."[14]

The illusion could not continue forever, however, and after the first summer, people began to see that the war was affecting their daily lives. From an economy of plenty, they were being confronted by an economy of scarcity. A few began to take the view that maybe the privations were "all for the best." Perhaps the purpose was to teach the extravagant the lessons they needed to learn.[15] There were also those staunch souls who approached the problem with the attitude of making the best out of the situation. They did not have that carefree attitude exhibited by so many in the early days. Rather, they remained serious but pleasant as they went about the business of devising substitutes for the shortages that suddenly appeared.[16] Economy became the watchword in those households that never before had known its meaning.[17] Even the press began to pull together as the problem of shortages presented itself; and editors urged economy in all things. During the fall of 1861, real concern was evident about the shortages at home as well as those in the army circles,[18] and with each passing month the problem became more acute. There was no respite from it during the war.

If economy was the watchword, ingenuity became the password to mere existence in many households. The southern people surprised even themselves with their resourcefulness. With only a few exceptions they devised substitutes and makeshifts for those everyday items that became more and more scarce with each passing month. One woman, when asked how the people found substitutes so quickly, replied that memories were put to work to recall the stories told them, in an earlier year, of the American Revolution. She said that many substitutes used in the Civil War were those tried in the 1770's.[19] Be that as it may, one fact is certain, ingenuity was "taxed to the utmost" in Confederate households.[20] It has been estimated that the southern women had to "manufacture or devise a substitute for three-fourths of the articles in common use."[21] One witness of the period of scarcity wrote in later years:

> If that era of home life had to be characterized by one word, there could be no choice as to the term 'substitute.' . . . There was hardly a tree or a plant that did not in the long run furnish a substitute; being laid under tribute to feed or clothe the people, or to cure their ailments. Of these substitutes, some were in the beginning the rage, but each in the end [became] a necessity. The absorption of the southern mind in the war issue, coupled with its inherent non-inventiveness, or more accurately, its non completiveness can alone account for the paucity of permanently useful inventions that have arisen from that period of ceaseless experiment.[22]

The shortages in food, clothing, housing, medicine, and a hundred "little things" at first created only inconvenience. But soon this inconvenience developed into hardship and suffering. Nearly all people were affected in some way. The war spared no one group from the necessity of taxing its ingenuity. Whenever a useful substitute was found for some scarce item, the news was published in the local papers. Thence it found its way into other papers and into various magazines and journals. The people were usually willing and ready to spread the results of their amateur experiments. Their friends and fellow citizens were very anxious to have them. To such substitutes and expedients was applied the term "Confederate." It was said that "Confederate," so used, might be defined as anything "that is rough, unfinished, unfashionable or poor."[23] There were "Confederate" dresses, "Confederate" candles, "Confederate" flour, and many other "Confederate" items.

While the men of the South were fighting the war on the battlefields of the Confederacy, the women were fighting the war of substitutes at home. Their "minds were so taxed in devising temporary expedients" and "their hands so busy carrying them into effect" that there was no time to brood. Some grew so accustomed to the substitutes that "they scarcely seemed privations."[24] While all were slow in facing the problems created by possible shortages, they realized that the stocks on hand were dwindling. Finally the stockpile disappeared entirely. Then it was that the people began to awaken to the fact that shortages were obstacles in the path of victory. They set to work to remove the obstacles. In many cases they found they had awakened too late, for while some commodities were replaced with fairly successful substitutes, others loomed as enigmas.

II

CAUSES OF SHORTAGES

PRESIDENT LINCOLN WAS AWARE OF THE DEPENDENCE OF THE SOUTH on outside help if its needs were to be met. When he blockaded the southern coast, he had a twofold purpose: to exclude manufactured goods, especially munitions of war, from the Confederacy; and to prevent the exportation of cotton to European countries. Established first on April 19, 1861, and later extended to include Virginia, North Carolina and Texas, the blockade was not at first effective. Thomas Cooper DeLeon wrote that it was, in the early days, so inadequate that traders "ran in and out [of southern ports] with greater frequency than before those ports were closed."[1] Francis B. C. Bradlee points out that "nearly everyone, including the highest naval authorities . . . considered that the blockade could not possibly be rigorously enforced, and that it would result in . . . a 'paper blockade.'"[2] There was expectation in some circles that the blockade would be raised at any time, so useless would it prove.[3] Even the cautious Jefferson Davis, in his inaugural address in February, 1862, expressed the opinion that the blockade would be ineffective.[4] J. D. B. DeBow, in an editorial published in his *Review*, outlined the possible rewards that might spring from the blockade. He believed that the South would some day "Thank God for it"; he visualized industry springing from the Southland, so confident was he that "necessity is the mother of invention," and he believed that the blockade would create the necessity.[5] What he failed to see was that the major energies of the South would be channeled into warfare. Only secondary efforts could be expended on industry. Yet there was a tremendous growth of small industries during the war, most of these being the direct outcome of the blockade. But never did these establishments supply all the needs of the South.

11

These first attitudes regarding the effectiveness of the blockade were soon changed, for the stranglehold became closer as the war years wore on, and it finally succeeded in "commercially throttling the South to death."[6] By the end of the second year, the blockade was being felt, and only specially built "runners" stood much chance of getting through and into port.[7] The opinion has been expressed that this blockade "contributed as much to the final issue as the victories of the Union Army in the field."[8] Certainly, it was a major cause for many of the shortages. The diaries and letters of the period give evidence that the people who lived through those years of conflict blamed the blockade for many of their woes. One diarist called it "a stockade," asserting that it "hems us in with only the open sky above us."[9] Another writer made the exaggerated statement that the blockade "for extent and effectiveness . . . stands without parallel in history."[10] Those imports that did manage to come into Confederate ports were said to be "only a drop in the great empty bucket of want."[11] The blockade "proclaimed its own substitute law."[12] Writing years after the Civil War became history, Thomas Cooper DeLeon had the following to say about the blockade: "If I were asked the most active cause in the Confederate collapse I should say: the blockade whipped us."[13]

Regardless of the varying opinions on the effectiveness of the blockade, it is common knowledge that runners did get through. The stories of these blockade-runners form one of the most colorful chapters in the history of the Confederacy. Until February, 1865, when Fort Fisher fell, there was always some port that remained at least partially open to receive cargoes from abroad. New Orleans fell early in the war, but as long as it was open to southern trade, there was nearly complete disregard of the blockade there.[14] Its loss to Federal forces was a serious one, but even after it fell such ports as Wilmington, Charleston, Savannah, Galveston, Mobile, and Brownsville remained. Of these, Wilmington played a leading role longer than any of the others. Into this Carolina town were imported luxuries long after they had disappeared from other places. Because of the abundance of prewar luxuries, Wilmington was called "the fairy-land" of the Confederacy.[15] Into the various ports came ships laden with expensive merchandise from Bermuda, Nassau, Havana, and Matamoras, the intermediary points, used primarily as deposit places for goods originating in

Europe or the North. From these southward ports shipments were made by the daring and well paid captains of the blockade-runners. In this way, the Confederacy was able to import varying quantities of goods until almost the end of the war.[16]

Texans, especially Germans living there, and they were numerous, profited greatly from the blockade-running across the Rio Grande River. This trade was unique. Relatives and friends in Germany would send them scarce items by way of France and Mexico. Thus it was that "the little German girls strutted about in imported dresses to the envy of little native born lasses, who had to don homespun."[17] The Federal authorities were well aware of the value of the Rio Grande to the Confederacy, and they were encouraged by the northern press to take possession of the river at the earliest possible moment.[18] By late December, 1863, General Kirby Smith considered that the Rio Grande was closed to the South.[19] After that date, the problem of shortages became more severe in Texas and the entire Trans-Mississippi area.

The task of running the blockade was undertaken by the Confederate and State governments as well as by individuals. It was a profitable business, especially when carried on by private runners. The men engaged in the business were not only paid high wages, but they usually received a bounty.[20] It was estimated that a successful investment in blockade-running might net from "fifteen hundred to two thousand per cent on its first cost."[21] This tremendous profit was due to two factors, the first being the risk taken and the loss sustained, for it has been estimated that two out of five cargoes never reached their destination.[22] One student of the blockade estimated that 1,504 of these vessels were captured or destroyed in the war.[23] The second factor was the hunger of the South for imported articles, and consequently the willingness to pay any price for them. After the captain of a runner had disposed of his cargo and received his money, he was "well-supplied with coin" and managed "to live in comfort," even though those around him suffered privations.[24] As a result there was much criticism of the runners. Not only were their immense profits the target of the critics, but also the types of cargoes they carried. J. B. Jones quoted an Alabama judge as saying that the blockade-runners were ruining the country, "supplying the enemy with cotton and bringing in liquors and useless gew-gaws."[25] Another wrote in later years that a stronger hand "should have been used to prevent misuse of the blockade."[26]

The criticism of cargoes seems justified. Generally the shipments consisted of commodities that were light in weight and that were apt to bring greatest returns. Thus, the shortage of such items as boiler iron, steel, copper, zinc, and machinery of all kinds was not relieved to any great extent by blockade-running. Such things as quinine, morphine, expensive dress materials, laces, and miscellaneous items were brought in greater quantity.[27] The majority of articles brought by private runners were luxuries, while articles of great necessity came in slight quantity or not at all. The South was so desperately in need of necessities that the Confederate Congress made it illegal for luxuries to be imported.[28] This law was not well enforced, however, and the flow of expensive luxuries continued.[29]

Blockade-running was not confined to ships and the sea. Individuals ran the land blockade. Men and women would get through the lines, secure scarce provisions in an area held by the Federals, conceal them in various ways, and then slip back into the Confederacy. Ladies from some of the most prominent families were among those who ran the blockade. Misses Hetty and Constance Cary crossed the Potomac several times and brought back much needed articles.[30] Medicine was the most common cargo brought through the lines, for it was needed and was easy to conceal because of its small bulk. The usual method of concealing quinine, morphine, and other drugs was to sew them into one's clothing.[31] It was an easy task for a woman to do this, styles being what they were in the sixties. Although medicine was the most common article brought in this manner, needles, thread, small quantities of sugar, tea, salt, cloth, gloves, ribbons, and buttons were concealed in linings and under hoop skirts.[32] Two Tennessee women found that Memphis, after its capture by the Federals, was "hard to get in and ten times harder to get out," but they disguised themselves as country women, taking a wagon load of greens into the city to sell. Once inside the town they purchased some much desired merchandise that was unobtainable in the community in which they lived. This they hid in their bustles and in their hair, and successfully got through the lines and back to their homes.[33] Whenever and wherever individuals succeeded in getting into the Confederacy laden with scarce items, they were "hailed with delight by their friends."[34] So prevalent was individual running of the blockade that a parody on "Maryland, My Maryland" became very popular. It ran as follows:

> We rowed across the Potomac,
> Maryland!
> We put up cash and then rowed back,
> Maryland!
> We're loaded deep with hats and shoes
> Or medicines the sick can use—
> At prices that just beat the Jews!
> Maryland, My Maryland![35]

Of equal importance with the blockade, in the list of causes which aggravated the problem of shortages, was the inadequate transportation system of the Confederacy. This is an example of a shortage causing a shortage, and it shows something of the complexity of the general problem. As a separate and distinct item, a more detailed study of the transportation shortage is relegated to a later chapter. However, there are some general points that should be brought in here.

The railroads of the Confederacy proved to be a necessity in the waging of the Civil War. They were required to transport troops, as well as munitions, food, and clothing to the many fronts. But they were needed as well in supplying the homefront, especially the city dwellers. The back country had to be tapped, and it was the job of the railroads to do this. The roads were, as a rule, "short, local lines inadequately financed by local capital, cheaply constructed, poorly equipped, . . . and they were wholly unprepared for the task suddenly thrust upon them by the war."[36] There was a shortage of engines and cars on every line during the entire conflict. Roads most in use were least able to bear the burdens.[37] The lack of uniform gauge, the poor facilities for transporting cargoes from one rail terminus to another, the cutting of the railroads by both armies, all had a direct and severe effect upon the feeding and the clothing of the civilians as well as the soldiers.[38] Nor did the government's policy of using the railroads for transportation of necessities of war aid in solving the problem of homefront shortages. All recognized the importance of feeding and clothing the army in the field, but to do this created shortages, especially food shortages, among the civilians. The railroads found it impossible to transport food for both. There were times when the railroads could supply neither; and the roads became more inefficient as the war continued. An authority on the problem wrote that "For more than a year before the end came, the railroads were in such wretched condition that a complete breakdown seemed always imminent."[39] While some sections of the Confederacy had more food and supplies than their needs required, others, especially that area around Richmond, suffered acutely.

Many efforts were made to remedy a situation that was, in reality, hopeless. Not a year passed but saw attempts of the government and railroad men to reach a solution. Railroad conventions met and passed resolutions, but failed to put them into "general execution."[40] In 1862 Colonel William M. Wadley was assigned "to the supervision and control of the transportation for the Government, on all railroads in the Confederate States."[41] After he had been engaged in the immense task for five months, the Senate, in the spring of 1863, belatedly rejected his name,[42] and Captain F. W. Sims was appointed to the post. Captain Sims continued in this work until the collapse of the Confederacy, but his major concern was the provisioning of the army, and he did little to alleviate the problem of shortages among the civilians.[43] After June, 1862, the overcrowded city of Richmond was never sure of receiving farm produce from great distances except over the Danville and Richmond Railroad.[44] It is small wonder that provisions were so scarce in the capital of the Confederacy.

The conditions of the railroads had a serious effect on the transporting of the essentials of life to the people of the war-torn South. The wagon roads, too, affected the transportation of supplies. Most roads were impassable during a greater part of every year. Little repair work was done on them from 1861 to 1865 and, as a result, they were washed into gullies, and it was a common occurrence to find holes in the road knee-deep.[45] Even when it was possible to limp and jolt along these poor roads, one never knew when he would find a bridge gone—the result of decay or destruction.[46] Thus, to bring supplies overland by way of the roads was sometimes impossible and always improbable.

Even if the roads had been in excellent condition, the shortage of beasts of burden, as well as of wagons and carts, would have hindered travel and transportation. Poorly fed, impressed for service with the Confederate Army, killed or captured by enemy forces, there were never enough horses and mules to pull the farm wagons to market. Many were the odd objects that the few remaining animals pulled along the roads of the South, for the shortage of wagons and carts taxed the ingenuity of the Confederates. Most substitutes proved inadequate.[47]

The government was criticized severely for its inability to solve the transportation problem. It was said that "no department was worse neglected and mismanaged."[48] The problem of transportation was never solved, but was as nearly insurmountable as any faced during the war. Had some solution been found, however, the problem of shortages, both in the army and at home, would have been less in all cases and nonexistent in some.

The twin evils of speculation and hoarding were important contributors to shortages. No part of the Confederacy was immune to them. Of the two, more was written in the diaries, letters, and newspapers about speculation. This was a public matter, easily seen and detected. Hoarding was more or less a private affair.

Most people condemned speculation, but it was never checked to any great degree. It began early in the war, and continued to the end. As soon as the war commenced and the blockade was established around the southern coast, the speculators started "buying up" stocks of scarce items. Such commodities as salt, bacon, and leather were particularly attractive to them, and "a clique of half a dozen men obtained and held control of the only two nail factories in the Confederacy."[49] The war was scarcely seven months old when the Vicksburg *Sun* urged the people not to buy the flour in the hands of the speculators,[50] and the war was less than a year old when the Wilmington *Journal* accused the speculators of having done "more harm than the enemy."[51] But the worst was yet to come, for the scourge continued throughout the war. Emma, daughter of Joseph LeConte, recorded in her diary on December 31, 1864, that "speculators and extortioners" were "starving us."[52] It was only when the end of the conflict became a matter of days that speculators in Richmond thrust their stocks on the market, but even then they refused to lower prices.[53]

People complained about speculation more than any other of the war evils. The newspapers were heavy-laden with editorials, articles, and letters-from-the-readers protesting against this evil. One editor wrote, in December, 1862, that he had "scarcely perused a paper published within the Confederacy" during the past six

months, which had not something to say in relation to speculation.[54]   The newspapers called upon the leaders of both the
Confederate and state governments to alleviate the suffering resulting from speculation and extortion.   That half-hearted efforts
were made to remedy the situation may be attributed largely to the
scorching condemnations published in every one of the Confederate States.   For example, the *Southern Confederacy,* outspoken
Atlanta paper, reminded the Georgia government that it was its
duty to do something about the problem;[55] and when Governor
Joseph E. Brown ordered that all salt held in the depot at Savannah be confiscated and sold to the public at $5.00 a sack, the
newspaper reminded the Governor that salt was not the only
prime necessity of life.   "Impartial justice requires the Governor
to deal with all alike and put down all unpatriotic speculation,"
wrote the editor.   He added that the Governor should remember
that the "constitution of Georgia says that private property can be
seized for public use."[56]

The Richmond *Examiner* approached the problem in a slightly
different manner.   It appealed to the pride of the people of Richmond.   The editor reminded them that Richmond was the capital
of the Confederacy, and as such, it would have many visitors.   He
raised this question with his readers: "Does Richmond want a repu-
tation [for extortion] throughout the South of a Yankee town?"[57]
A North Carolina paper tried still another means of appealing to
speculators.   It urged that these men read and follow the teachings
of the Bible;[58] and the Petersburg *Daily Express* referred to the
speculators as "traitors" deserving "the denunciation and condem-
nation of every good citizen."[59]

The newspapers were not alone in tackling the problem. People
throughout the length and breadth of the Confederacy were
aroused, and they discussed the problem among themselves.   Speculation made the lot of the plain people very difficult.   Finally
they began to call upon the government to do something about
it.   One lady wrote to her husband, who was in government circles
in Richmond at the time, and asked him why the government did
not "put down the screws" and force the speculators to release
their stores.[60]   J. B. Jones, who always managed to keep his
finger on the pulse of the Confederacy, recorded that the government might remedy the evils and "remove the distresses of the
people," but it refused to take a strong hand in the situation.[61]

Because of the hundreds of complaints, the state and Confederate governments were forced to look into the situation. The governors and mayors took action first, trying to remedy matters by proclamations and appeals. These failing, more direct action was taken by the state and Confederate governments.[62] Jefferson Davis voiced his concern over the "gigantic evil" of speculation, saying that it had "seduced citizens of all classes from a determined prosecution of the war to a sordid effort to amass money."[63] Despite appeals and legislation designed to punish extortioners and speculators, it was generally conceded that the government was no match for them.[64]

Just who were the speculators? Accusations flew thick and fast. The "Yankees," and this term might apply to those of the second generation, were often blamed;[65] but the worst and most frequent accusations were made against the Jews. One woman wrote that she felt as though Richmond were a foreign city, for many new names appeared in Richmond during the war. "Israel and David, and Moses and Jacobs, and Hyman and Levy, and Guggenheimer and Rosenheimer, and other names innumerable of the Ancient People were prominent . . . The war was a harvest to that class . . . Many of them were . . . the future Rothschilds of the South."[66] In an attempt to clarify the question of "Who are the speculators?" the Wilmington *Journal* boldly commented that "the disposition to speculate and monopolize is not confined to the professional trader but is found to exist with farmers and others, who hold back for fabulous prices."[67] And evidence shows that speculation was limited to no one ethnic, national, or religious group. Anyone might purchase an article one day and profit by its resale the next.[68] Private Theodore Honour, encamped near Charleston, wrote to his wife in 1863 that her father had confessed that in a month of speculating "in the necessaries of life" he had made enough to pay for a house and "expected to make much more." Private Honour indignantly warned his wife not to engage "in any way . . . in this terrible vice" for "money made in that way will be a dreadful curse to the maker."[69]

The farmers were often criticized for holding their crops for higher prices.[70] One observer dared to venture the comment that a bill making speculation illegal could not be passed by the state legislatures because most of the members were agriculturists.[71] A most unusual story about speculators came from Nashville, Tennessee. A local druggist heard that plans were being made to blow up the city. He immediately bought all the plate glass in town and stored it in a place of safe-keeping. When the city was rocked by a series of explosions several days later, over half of the windows were broken. The druggist sold his glass and made a fortune.[72] A story that originated in New Orleans was circulated throughout the Confederacy. According to the account, people of the city made the rounds buying "all the mourning goods for the purpose of speculation, in anticipation of a great battle at Corinth."[73] An Arkansas editor wrote that speculation was confined to "no one group, commodity, or locality, for it . . . [was] like an epidemic throughout the limits of the Confederacy."[74] A Virginia paper urged everyone to ask himself: "Am I an extortioner? . . . Am I demanding exorbitant prices for anything?" If he could answer in the affirmative, then the editor said that he might also say of himself that he was "an enemy to his country."[75]

Hoarding was also prevalent in the Confederacy. The extent of the practice is unknown, but its presence is reflected in many contemporary writings. Some were hesitant to admit that they hoarded scarce items; others brazenly acknowledged it. But hidden or not, the fact remains that hoarding did remove from circulation items of necessity, placing much in the hands of a few, while others had none. People, who themselves lacked the ability to look ahead and predict what articles would become scarce, were sometimes encouraged to hoard by the salespeople in the stores. A Richmond lady was told in May, 1861, that all piece goods would be scarce and the prices high, therefore she had better buy a year's supply while she could. The saleslady told her that she doubted whether there would be any cloth left in Richmond by fall. Grocers often encouraged their better customers to stock up on coffee and other rare items by whispering of future shortages and higher prices.[76] But those who had the inclination to hoard usually needed no such stimulation. They foresaw the scarcity and high prices, and bought anything and everything they could find and afford.

Many individuals laid in supplies sufficient to stock a small shop.[77] A lady tutor told of her patron bringing in supplies by the wagonload, until "the lawn and paths looked like a wharf covered with a ship's loads." She counted thirty barrels of dried fish, three hogsheads of molasses, and many more containers of sugar, coffee, soap, and whiskey.[78] All of these items became scarce during the war. In addition to the above articles, an Alabamian watched his employer hoard flour, tea, wine, spices and other condiments, calico, linen, domestic, linsey, and Osnaburgs. He remarked that they were bought "in wholesale quantities and stored away in spacious storerooms."[79] Some people purchased the stock of an entire store in order to get scarce commodities. A man in Warrenton, North Carolina, bought the contents of a store early in the war, and transferred the stock "to his own cupboards and pantry."[80] His home remained a Utopia in the midst of want and privation. A Louisiana family bought the contents of a country store on Bayou Plaquemine; the women were delighted to find that its stock included a "large supply of needles, thread, buttons, and dress materials."[81] A merchant in Charleston wrote to his mother in Greenville, South Carolina, regularly during the war urging her to purchase scarce goods in quantity. He made use of his contacts in the business world to secure for her tremendous quantities of foodstuffs and clothing unobtainable by most people. He warned his mother not to speak "to anybody of these things."[82] However, from September, 1863, until January, 1864, he sent her over two barrels of salt, several hogsheads of sugar, and quantities of black pepper, tea, rice, coffee, cloth, and stockings.[83] In the same period he urged her to buy "fowls and chickens . . . while you can," assuring her that he was endeavoring to buy bacon.[84] In October, 1863, he suggested that she purchase at least fifty loads of wood if she could get it, adding "Do pay attention to it at once."[85]

Such large scale hoarding was unusual, for there were not many who could afford such an outlay of money. It was more common to hoard one or a few items. Soap was bought in quantity by some,[86] codliver oil and medicine by others.[87] Clothing of all kinds soon disappeared from the stores, having been purchased in quantity. Of all the food items, coffee was most often hoarded.[88] Fuel was also stored up to be used at a later date.[89] Whenever such cases of hoarding were brought to light, the press usually had much to say about them. The Richmond *Enquirer* told of a man who had hoarded seven hundred barrels of flour, having them stored in his cellar, parlor, and attic. The editor vehemently added that all hoarders should be hanged "to the nearest lampposts."[90]

Along with those who speculated and hoarded the necessities of life were the hundreds of generous, patriotic citizens who not only gave, but gave until they were forced to do without those things they really needed. And this very generosity, unselfishness, and patriotism sometimes further increased the problem of home-front shortages. So lost were the majority of the people in the war fever during the early months of the war, and so confident were they of the early victory of the Confederacy, that they were ready and willing to part with anything in order that the soldiers might have enough. This spirit was manifested in gifts, both to the men at the front and to less fortunate friends at home. But the sheer inability to give because of a lack of items for giving caused a lessening of donations from the most generous toward the end of the war. But there was never complete cessation. Those who could, and who at the same time had the inclination to give, continued to divide with the less fortunate. A lady living near Lenoir, North Carolina, made clothing for soldiers and sent gifts to them until the end of the war.[91]

People were encouraged by the press to give to the Confederacy. Early in the war, before the paper shortage cut down their size, most newspapers listed those who donated articles to the cause. This always had an effect on the people, especially those who enjoyed seeing their names in print. The leaders, too, made appeals for gifts to the soldiers. Governor Zebulon Baird Vance of North Carolina was among the first. Both he and Governor John Letcher of Virginia asked for donations of blankets to state troops.[92] General Beauregard asked that bells and brass utensils, not absolutely needed on the homefront, be forwarded to him to be remade into weapons of war. Answers to his plea were many. The legislature of Arkansas passed a resolution that churches and planters "who may be owners of brass bells, be earnestly and respectfully requested to make a tender of the same to the Confederate States of America, for the purpose of having the same converted into cannon, to be used in defending their homes and obtaining their liberties."[93] These and other appeals were usually answered immediately and without further encouragement. The spirit of giving was prevalent as long as there remained anything to give. But giving often caused hardships at home.

It was said that "to do without was part of the southern woman's religion,"[94] and many civilians denied themselves "that they might

give."[95]   In all sections of the South women gathered together
at regular intervals to sew, knit, and pack boxes for the soldiers.[96]
To these gifts, sent to the front and to hospitals, were pinned the
names of the donors, and often a correspondence developed between donor and recipient.[97]   The generosity of the people was
commended by the leaders.   A committee appointed by the Senate of the Confederate Congress to examine the Medical Department of the Army, closed its report with these words:

> The Committee cannot close . . . without a testimonial to the
> kindness and patriotism of our citizens at home, manifested in
> their unremitting efforts to supply the wants and relieve the suf-
> ferings of the soldiers, sick and well. The supply of money, clothing
> and hospital stores derived from this generous source is not only
> of immense value in itself, but the most cheering indication of the
> spirit of our people.[98]

Everything desired or needed by the Confederate soldiers and
obtainable by civilians was given.   Food was the most popular
gift that could be sent.   Boxes went to the men at the front and
in the hospitals, but the poor transportation facilities and the distances between homes and the battlefield caused much of this
food to spoil.   Most of the women therefore gave up the idea
of sending a box to their own loved one, especially if he were some
distance away.   Instead they began to form clubs and meet troop
trains.   They fed the troops on these trains, some of the women
taking the dinners from their own tables as the train approached.[99]
These dinners were often so meagre and simple as to make the
soldiers feel hesitant to accept them.   They often consisted only
of cornbread, bacon, and water or milk.[100]   The women of Columbia, South Carolina, had a very efficient system worked out,
so that all trains would be sure to be met by someone.   Several
ladies were always at the station, and at "no hour of the day or
night could a train come and find no-one" to serve the travelers.[101]
   The soldier on foot had his friends, too.   Entire meals were
sometimes served these men from pathetically dwindling pantries.
A patriotic woman in the hills of Arkansas "always kept her table
ready-set"; and no matter what hour of the day or night a hungry
soldier came past, he was called into the humble home and given
the best his hostess had.[102]   William H. Clark endeared himself
to the weary foot soldiers, who passed through Halifax, Virginia,

in the summer of 1861, by providing them with buckets of mint juleps and bottles of fine old Madeira wine.[103]   These gifts of food gave proof that there were generous folk in the South, but they also helped to lay bare the larders.

Like food, clothing was shared.   Much of it was given to cover the soldiers,[104] and some of it went into much-needed bandages.[105] The story of Miss Lou Taylor, of Florida, received much publicity during the war and after.   When she saw a young soldier marching along without shoes, the sight of his bleeding feet was too much for her.   She gave him her only pair of shoes, and he marched on proudly wearing a woman's shoes.[106]

Household articles were donated to such an extent that carpets were practically nonexistent by 1865; even bedding was not sufficient for homefront needs.   Sheets, pillow cases, tablecloths, and furniture covers were torn into strips and rolled into bandages, and material was woven especially for use in the hospital.[107] Lead weights from windows were donated to the cause,[108] as were copper kettles, bells, and brass door knobs and knockers.[109]   Some generous people gave their horses to the army early in the war, one man relinquishing his stables for use of the cavalry.[110]   It is not surprising that so many homes were stripped bare.

Those who had more than was absolutely needed by their own families were often generous in dividing with their less fortunate friends and neighbors, as well as with the servicemen.   J. B. Jones recorded many contributions to his pantry, made by his rural friends.   They brought him fresh vegetables, fruit, butter, or meat regularly during the war.[111]   Those who could not afford to make outright gifts frequently exchanged their surplus commodities for items they did not possess.   Such a spirit of helpfulness to one's fellowman offset somewhat the more selfish attitude exhibited by speculators and hoarders; but strange as it may seem both aggravated the problem of shortages.   Many a person who gave freely in 1861 lived to see himself in want by 1865.   Yet the gratification felt from the generosity must have been worth something, even in time of need.

In the prosecution of the war, the people at home were forced into a secondary position.   The first thought of the Confederate government centered around winning the war; and the problem of supply was one of the gravest the government faced.   So serious did it become that a program of impressment was begun.[112] This policy helped to feed and clothe the army, but it also affected the supply on the homefront. It was certainly a contributing factor to the shortages of the civilians. Since the program was under the direction of the War Department, that agency received hundreds of letters of complaint from indignant citizens. The impressment policy was one of the most unpopular resorts of the Confederate government.[113] Its enforcement caused many, heretofore generous in gifts to the armed forces, to refuse to meet their allotments. There was widespread resentment against arbitrary seizures and, although there were those who continued their voluntary contributions whenever possible, these same people often condemned and denied the right of the government to impress commodities.

Since interior Georgia, South Carolina, and North Carolina were more plentifully supplied than some of the other states, they were favorite sources of supply for the government agents. Too, their products could be more easily and directly shipped to the battlefields than those of some other states. Impressment agents swarmed over Georgia and the Carolinas, but they were never cordially welcomed by the people. L. B. Northrop, Commissary-General of Subsistence, wrote Secretary of War James A. Seddon that the "people in both the Carolinas and Georgia have vehemently opposed impressment."[114] When circulars were distributed informing the farmers of the policy and offering market prices for produce, the farmers refused to bring this produce to market. Many towns were thereby forced to do without needed farm products, for the farmers were afraid to venture out for fear of having their produce seized by impressment agents. Governor M. L. Bonham of South Carolina wrote Secretary of War Seddon that the effect of the policy had been to cause suffering among the people. Said he: "The people of the towns and cities, many of them refugees from States now in the hands of the enemy and from our own sea coast, are absolutely in want of the necessaries of life."[115] Such conditions were general wherever the agents were found.[116] Some farmers even threatened to plant no more corn, wheat, peas, or "anything liable to impressment." One group thought of growing nothing but cabbages, which had "no place in the schedule of government prices."[117]

As the policy was expanded, scarcely anything was spared. Not only was food taken, but other commodities as well. Horses, mules, and wagons were greatly needed by the army and were frequently impressed.[118] A Richmond editor indignantly wrote that "Lee wants 10,000 horses . . . and must have them. So Richmond must furnish them if her citizens have to draw the hearse to the funeral."[119] The same editor estimated that farmers were deprived of one-third of their horses and mules, "thus leaving them without sufficient force to cultivate even ordinary crops."[120] Such practices necessarily affected the amount of food produced; and there were times when merchants in towns could not deliver even so necessary an item as firewood because a government agent had taken their horses and mules.[121] Transportation was further hampered in parts of the Confederacy by the seizure of railroad iron and equipment. Governor Joseph E. Brown of Georgia wired General Josiah Gorgas of the Ordnance Department that unless "the Confederate authorities cease to impress rolling stock of the State Road, I shall be obligated to stop entirely the transportation of coal over the road."[122] This and other impressment continued, however, until many railroads were without either rails or rolling stock.[123]

A major argument for the continuation of the policy by the Confederate government was that it would force the speculators to disgorge.[124] Whereas it was successful in accomplishing this in isolated incidents, it was not generally successful. But it did aggravate the problem of supply for the homefront and it caused shortages. The editor of the Richmond *Examiner* wrote that the people of that city were being reduced "to a point of starvation. Neither corn nor meal can be obtained here for love nor money."[125] In the attempt to feed the fighting men, the government created a homefront problem.

Depending upon victory in the war to perpetuate its very existence, the Confederate government often worked counter to the welfare of the people at home. In draining off the manpower to fight the war, production of essential items was slowed down and sometimes halted. Upon the women and children of the South fell the burden of running farm and plantation, for not only masters but overseers as well often joined the armed forces. Those who cultivated small farms with few or no slaves were the men that made up the bulk of the army, and they, too, left their land without sufficient hands to till it.[126] Because overseers were sometimes exempt from service, some of the larger plantations managed to maintain them,[127] but on some Negroes took complete charge.[128] On the thousands of small farms, however, the main burden of tending the crops fell upon the women. "Many a woman who never held a plow" found her family dependent on her,[129] and she therefore learned to plow, hoe, bind and thresh grains, gather and shuck corn,[130] and do many of the chores that were thought to be men's jobs. She cut wood,[131] cleaned wells,[132] and even buried the dead,[133] as well as performed the usual woman's tasks. With this inexperienced labor and too little even of that, food production was decreased at a time when greater production was needed. The "shortage of manpower was a paramount factor in the scarcity of food."[134]

The industrial output, as well as that of agriculture, was handicapped by a shortage of laborers. Newspapers carried numerous advertisements for artisans and skilled laborers. These men had gone to war or had hired themselves out to the government as workers. Some of the skilled workers employed in the South in 1861 were northerners by birth. When the war came, many returned to the North.[135] The Marietta (Georgia) Paper Mill furnishes an example of how the lack of laborers affected the output. This firm was forced to close completely in September, 1863, because of the want of laborers[136] and, although it opened again in a few months, its output was restricted because of the manpower shortage.[137] A similar situation existed in other industries over the South. The lack of sufficient agricultural and industrial workers curtailed production and was, therefore, a contributing factor to the general problem of shortages.

Another factor lay in existing wartime conditions. General effects of the conflict, such as devastation, abnormally overcrowded communities, and the loss of productive areas, made the task of the people far more difficult than it would have been otherwise. Property damage and destruction amounting to millions of dollars, irreplaceable in time of war, created further grave problems. The Confederate and Federal armies, marching and countermarching over the South, laid waste its fields and destroyed its buildings. In the wake of General Sherman's "March to the Sea" in the fall and early winter of 1864, "everywhere the houses . . . were pillaged, clothes torn up, beds torn to pieces, barns and gins and

their contents given to flames."[138]   Similar scenes were enacted
hundreds of times, but it was not always the northern invader who
destroyed, but the Confederate army as well.   A Georgian told
J. B. Jones that his friends flew before the Confederate cavalry for
"they devastate the country as much as the enemy";[139] and Governor Vance complained of damage done by this same branch of
the service.[140]   The Confederate forces were urged by the newspapers to take greater care and not destroy or deface buildings,
fences, and other property.   The Richmond *Enquirer* warned that
the war might be long, therefore resources should be "nursed . . .
or we shall break down."[141]   Despite such warnings destruction
continued and in the last years of the war it became more difficult
to replace anything.   Shortages appeared as a natural result.

Certain areas were seriously overcrowded by the war.   Richmond, particularly, had more people than the town could accommodate.   There were shortages of food, housing, fuel, and other
items in the capital; other towns, too, felt the press of abnormal
conditions arising from overcrowding.   Where such conditions
existed, the area usually tapped for food proved to be insufficient.   Hunger was thus more widespread in and around the
towns than in rural areas.   Whenever a town was near the battlefront or near a camp, food was apt to be scarce, for the soldiers
were usually given first choice.   Betty Herndon Maury recorded
in her diary in March, 1862, that the presence of the Confederate
soldiers in the vicinity of Fredericksburg made it impossible for
her to get meat, butter, or eggs.   The soldiers took everything.[142]
Similar complaints were numerous.   A South Carolinian complained
to Governor Magrath that the soldiers were eating all the provisions in the Abbeville area.[143]   Although their presence was recognized as a necessity, the soldiers helped to create a shortage of
foodstuffs otherwise available to civilians.

When certain rich and productive areas fell into the hands
of the enemy or became isolated from the rest of the Confederacy,
a shortage of products indigenous to that area naturally followed.
Of all such losses, none created greater grief than the bisecting of
the Confederacy along the line of the Mississippi River.   The
great shortage of sugar in the eastern part of the Confederacy
after 1863 is mentioned frequently by the diarists and newspapers of the period.   Meat, too, became more scarce after the
fall of Vicksburg, for Texas cattle were no longer available.   One

observer thought that this splitting of the Confederacy was "al-most as damaging as the blockade."[144]   As valuable in its own right, as the western part of the Confederacy, was the Shenandoah Valley. It was the "bread-basket" of Lee's army, and many were the battles fought to protect this rich area. Its loss was a serious blow to the South. With the steady contraction of the Confederacy, the supplying of even the barest necessities became an impossi-bility. It was then that the Confederacy finally and completely collapsed.

Included in the list of causes must be those events that might have been disastrous in any year, but occurring as they did during the war, they proved to be catastrophic. Among such events was the inclement weather. It often prevented the production of bumper crops. Droughts occurred at various times, notably in June, 1862, in southeastern Alabama. So serious was it that min-isters in Selma set aside June 24 as a day of prayer and fasting.[145] A year earlier, there had been a serious drought in parts of Texas,[146] and a year later there was one in North Carolina.[147] Floods, too, hampered the production of food. The Mississippi River went on a rampage in the late spring of 1861 and again in the early sum-mer of 1862. In both years the levees broke at various places along the river and destroyed newly planted crops. The broken levees in 1861 in Chicot County, Arkansas, did damage in excess of $1,-000,000[148] while in 1862 the flood of the Mississippi created havoc in Arkansas, Mississippi, and Louisiana. It was possible to row boats over cultivated fields as far as seven miles back from the river.[149] In the spring of 1864, the Appomattox River overflowed, causing not only destruction of crops but also the loss of food stores in a government warehouse in Petersburg.[150] While the spring floods and the summer droughts affected the production of food crops, the winter snow and ice storms prevented their transporta-tion to market. One diarist recorded that "the snow laid an em-bargo on the . . . supplies brought to market, and all who had no provisions for such a contingency are subsisting on very short commons."[151] Late freezes were sometimes disastrous, especially to fruit crops.[152] All of these elements affected the production of food, and they seemed especially numerous during the Civil War, although this was due in part to the fact that such things were noticed more in those times of stress.

Closely akin to weather problems were epidemics of both plant and human diseases. When the supply of northern wheat was cut off, southern farmers attempted to increase their yield, but they found their crops plagued with rust. So serious did it become in the spring of 1862 that the *Southern Cultivator* published an article in the May-June issue, urging the farmers to abandon wheat and turn to peas, corn, and potatoes.[153] Like wheat, oats were infested with rust, and farmers were urged to plant corn in their stead.[154] It is evident even to the most casual reader of the contemporary sources that plant diseases and blight caused a diminution of production, but to blame a food shortage on human diseases might seem a trifle far-fetched. Yet such diseases, especially when they reached epidemic proportions, did affect the supply of food. Not only did they cut down the output of those who were affected, but they sometimes prevented farm produce from being brought into town. During the terrible yellow fever epidemic at Wilmington, North Carolina, in the fall of 1862, the rural folk refused to bring either food or fuel into the city. The local paper said that the townspeople could "hardly obtain any article, even of the most common necessity." Stores were closed and even speculators refused to come into town and bid on the cargo of a blockade-runner.[155] Fuel was badly needed, but none was available at the height of the epidemic; and in late November, when the disease was about under control, the editor of the local paper begged that "country friends . . . have some mercy on . . . [them], and bring in produce, such as pork, beef, eggs, butter, poultry, meal, flour, cabbages, etc., for the inner man, and wood to keep . . . [them] warm."[156]

Fire was also a cause of certain shortages. There were hundreds of conflagrations throughout the South during the war. Shells fired at buildings often started fires. Homes, business houses, warehouses, and factories were burned and their contents lost. The worst fire during the war was in Charleston in December, 1861. It burned for several days and nights before it could be brought under control. A large portion of the city was destroyed, and hundreds of people were made homeless. In an effort to alleviate the sufferings of the burned-out victims, towns all over the Confederacy sent aid.[157] Among smaller fires that destroyed buildings and produce was the burning of a warehouse in Richmond where a large quantity of flour was destroyed.[158] The burning of the Bath Paper Mills had its repercussions. Several newspapers and journals were dependent upon this mill for their paper. Among these was *Southern Field and Fireside*.[159] Two of the most important factories in the South, the Tredegar Iron Works and the Crenshaw Woolen Mills, both in Richmond, were almost destroyed by fires on the night of May 14, 1863. The damage caused a considerable decrease in production.[160]

Lack of self-sufficiency, the blockade, inadequate transportation facilities, speculation, hoarding, generosity, government impressment, an insufficient labor force, destruction by fire and sword, and a host of natural phenomena stand out as the major reasons for homefront shortages. Yet these factors are interrelated. Seldom did a community suffer from the presence of only one of these, but rather from a combination of them.

III

GOVERNMENTAL POLICIES

SHORTAGES, CAUSED AS THEY WERE BY A MULTIPLICITY OF FACTORS, affected everyone in the Confederacy in some way. For many they brought suffering and hardship. Some took the only course of action they felt would help them. They wrote to President Davis, to congressmen, and to state, county, and city officials. In these letters they asked that something be done to bring relief to them. The desks of the members of the Confederate Congress, as well as those of the state legislatures, were piled high with petitions, suggestions, and pleas from citizens of the Confederacy. Early in the war these evidences of discontent were largely ignored, for the individual problems of the civilian seemed minute in comparison with the military, diplomatic, and governmental problems of the young nation. Nor did the Confederate government ever become very sympathetic or helpful in solving the problem of shortages on the homefront. Most of what was accomplished was done through the channels of state legislation, gubernatorial proclamations, and city ordinances.

President Jefferson Davis, was disturbed from time to time about the feeding, clothing, and housing of the noncombatants, but he never took any positive stand on any definite program. Like most citizens, his outlook early in the war tended to be one of false optimism, which, in turn, affected the attitudes of the people. In his address to Congress in July, 1861, he was very optimistic about the production of food, a subject that was always dear to him. At that time he announced that the supply was adequate for "two years consumption."[1] In the following November he sounded another optimistic note as he referred to the abundant yields of summer and fall.[2] It was not long, however, before he realized his false optimism and misinformation, for it soon became evident that the harvest of 1861 was not sufficient for "two years consumption." By

33

early spring, 1863, he was forced to make a plea for the greater production of crops. In addressing the people of the Confederate States on April 10, 1863, he admitted that an overconfident attitude had been assumed by most people early in the war, and that, unless food crops and livestock were immediately substituted for cotton and tobacco, "the consequences . . . [might] prove serious if not disastrous." He further urged that the "fields be devoted exclusively to the production of corn, oats, beans, peas, potatoes, and other food for men and beast."[3] He praised state action that partially prohibited the growing of cotton and encouraged food crops,[4] and from 1863 until the end of the war his attitude was one of grave concern over the supply. Usually, however, this worry revolved around the subsistence of the army rather than the civilians.[5]

President Davis was interested in the general subject of transportation, so vitally connected with that of supply, but he was mainly concerned with the conveyance of supplies to the army. Early in the war, he delivered an address in which he expressed hope that these supplies could be furnished the army in such a manner "as not to interrupt the commercial intercourse between . . . [the] people"[6] but as transportation facilities began to show signs of breaking, this became an impossibility. He urged that corn and other food crops be planted near the railroads, rivers, and canals, thus simplifying the problem of carrying these commodities to the battlefronts. In the same speech, he urged that something be done about the roads of the Confederacy, for he recognized that they were affecting the passage of supplies.[7] He condemned speculation as a "gigantic evil."[8] He gave support to the impressment policy of the Confederate government, hoping that it would put an end to speculation, extortion, and hoarding.[9] He encouraged more extensive industrialization in the South.[10] In an address to the Confederate Congress in January, 1863, he noted that "Cotton and woolen fabrics, shoes and harnesses, wagons and gun carriages are produced in daily increasing quantities by the factories springing into existence," while at the same time "the noise of the loom and spinning wheel may be heard throughout the land."[11] His distress over the importation of luxuries in times of want had an effect on Congress and was partially responsible for legislation on the subject.[12]

Davis was often criticized for his dictatorial attitude, but this spirit was not evident when he dealt with matters on the home-front. The specific problem of shortages there interested him but slightly. Although he spoke of them and made a few mild suggestions for reform, he did virtually nothing to alleviate the situation. It was because of this apparent lack of concern at a time when part of the civilian population was actually suffering, and most were sorely inconvenienced, that one diarist wrote that the situation could be eased if the Confederacy had a "Roman dictator."[13]

The Confederate Congress only indirectly helped to relieve the suffering caused by the shortages at home. With few exceptions, its legislative program was drawn up and administered with only the idea of successful defense and the hope of victory on the battlefield. Civilian problems arising from the shortages were never completely solved by either the Confederate or state governmental agencies, but the latter came nearer to a solution than the former.

Although the southern states had opposed the protective tariff of the United States, the Confederacy found it necessary to establish a revenue tariff. One of the first acts passed by the Provisional Congress, in February, 1861, related to this tariff. The measure included a long list of agricultural products, munitions, and materials of war that were to be admitted duty free. It did not attempt to throttle the ingress of such items, but rather, encouraged importation.[14] To this original law were added various adjustments from time to time, but only a few bore directly upon the problem of shortages. On March 15, 1861, an ad valorem duty of fifteen per cent was imposed on all imported "coal, cheese, iron in blooms, pig iron, bars, bolts and slabs . . . on all iron in a less manufactured state; . . . on all railroad rails, spikes, . . . papers of all sorts . . . [and] wood."[15] Every one of these items became scarce in the Confederacy.

One of the first major shortages to become apparent was that of building material for railroads. The construction of the line from Selma, Alabama, to Meridian, Mississippi, was brought to a halt because of the lack of iron. Congress, therefore, remitted the duty on all iron imported for the specific purpose of completing this railroad.[16] In the late winter of 1863, the shortage of machinery for the manufacturing of clothing became apparent; the clothing situation became so grave that a law was enacted whereby "all machinery for the manufacture of cotton, or wool, or necessary for carrying on any of the mechanic arts . . . be admitted free of duty until the ratification of peace between the Confederate States and the United States."[17] In 1864 the transportation problem became even graver than it had been two years previously, and Congress passed a law declaring that "all machinery and materials needed and in any wise necessary for the construction, equipment and operation of railroads, imported by any railroad company for its own use, and engines, cars, and other rolling stock for use upon any railroad, be admitted free of duty during the existing war."[18] These few concessions to the shortage problem were all that Congress made in the tariff policy, and they were of such nature as to do little to relieve the situation. Machinery and railroad equipment were too heavy to be imported in quantity by the blockade-runners. The effectiveness of the blockade led the Confederate Congress to enact a law whereby vessels could unload their cargoes anywhere on the Confederate coast, rather than in designated ports only.[19] Whereas there was a relation between the government's tariff policy and shortages, it is doubtful that the latter was a result of the policy to any great extent, and yet the failure definitely to encourage much-needed importations might be a point of criticism. During the first eighteen months of the war, the rates on many necessary items were prohibitive. Gradually the policy became less restrictive and after 1863 some schedules were eased, but by that time the blockade prevented importation of those same commodities.

Such things as silks, satins, laces, jewels, cigars, and liquors always had a ready market in the South even in the war years, but in February, 1864, Congress prohibited the importation of these items as well as canned foods and other articles considered luxuries.[20] Four months later, however, that part of the act prohibiting importation of "prepared vegetables, fruits, meats, poultry and game, sealed or inclosed in cans or otherwise, and brooms and brushes of all kinds" was repealed.[21] These laws regulating the importation of luxuries unfortunately came late in the war, and were not very effective. The damage had already been done.

The Confederate government, in the spring of 1863, passed a law to regulate impressment, hoping by so-doing that speculation might be done away with and that the armed forces might be better fed. But the policy of impressment affected the speculators only slightly, and failed to solve the problem of feeding the army. On the other hand, it created discontent among the civilian population and was a chief cause of shortages in certain areas of the Confederacy. Under the act of March 26, 1863, the seizure of forage and all articles needed for the subsistence of the army was to be made by officers appointed for each state. Appraisement of the impressed commodities was to be made by a committee of two "disinterested persons," one chosen by the owner of the goods, the other by the impressing officer. A certificate of payment was to be given the owner. Another clause of the law, very odious to many people, gave to the Secretary of War the authority to take private property for public use, making compensation for such seizures.[22] Although discontent was widespread, the government found it absolutely necessary to continue the policy throughout the remainder of the war. Its enforcement became more severe with each passing month, but protests against and disobedience of the law became more general. Foodstuffs, taken in wholesale quantities, horses, mules, and wagons were seized. The original law was amended in 1864 and 1865. The amendment of March, 1865, declared it unlawful to impress "sheep, milch cows, brood mares, stallions, jacks, bulls, breeding hogs or other stock . . . necessary for raising sheep, hogs, horses, mules or cattle." The act also declared that the market price was the "just price."[23] Many farmers refused to sell at this price when inflation was running wild. So fearful were some that their produce would be seized that they refused to bring it to market. Thus a shortage was created in two ways by the impressment policy of the government: first, it removed from civilian consumption many things needed at home; and, second, it created false shortages because people refused to make their produce accessible, through fear of seizure.

Closely akin to the impressment policy of the Confederate government was the "tax-in-kind," or "tithe law," as it was sometimes called. The law was approved by the Congress on April 24, 1863, and it went into immediate effect.[24] It required the payment of one-tenth of all farm produce that could be transported over long distances.[25] There were certain exemptions from this sweeping tax law, but they affected only the very poor, the disabled servicemen who were not "worth more than $1,000," and the widows of men who had lost their lives in the war, who were not "worth more than $1,000."[26] The agents in charge of collecting the "tax-in-kind" were often as disagreeable as impressment agents. Their arrogance was sometimes unbearable. In many areas resentment to this enactment was widespread but it was especially so in western North Carolina. Meetings were held in August and September, 1863, in these mountain counties, and resolutions were passed condemning the hated "tithing law." Some of the resolutions suggested that the government take the money instead of produce, and others insisted that such a tax could not be borne in either money or produce. One set of the resolutions declared, that the tithing law was "not only unconstitutional, anti-republican, and oppressive, but unnecessary—unnecessary, for the simple fact that if the Confederacy will furnish the people with a sound currency, the government will at all times be able to purchase such supplies . . . , provided the people have them to spare."[27] A large number of mountain farmers absolutely refused to pay the tithe.[28] In December, 1863, the "tax-in-kind" on sweet potatoes was withdrawn in lieu of money payment, but otherwise the detested law remained in force, and much food was drained from an already hungry civilian population. The same areas suffered seizure of provisions over and over again. Those areas near a railroad, river, canal, or the front were most frequently plagued with impressment and tithing agents. These laws had little effect on some areas, but they bore heavily on others. They aggravated the problem of shortages in the regions that were more accessible, but hardly affected the more remote sections.

The Confederate government made some attempts to encourage manufacturing but, in this instance as in others, the primary motive behind such encouragement was the furnishing of the army. Cotton cards, which were always needed in the Confederacy, as well as machinery and materials for clothing, were admitted free of duties, provided they were used "for increasing the manufacture of clothing for the army."[29] The appalling shortage of shoes in the army caused Congress to authorize the Quartermaster-General "to detail from the Army persons skilled in the manufacture of shoes . . . and employ them diligently in the manufacture of shoes for the Army,"[30] but nothing was done by the Confederate government to help solve the shoe problem among civilians. The central government took under contract many of the factories of the South, thus absorbing their entire output for the use of the armed forces. Civilians found it difficult to pro-

cure the products of these factories. For example, Mrs. Cornelia
McDonald, a refugee in western Virginia, wanted to get some
wool carded, but she found that it "could be carded at no factory
in the neighborhood except by consent of the authorities, as the
government had all the factories in its employ."[31] If civilians
desired anything made, it was fairly safe to assume that they would
have it made at home, not in the factories controlled by the government.

The Confederate government encouraged ingenuity and made
an overall contribution to the Confederacy by setting up the
Patent Office, on May 21, 1861. Rufus R. Rhodes was appointed
Commissioner of Patents.[32] Annual reports were made to Congress by the Commissioner. These reports gave a résumé of the
business of the office and listed all patents granted during the
current year. Hundreds of patents were issued to the people of
the Confederacy. About one-third were for war equipment, while
the other two-thirds were mostly for agricultural inventions, such
as a cotton cleaner, ploughs, hoes, seed-planters, compounds for
expelling insects, hullers, and churns. Patents were also issued
for miscellaneous items, including sewing machines, leather-tan-
ning processes, fire tongs, looms, soaps, and wooden soled shoes.[33]
The Patent Office encouraged inventions, both military and non-
military, and no partiality was shown the former.

At various times during the war, several suggestions were made
to Congress for the relief of shortages on the homefront. The few
of these reaching the floor of this body were discussed and debated,
but none were enacted into law. Among the suggestions frequently made was one involving the production of food crops instead
of cotton. Many citizens thought that Congress should legislate
on the subject. A bill curtailing cotton production was discussed
in the Senate in the spring of 1862. It provided that cotton production should be limited to three bales of cotton for each planter
and one bale for each hand employed. A fine would be imposed
on anyone breaking the law. This bill, however, was rejected by
a vote of eleven to eight.[34] Several weeks later, Congress passed
a resolution which stressed the possibility of a long war and recommended that the people should "direct their agricultural labor
mainly to the production of such crops as will insure a sufficiency of
food . . . for every emergency." It also suggested that the President issue a proclamation urging the necessity "of guarding against

the great perils of a short crop of provisions."[35] A second measure suggested to the Confederate government at various times, dealt with the making of alcoholic beverages from grains. Many people wanted a stringent law passed that would prohibit such distillation for the duration of the war. However, this remedy was left to state action. One authority has given as the reason for the "hands-off" policy of the Confederate government the idea of state rights that was so deeply imbedded in the thinking of the Confederate leaders and people.[36] The Confederate government aroused much indignation and brought down on its head the wrath of many when it continued to manufacture alcohol and liquor for use in hospitals and in the army. This was carried on in laboratories over the South during the entire war, but it was specifically legalized in the early summer of 1864.[37] Although provisions were inserted in the law to prevent liquor from being diverted into any but lawful channels, the attempt proved unsuccessful. Many civilians who were hungry for bread resented the fact that grain was being made into alcohol.

A third problem often discussed by governmental leaders was that of speculation. Although the War Department carried on extensive correspondence and received many suggestions for the solution to the problem, little was done. It was hoped that the impressment policy would ease the situation, but it failed to do so. In December, 1863, "a bill to prevent speculation, hoarding and extortion . . . [was] referred to the Committee on Judiciary" in the Senate. On January 5, 1864, this bill was reported back from the committee by Senator Benjamin H. Hill of Georgia. The committee announced its opposition to the bill, and on January 19, it was tabled and nothing further was done about it.[38] It was suggested that Congress put into effect some form of price-fixing, but nothing was done except in towns where martial law was declared. The War Department occasionally tried to enforce a form of price-fixing, but it was never satisfactory.

Congress was often criticized by the civilians for the course it took in regard to shortages. Newspapers carried scorching editorials; news items, diaries, and letters were filled with denunciations; and orators often rebuked the government for its do-nothing policy. An editor of a Columbia, South Carolina, newspaper asked the people to call on the Lord for help, since none could be had from "our rulers."[39] The inveterate critic, J. B. Jones, lashed out against governmental inefficiency. One of his most stinging charges was made against government contractors;[40] when things were at their worst and Congress still remained complacent, he called for martial law "everywhere in the Confederacy." In late November, 1863, he bitterly criticized the policy of impressment and the unfair administration of the law.[41] He always became irate when he heard of waste, for he was dependent upon the salary of a government clerk and saw this pitiful stipend shrink until he could scarcely feed his family. In the fall of 1863 he heard that forty thousand bushels of sweet potatoes, taken as tithes by the government, were rotting in warehouses, "between Richmond and Wilmington." He saw hunger around him every day and it was hard to take such news as this calmly. He confided to his diary that "a lethargy had seized the government, and no-one may foretell the consequences of official supineness."[42] Another critic of the government wrote that the lack of a forceful policy by the government brought about a "dimunition of supplies to the point of starvation. It was a policy of blunders; it lacked some steady and deliberate system; and, it . . . got to that point where the whole system of Confederate defense was bound to break down by the want of subsistence, even without a catastrophe of arms."[43]

Critical though the people were of Congress and the governmental policy in general, it was the War Department that was most frequently the object of vituperative attack. The primary object of this department was to win the war, consequently it was forced into a strong, domineering position. Fighting off the enemy as it was, it could not and did not stand on ceremony. It had little time or inclination to think of legal aspects, the feeling of the people, or the repercussion of its action, when the enemy was at the door. The War Department, responsible for administering the impressment program, and for feeding and equipping the army, frequently aroused the animosity of the people. It seemed, even to the most passive civilians, to creep into their daily lives and into their family circles. Thousands of letters of complaint were sent to the Secretary of War and preserved in his letter-books. One, written to Secretary Seddon by a group of Georgia citizens, expressed resentment at having their corn impressed to be used in government distilleries. These Georgians wrote that they were in want of bread. To this letter Seddon replied, "The whiskey must be distilled somewhere, and nowhere

can corn be found more abundantly."[44] Such answers did little
to appease the people. Much of the corn paid to the government
as tithe was weevil-infested and, according to Major J. F. Cummings, Commissary of Subsistence in Georgia, it was this corn that
was being distilled.[45] This information was not generally circulated nor was it believed by those who heard it, and criticism continued. The War Department did prohibit officers, contractors,
and agents of the government from feeding wheat to their horses,
and it forbade the impressment of food collected by the county
and district agents for the use of the poor.[46] The War Department was harsh, dictatorial, and at times unreasonable, but it
had its difficulties, too. The price of any article was considerably
enhanced if it became known that the purchasers were government
agents. Consequently, the government attempted to conceal its
purchase.[47] So unpopular were impressment officers and tax-
collectors that the people, when dubious as to whom a stranger
was, were said to "receive him like a tax-collector."[48]

One of the problems that gave concern to the War Department
late in the war shows something of the conditions on the homefront. The soldiers often found it profitable to sell their clothing
and food to civilians. There were those who had a surplus or
who felt that they could get more at the nearest Quartermaster's
Depot. The people on the homefront would pay them well, or
exchange some desired commodity with them. The practice was
extensive, and General Samuel Cooper, in September, 1864, issued an order making it an offense for a private or non-commis-
sioned officer to sell his rations.[49] In March, 1865, General Cooper
issued another order reminding both the soldiers and the civilians
of an act of Congress passed in January, 1864, stating that "any
person not subject to the Rules and Articles of War who shall
purchase . . . from any soldier or person enrolled in the service
any portion of his clothing . . . or any property belonging to the
Confederate States, shall, upon conviction . . . be fined not exceed-
ing $1000 and be imprisoned not exceeding two years."[50]

It might be asked why it was that the Confederate Congress
failed to legislate for the benefit of the people as a whole. There
are several explanations. The winning of the war was the all important single goal of the government, and, whatever the cost
might be to the civilians, it was for their best interests in the
long run. Consequently, the welfare of the civilians was secondary

to the war effort. As the war went from bad to worse, and the Confederacy was gradually overrun, only those things of prime importance could be dealt with by the leaders. There never seemed time to consider civilian problems. A second explanation strikes more deeply, touching the very core of the ideology of the southern people. The people had become convinced that such matters as economic legislation should be left to the states, which were the direct agents of the people. One authority stressed the importance of the principle of state rights in the government of the Confederacy.[51] Believing everything not specifically included in the Constitution to be unconstitutional, and the government to be one of delegated powers, the people threw tremendous obstacles in the path of Congress, making it practically impossible for this body to legislate on the many and diverse homefront problems. A third explanation lay in the fact that the Confederacy was a newly organized nation faced with tremendous problems. The machinery of the government had to be started and kept rolling. A place among nations had to be found. A spirit of indifference and animosity within the Confederacy had to be overcome. A war had to be won. These problems would have been tremendous in time of peace, but they proved insurmountable in time of war. For these reasons the Confederate government was unable to relieve the homefront to the extent that might normally have been expected. Remedial legislation affecting this area was left to the states, and they went much further in the attempted solution than did the Confederate government.

The governors of the various states were most sympathetic to the needs of the people. Being nearer to the scene of want and privation, they led the movement to alleviate shortages and to feed and clothe their constituents. All the southern governors spoke and wrote of the problems arising from the shortage of food, clothing, and transportation. All concerned themselves, with varying degrees of energy, with the solutions of these problems. All showed themselves to be interested in the people of their states, but none was as belligerent in tone and aggressive in action as Zebulon Baird Vance of North Carolina and Joseph Emerson Brown of Georgia. These outspoken leaders were constantly sparring with the Confederate officials. They took matters in their own hands and steered a clear-cut path for their people.

Governor Vance determined to remedy the effects of the short-ages by running the blockade and bringing into North Carolina much needed commodities. The state owned runner, *Ad-Vance,* became famous for the cargoes it brought safely into port. In his message to the General Assembly on November 25, 1863, Governor Vance reported that the running of the blockade had "proven a complete success." Such things as leather, shoes, lubricating oils, iron, tin, medicines, dye-stuffs, blankets, cotton bagging and rope, spirits, coffee, as well as arms and ammunition had been imported.[52] Governor Vance interested himself, too, in the problem of specu-lation, for he was conscious of the effects of this evil on the people of his state, civilian and military. In the fall of 1862 he expressed his consternation over rapidly increasing prices of the necessities of life. Writing to Weldon N. Edwards of Ridgeway, North Carolina, he said, "It is a subject that distresses me beyond measure, the more as I feel powerless to remedy any of its evils." He urged the convening of the Assembly to help solve the prob-lem.[53] When the Assembly did convene, he addressed that body on November 17, 1862, saying, "Next to the defense of the State from the enemy in importance is the defense of our people against extortion and starvation." He told the legislators that "Flour . . . can now be used only by the rich," and clothing was both scarce and high. He was concerned about those speculators who came from without the state, and he urged the Assembly to prevent ex-portation of rare or much needed items from the state. He called for the establishment of depots at various points in the state where food could be stored and sold to the poor at cost.[54] The legisla-ture, five days later, by joint resolution, authorized the governor to lay an embargo upon articles of prime necessity and to prevent their being exported from the state, except in certain specified cases. Governor Vance immediately issued a proclamation for-bidding such exportation. He also wrote Confederate officials, notably the Secretary of War, reprimanding governmental agents for engaging in speculation.[55]

Governor Vance also took a firm stand against the use of grain for the distillation of liquor. He asked the General Assembly to prohibit such distillation, for he felt it was "much better for the soldier to go without spirits than his wife and child to go without bread."[56] He constantly contested the right of the Confederate government to build distilleries and impress grain for the purpose of distillation within North Carolina; and weighty correspondence was carried on between Governor Vance and the Confederate officials over the issue.[57] As late as February, 1865, he was still vehemently contesting the right of the Confederate government to use grain in the making of liquor in North Carolina.[58] He urged citizens of his state to see that the law forbidding distillation was enforced.[59]

Governor Vance was also interested in helping the poor, especially the families of soldiers. He realized that there was acute suffering among many of this group. Legislation regarding aid to the poor in North Carolina came partially as a result of his requests. "Granaries were established at certain points in the State, and corn was distributed to the most needy districts" largely because of the interest the Governor had in the "common folk" of the state.[60]

Governor Brown of Georgia was even more critical of the Confederate government's policies than was Governor Vance. He wrote a large number of letters to the Secretary of War and to other officials, who seemed to him to be encroaching upon the rights of the state of Georgia. He watched after the welfare of the Georgians and tried to keep them adequately clothed and fed. Whenever the policies of the Confederate government cut across his plans, he protested in the strongest terms. He was particularly bitter about the impressment policy of the central government. He predicted rebellion in certain areas of Georgia unless impressment ceased, and he wrote President Davis that if the poor continued to suffer as a result of this program, soldiers would desert the army and "go to the relief of their suffering families." He frequently criticized the impressment officers, making clear his contempt for them.[61]

Like others, Governor Brown was greatly concerned over the distillation of spirits. In the early spring of 1862, he "issued a proclamation commanding every distiller in the State to cease manufacturing ardent spirits after the 15th of March . . . under penalty of seizure of property thus employed."[62] Furthermore, he carried on an extensive correspondence with the Confederate government about the use of tithe corn in the distilling of liquors. In a letter of February 6, 1864, to Major J. F. Cummings, he wrote that if the Confederate government could thus use tithe corn, "it might impress the bread . . . [from] the mouths of the wives and children of soldiers." He added that "the demand for bread is much greater" than that for liquor. In the same letter he told of a trip through upper, middle, and southwestern Georgia, where "the prospects of suffering for bread . . . were alarming."[63]

The governors of other Confederate states were also greatly concerned about the welfare of their constituents. They made appeals to their respective legislatures to do something about speculation, extortion, transportation, and distillation. They carried on a system of state blockade-running when this was possible, and all governers favored aid for the indigent families of the servicemen. Many wanted some sort of crop control, but Governor John Milton of Florida opposed such legislation. He doubted whether or not it was constitutionally possible to legislate on this subject. He believed that "reliance must be placed on the good sense and patriotism of the people."[64] Even though the governors protested the impressment policy of the government and criticized the officials, there were instances when they favored a form of impressment if it meant proper distribution of scarce items. Governor John J. Pettus of Mississippi caused to have written a letter to General John C. Pemberton, offering to seize the corn that had been bought by the distillers, if such corn was needed by the army.[65] The governors were often driven to impress items for the use of the state troops. Governor John Gill Shorter of Alabama seized leather for the use of the Alabama soldiers.[66] State impressment sometimes created shortages of certain commodities, but such action was not general and it was not as odious to the people as Confederate impressment.

Whatever might be said in criticism or praise, the governors of the Confederate states tried to help the rank and file of the people as they experienced the inconveniences and sufferings of wartime living. Much of the remedial legislation enacted by the states was first outlined by the governors, for it was the governor to whom the people turned in their time of need. Thousands of letters reached the desks of the governors, and hundreds of editorials were addressd to them. Committees of people met together to discuss their trials and tribulations, and they frequently addressed complaints and suggestions to their governors. Out of these letters, editorials, and public meetings, the governors formulated their ideas, plans, and appeals. These they submitted to their legislatures.

It was in the halls of the state legislatures that the laws were born that were to aid in the solving of many civilian problems. What was done by the legislatures was diverse and varied. There was only one law affecting in any way the problem of scarcity passed by all eleven of the Confederate states. That was the law to aid destitute families of men in the service. Prohibition of the distillation of liquors was passed by ten of the states, and it was requested in the eleventh.[67] Other laws were passed by a number of states. Georgia passed more laws and resolutions that might be listed as in some way alleviating shortages than did any other state. Ten different categories of such laws were enacted by the Georgia General Assembly. Alabama followed close behind with nine, Florida with eight, and North Carolina with seven. Tennessee enacted fewer than any other state; this may be explained by the fact that the state was early overrun by Federal troops.

All states passed laws giving assistance of various kinds to the families of soldiers. Alabama, the first state to act, passed such a law on November 29, 1861. This act did not set up any new fund from which money was to be used for care of the poor; it merely authorized court and county commissioners to use any part of the funds then in the county treasury for the relief of indigent families of soldiers.[68] Mississippi and Florida were not far behind Alabama in passing similar legislation. Florida's bill, approved December 13, 1861, called for a tax of fifty per cent on the state tax, to be collected and distributed by the counties.[69] Mississippi's bill, approved December 16, 1861, called for a special tax of thirty per cent upon the regular state taxes, to be levied each year of the war and to be called a "Relief Fund." It was to be apportioned and collected through the county agencies.[70] An act calling for a percentage tax was passed in South Carolina, which incidentally, was the last state to begin such a program.[71] Georgia, Tennessee, Louisiana, and Texas appropriated various sums of money to be used to defray the expenses of their relief programs. These appropriations ranged from $450,000 in Tennessee to $5,000,000 in Louisiana.[72] In Virginia, North Carolina, and Arkansas, no mention was made of any tax percentage or fixed sum. Rather, the laws were couched in such general terms as "an allowance,"[73] "some provision,"[74] or "sufficient tax."[75] After these first enactments, the states enlarged their appropriations. North Carolina, Georgia, Virginia, Florida, Texas, and Tennessee made annual money grants, while other states raised theirs by taxes, both money and produce taxes. As unsatisfactory as were impressment and the tax-in-kind, when administered by the Confederate government, several states resorted to both these means of relieving the poor. Mississippi permitted a part of the tax levied for the poor to be paid in kind,[76] and also ordered impressment of surplus provisions, these to be used for the needy. The law ordering such seizures stated that if the county commissioners could not find such provisions in their own county, they might go into another county, make application for surplus provisions and impress these.[77] Tax-in-kind as payment of relief taxes became fairly universal. Food, clothing, medicine, and transportation facilities were all impressed, bought, or taxed-in-kind or otherwise to help the poor families. The collection and distribution of the money and commodities were relegated to the county government. Usually appointed commissioners or county courts took charge of the problem, and there was a sincere effort expended in every state for the relief of families, who found that because of war conditions they were unable to support themselves.

Ten states of the Confederacy passed some sort of legislation prohibiting the distillation of liquor. Cut off from the foreign source of supply by the blockade, the southern people were forced to do without their intoxicating beverages or to resort to domestic products which had long been familiar to the poorer people and those in remote areas. These domestic products were distilled chiefly from corn, but other grains and fruits were also used. At a time when the grain was more than ever needed for bread, distillation was increasing. To put a stop to this, the states enacted laws forbidding distillation, making it an offense for which various punishments were provided. The first laws generally prohibited the use of such grains as corn, wheat, rye, and barley. But as the war progressed and the people proved themselves ingenious at finding substitutes, laws prohibiting the use of other items were enacted. In addition to grains, Louisiana and Mississippi prohibited the use of sugar, molasses, and cane juice;[78] Virginia, Florida, and Alabama added fruits and vegetables to these items.[79] Georgia added to her prohibitive list "honey, sweet potatoes, pumpkins, peas, and Irish potatoes,"[80] while North Carolina found it necessary to restrict the use of all the above items, as well as oats, peanuts, seed of sugar cane, and "any mixture of any or either of them";[81] later buckwheat was also added to this list.[82] Penalties for disobeying the laws varied from state to state and from time to time. In practically all states, punishment consisted of both fine and imprisonment. The fines and imprisonment clauses varied, however. In Virginia the fine ranged from $100 to $5,000.[83] Arkansas and North Carolina set their minimum fine at $500.[84] In Louisiana anyone caught distilling the products prohibited by law might have to pay a fine amounting to $15,000.[85] The length of imprisonment also varied. Always the term must be served in the county jail, or, in the case of Louisiana, in the parish jail. Most bills merely called for imprisonment of not more than twelve months, but in South Carolina, one might have to serve twenty-four months.[86] In Texas there was no mention of imprisonment, and in Arkansas, the minimum sentence was one month.[87]

Although these laws prohibiting distillation met with only partial success, the seriousness with which the legislatures approached the problem and outlined their program is evident in the many and unusual measures incorporated in the bills. Several states included in their enactments specifications that the person informing the state government that distillation was taking place would be rewarded. The amounts paid the informer varied. For example, in Louisiana and Alabama[88] one-half of the fine collected was paid, while in South Carolina the flat sum of $250 was set as the reward.[89] Officers who refused to bring a suspected person to trial were subject to fine and imprisonment in Florida.[90] The state of Texas not only punished those who made alcoholic beverages, but placed a graduated income tax on any person selling "any distilled spirit, fermented liquor or wine." These taxes were based on the amount sold.[91] In Virginia and Georgia all stills were forfeited to the state when a person was convicted.[92] In an effort to prevent distillation of illegal alcohol and liquor and at the same time permit their being made for hospital use, Virginia, Mississippi, South Carolina, Georgia, Florida, and Alabama excepted the distillation of these items when they were to be used in hospitals or as medicine, but rigid systems of licenses were es-

tablished in these states.[93]   The passage of these laws is evidence
that many were concerned with the shortage of bread; but despite the laws, distillation continued.   It was never stopped, but
manufacture of alcoholic beverages was checked.

A third program entered into by several states was that of
crop control.   This was one of the most widely discussed topics
of the day.   The aim of the state program was to restrict the
planting of cotton and tobacco and encourage the production
of food crops.   The first state to legislate on the matter was Arkansas.   On March 21, 1862, a bill was approved that made it
illegal for anyone "to plant or cultivate more than two acres"
of land in cotton for every hand over fourteen years of age that
was used on the farm or plantation.   A fine of not less than $500
nor more than $5,000, with imprisonment until the fine and costs
were paid, was the penalty for illegal planting.[94]   Three other
states legislated on the subject: Georgia, South Carolina, and
Florida.   Florida permitted the planting of one acre for every
hand between fifteen and sixty years of age with a fine of $1,000
for each acre planted over the legal amount.   But any excess cotton grown was exempt if manufactured on the place.   By the
same law, one-fourth an acre of tobacco per hand was permitted
to the planter.[95]   Both Georgia and South Carolina allowed three
acres of cotton for each hand between the ages of fifteen and
fifty-five.   Both set a fine of $500 for each acre planted over the
legal amount.[96]   Georgia, Florida, and South Carolina allowed
payment of one-half of the fine to the person who had informed
the state officials of the illegal planting.[97]   Even in those states
where crop control never reached the point of legislation, there
was much discussion of the problem, and many felt that such
legislation would help to alleviate the food shortage.

A program aimed at protecting the resources of a state for the
use of the citizens of that state was responsible for legislation
prohibiting the exportation of provisions beyond the bounds of
the state.   Florida was first to enact such a law.   On November
28, 1861, the exportation of meats, corn-meal or corn, salt, "or
provisions of any kind" beyond the limits of Florida, "except for
the use of the State of Florida or the Confederate States," was
prohibited.   The penalty for disobedience was $1,000, one half
of which was to go to the informer, and imprisonment of not more
than twelve months.[98]   The North Carolina General Assembly re-

solved, on November 22, 1862, that the governor be authorized to lay an "immediate embargo on all articles of clothing, wool, shoes, leather, cloth of any kind, cotton yarns, . . . wheat, flour, meal, . . . salt and meat." The exception was the same as the Florida law.[99] South Carolina and Alabama also passed similar legislation on the subject of exportation of food.[100]

Two states, Florida and North Carolina, passed acts regulating the use of farm animals. In Florida, the milking, penning, or separating of calves and cows belonging to another person was made illegal. The only exception was that one might first get the permission of the owner.[101] North Carolina attempted to protect cattle by imposing penalties on those owners who refused to erect fences. The poisoning of cattle was also specifically forbidden.[102]

Every Confederate state encouraged the establishment of factories within the respective state. Hundreds of corporations received their charters from the state legislatures during the war; few seem to have gone into operation, but this was largely due to shortages caused by the blockade. It was hoped that these manufacturing enterprises would help to alleviate the shortages. One of the scarcest items, and at the same time one of the most needed, was cotton cards. More than in the years before the war, the people were making their own yarn and cloth, and the shortage of cards was keenly felt. In an effort to help the people, eight of the Confederate states saw fit to legislate on the subject. These states were Louisiana, Virginia, Mississippi, Georgia, Florida, Arkansas, Alabama, and North Carolina.[103] In all of these states, money was appropriated to import cards through the blockade or from other southern states, or to set up machinery and encourage manufacture of cards within the states. Mississippi and Alabama encouraged their manufacture by providing a bonus to all who undertook the venture.[104] Cotton cloth and yarn were sorely needed in the Confederacy, and Virginia and Georgia sought to stimulate their production. Virginia passed a law in the spring of 1864 making it an offense for any factory in the state to refuse to manufacture raw cotton into yarn and cloth for the state. The fine for such an offense was $5,000. The yarn and cloth manufactured were to be deposited in Richmond and distributed at cost, direct to the needy.[105] The Georgia General Assembly appropriated various sums annually for the manufacture of cloth as well as cards. These items were made in the state penitentiary, as well as in factories privately owned, and were sold at cost.[106] Texas approached the problem of stimulating manufactures in a unique manner. Like Georgia, it utilized the labor of the state penitentiary,[107] but it went a step further than any other state in encouraging the establishment of manufacturing enterprises. It offered land grants to "any person, company or corporation, who shall erect and put into operation by March 1, 1865, new and efficient machinery for the manufacture of iron from ore, or the manufacture of cotton or wool into thread, or for the manufacture of fire arms, nitre, sulphur, powder, salt, cotton or woolen cards and spinning jennies, or paper and oil." The land grant would consist of three hundred and twenty acres of land for every thousand dollars worth of machinery so erected.[108] The states continued to encourage, in various ways, the establishment of industries throughout the war. It was the hope of the states that in this way shortages of manufactured goods might be eliminated.

Another problem, interwoven with that of shortages, was speculation. The Confederate government failed to handle this problem, although it was discussed in Congress. The attempt at a solution, therefore, rested with the states, and Georgia, Florida, Alabama, North Carolina, South Carolina, and Texas legislated on the subject.[109] These laws had teeth in them, yet it is common knowledge that speculation was never eliminated in the Confederacy. The laws were not cures but palliatives. In handling the problem, the legislators were not content merely to outlaw speculation in broad terms, they went so far as to list items in the bills. Georgia, for example, prohibited speculating in "clothing, shoes, leather, cloth of any kind, provisions, wheat, flour, corn, corn-meal, meat, bacon, hogs, cattle, salt, bagging, rope, and twine."[110] Florida worded her law in almost the same language, but added to the list "syrup, sugar or molasses."[111] North Carolina included in her law fish, cheese, coffee, tea, and saltpetre.[112] South Carolina added drugs, medicine, nails, hardware, gold, silver, wood, candles, and soap.[113] Texas included horses, wagons, and ambulances.[114] Since speculators usually disposed of their commodities at public auction, selling at auction was made illegal in Alabama.[115] To read the lists of items in these antispeculation bills is to get a fairly complete list of shortages. And the fact that many of the states legislated on the subject so early in the war gives evidence of the fact that shortages early appeared. All states legislating on speculation punished offenders with fine and imprisonment.

In an effort to get possession of needed articles held by the speculators, Georgia, Alabama, and Mississippi passed laws and resolutions authorizing the governors of these states or their agents to seize the needed items.[116] Yet these same states, and others, protested the impressment policy of the Confederate government. They were especially critical of the impressment officers, many of whom were arrogant and unfair. Seizure was unequal and some areas were left with a sufficiency while others lacked the essentials of life. In an effort to remedy this discrimination, Georgia, Alabama, and Mississippi legislated on the subject. Eight states officially lodged complaints against the central government.[117]

IV

FOOD AND DRINK

THE FOOD SHORTAGE WAS MORE KEENLY FELT BY A VAST MAJORITY of Confederates, both civil and military, than any other. The problem of sustaining the army and the civilian population proved to be a major task for both the leaders and the "common man." For one thing, the shortage of labor presented a grave problem. Many men from the farm joined the armed forces during the war. At the same time, acreage was cut as the farmland became battlefields. These factors made the problem of food production a serious one. Even when an abundance of produce was raised, the breakdown of transportation prevented its being sent to needy areas. The result was hunger and near starvation in some parts of the Confederacy, while in all sections substitutes were forced upon the people by the absolute inability to get certain commodities, such as coffee, tea, and salt.

Contemporary letters, diaries, and newspapers contain frequent reference to the food shortage. A few mention abundance of food in one section or another, but that was unusual. The rank and file seem to have felt the pinch of the times. While one family might have plenty to eat, next door there might be hunger. Such was the case in the Virginia village where Mrs. Cornelia McDonald lived during a part of the war. While she was forced to live upon the simple fare of bread and water, there were those in her neighborhood who could dine sumptuously.[1] Miss Constance Cary, later Mrs. Burton Harrison, wrote that she could not remember getting up from a single meal while she was in Richmond in 1864-1865 "without wishing there were more of it,"[2] while another young lady, who chanced to be visiting on a Virginia plantation that had been untouched by the war, found delicacies in bounteous quantities.[3] Although there were some who managed to have a sufficiency, there were others in the South who regularly

55

felt the pangs of hunger. One writer declared that "the Confederacy was always hungry."[4]

There was nearly always a food shortage in certain areas. Those near the battle lines were most often swept clean of all food. Foragers from both Confederate and Federal armies preyed upon the land. That section of Virginia, which was a battleground for four years, saw the food problem daily becoming more acute. Here the battle against starvation was fought during the entire war.[5] In other areas, the armies swept across the land at varying times, leaving hunger in their paths. Such a destructive march was that of General Sherman's army across Georgia and thence northward into the Carolinas. That section had felt little actual hunger prior to this time, but the destitution left by the Federals was widespread and severe. One young girl who witnessed the march reported that the people in Georgia eagerly sought stray bits of corn left uneaten by the horses;[6] another told of searching for stray Minié balls left on the field of battle and exchanging them for food at Confederate Headquarters.[7]

While civilians living near the battle areas keenly felt the shortage of food, those living in so called "refugee havens" likewise faced the problem. In an attempt to flee from the enemy, many thousands were swept into areas believed to be safe from invasion. As such areas contracted with each passing month, more and more people were herded into less and less space. The problem of feeding these people became immense and sometimes impossible. Then it was that shortages became widespread and hunger appeared where it had not been before.[8] In the cities, too, shortages created immense problems. Depending upon the surrounding rural areas for their subsistence, the city dwellers were sometimes forced to do without even the simplest food. Farmers often refused to bring their produce to town, even when they had it. The fear of the impressment officers, coupled with the poor roads, were most often the reasons for withholding the farm produce. So bad did the situation become in some cities that the inhabitants were seen eating the refuse from garbage cans.[9] One diarist wrote that the people of Richmond lived in a clean city, for "everything [is] being so cleanly consumed that no garbage or filth can accumulate." He added that the citizens of the capital were "such good scavengers" that there was "no need of buzzards."[10] Richmond felt the food shortage for a longer period of time, and more severely, than did any other city, for into the capital had come hundreds of government workers, military figures, on-lookers, seekers of favors, travelers, and men of fortune. The population grew to such an extent that even had normal amounts of produce come into Richmond they would have proved insufficient. But normal amounts did not come in during the war; therefore, the problem of food was a grave one.

Besieged towns, too, were often driven to great lengths to get enough food to keep the people alive. Vicksburg and Petersburg were in desperate straits while they were under siege. In both of these towns, all sorts of food substitutes were utilized. While the shortage was felt most severely in these and other towns and cities in the Confederacy, it was by no means absent from the rural areas. Some rural folk suffered, others did not. Some areas were without sufficient food a part of the time, while others usually had enough for their people. Few, however, were those people or places that had prewar quantities during the entire four years. The leaders often received letters from their friends and constituents in rural areas, telling of the hardships and asking that something be done. Secretary of War Seddon received such a letter in the spring of 1864, written by Thomas S. Babcock for a group of citizens in Appomattox County, Virginia. It declared that corn could not be found; the situation was described as "urgent." Seddon's aid was sought with the hope of easing a "sober and lamentable reality."[11] A particularly graphic plea was written by several county leaders of Rockingham County, Virginia, to the Honorable James B. Baldwin, in the late fall of 1864. Conditions in this county were described as "appalling and unparalleled," there was barely enough food "to sustain life," and people "were almost reduced to beggary."[12] The rural folk always evidenced much concern when there was a lack of food. They never seemed able to take it in their stride as did their city friends. One lady remarked that as she traveled about in rural areas of the South, the people seemed far more interested in "the non-arrival of a jug of molasses or a sack of meal than in the issue of battles."[13]

In determining what groups of people felt the food shortage most keenly, it is impossible to generalize. Evidence points to the fact that the poor people of the Confederacy found it extremely difficult to get enough to eat. Despite the generosity of many in helping the poor, most of the organized charities were found in

the larger towns, and those in remote areas were unable to benefit
by their charity. Others had too much pride to become beggars,
so they went hungry. There was hunger, however, among those
who were widely known in Confederate circles. Such outstanding
people as Joseph LeConte,[14] and his daughter, Emma, mention
the scarcity of food in their pantry.[15] Constance Cary, one of
the favorites of Richmond society during the war, went hungry
many times,[16] while Mrs. Joseph E. Johnston, wife of the Confederate General, at one time had only cornbread and sorghum molasses to eat.[17] There were many similar cases among the better
known and more affluent members of the Confederacy, but this
group, more often than any other, got the rare articles when they
were available. Mrs. Jefferson Davis admitted that the household
of the President had fewer deprivations "than those of persons
not holding such high official positions."[18] This is further veri-
fied by Mrs. James Chesnut, Jr., wife of the South Carolina Senator, who dined with Mrs. Davis late in the war. On the President's
table she found chicken, oysters, gumbo, duck, olives, salad, lettuce, chocolate ice cream, jelly, cake, claret, and champagne.[19]
Other persons of high rank benefited by their "connections."
Secretary of the Treasury George Trenholm assisted his friends in
securing from abroad various scarce and almost forgotten items,[20]
and Secretary of the Navy Stephen R. Mallory was accused of in-
dulging in a diet that would delight the most critical of the epi-
cures.[21] But these leaders and their circles of intimate friends
composed only a small percentage of the Confederates. The rank
and file fared simply on the most monotonous of diets; and coffee,
tea, salt, and sugar made their exits early in the war. The lack of
these items continued to be fairly general, except in those parts
of the Confederacy west of the Mississippi where sugar was grown.
Rich or poor, famous or little known, all people had to forego
their usual indulgence in these items. The more ingenious sought
and found substitutes for some of the items, others were unsuccessful.

Recognizing the food shortages, the newspapers and periodicals
of the time made room for recipes and the results of culinary research. When the *Southern Illustrated News* was founded in
Richmond in September, 1862, the promise was given the readers
that a place would be given "to all good recipes furnished by
experienced housekeepers."[22] Recipe books published during the

war stressed shortages and modeled the recipes to fit the times. Housewives cut these recipes from magazines and newspapers and made their own wartime recipe books. One kept by a South Carolina housewife is so typically "Confederate" that it merits description. Bound in the coarsest of homespun, the book contains recipes written on the blank side of Confederate money, old envelopes, and letters, all cut to a uniform size.[23] All of the war recipes were simple, and war names were given to the various concoctions, such as "Rebel Bread" and "Beauregard Cake."[24]

The same periodicals that gave so much space to the recipes also encouraged the planting of food crops in place of cotton and tobacco. State legislation on this subject was a direct outgrowth of the newspaper campaign. The papers made appeals to the farmers to meet together and discuss this topic. When they did come together and decide to forsake the planting of cotton for corn, they received publicity for their actions. Not only would the hometown paper publish the news of the farmers' unselfishness, but the story would find its way into newspapers far from the scene of the action.[25] The newspapers urged not only the planting of food crops, but the planting of more than the family could use. A South Carolina paper declared that farmers could whip the famine if everyone would plant one-fifth more than the family could consume.[26] The widely read *Southern Cultivator* told the southern people that the planting of food crops was not a matter of choice, but "a matter of necessity,"[27] and the Wilmington *Journal* subtly reminded the meat-loving and meat-hungry Confederacy that "corn is pork in the rough."[28] It was not only the big planter who was urged by southern editors to plant food crops. The people, both in city and town, were encouraged to plant gardens. The practice of growing vegetables on any available plot of ground became universal during the war. J. B. Jones noted, with great satisfaction, that on his lot in Richmond "Every inch of ground is in cultivation—even the ash heap is covered all over with tomato vines."[29] But this did not entirely satisfy him. When he wanted to grow vegetables through the cold winter months, he made a hotbed out of a flour barrel sawed in half, and in this he planted corn, cabbage, tomatoes, beets, and eggplant. Being portable, this ingenious device could be brought indoors in cold weather.[30] Women as well as men cultivated gardens with an uncommon enthusiasm. By so doing they assured themselves and their families of a supply of fresh vegetables in the time of scarcity. When Mrs. James Chesnut called on Mrs. Raphael Semmes in Richmond, she found the wife of the famous Confederate admiral working patiently with her lettuce and radishes.[31] Mrs. Robert Francis Withers Allston, upon the death of her husband, the former governor of South Carolina, planted a vegetable garden in order that the diet of her family might be supplemented. Her daughter proudly recorded that the products of her mother's labor were "wonderful."[32]

Whether a person cultivated a small plot of ground or many acres, the problem of obtaining seeds was a major one. During the war there was an acute shortage of all vegetable seeds. In former years, many of these had been imported from the North, and with that channel of trade blocked, it became necessary for the southern people to produce all of their own. One editor rebuked his readers for having depended upon the North for this item. He wrote: "There's no real necessity for this. We grow as good seed and as many of them as any portion of Yankeedom." He urged that the people in the South be careful to save all necessary seed.[33] Because of the shortage, a spirit of cooperation grew up among the people. Notices were published in papers by those who had a surplus of seed, and this surplus was sold, exchanged, or given away to those who needed it.[34] It became quite common to use the office of the local editor as a clearing house for these transactions. Despite this and similar efforts to distribute seeds, the shortage continued. In the spring of 1863, pea, bean, corn, and tomato seed were not to be had in Richmond,[35] and in February 1865, an amateur gardener in the same city bought a quarter ounce of cabbage seed at $10 per ounce.[36] While some seed came through the blockade, there was never enough to satisfy the demand.[37]

While the cultivation of food crops and the saving of seed were encouraged by the editors, the preservation of fruits and vegetables was also encouraged. Many papers carried instructions for the preserving and drying of surplus produce. One editor suggested that "Every apple should be saved, both for food and vinegar."[38] The recipe books of the war years give evidence of the increased interest in methods of preserving foods.

Among the most objectionable food shortages was that of meat. The lack of this essential item of diet caused concern among many.

The South usually consumed large quantities of pork, but even this domestic product proved scarce during the war. The scarcity of feed, the absence of many men accustomed to preside over the butchering and curing, and the lack of sufficient salt to cure the pork properly—all combined to produce the shortage. In the years before the war, much of the beef consumed in the lower South and the seaboard area had been brought from Tennessee, Kentucky, the Mid-West and the Trans-Mississippi region. Although these areas continued to supply the Confederacy in varying quantities through most of 1862,[39] by mid-summer of 1863 all of these sources were lost to the Confederacy, as far as supplying it with any great amount of provisions was concerned. The people living east of the Mississippi turned toward the raising of stock in an effort to produce their own meat.[40] But it took time to produce cattle for slaughter, and the lack of grain and of experience, combined with the time element and war destruction, made it impossible for the eastern Confederacy to produce its own meat in sufficient quantities. The meat shortage remained among the most acute during the entire conflict.

Many butcher shops closed their doors, and those that managed to stay open had little or no meat.[41] When it was available, it was well for the housewife or servant to rise early and rush to purchase some of the rare articles. The supply was usually exhausted in the early morning.[42] Under these circumstances, many were forced to forego meat, but their craving for it diminished not at all. It was said that in the prayers for daily bread, there was usually added, "And a little meat, too, O Lord."[43] Those who did manage to get meat got much less than was needed to feed the family, so a little was made to go a long way. In 1863 in one household a pound of meat was made to serve "seven hungry children," the parents, and a servant,[44] but by 1864 an ounce of meat per person daily was considered ample for the times.[45]

Under such conditions, there was nothing to do but use substitutes. The most common were fish and fowl. One diarist wrote that "fish became the staple article" of diet, but even to get this it was necessary to be at the market "before the break of day, and frequently . . . the crowd that pressed around the meat market was so dense that many were compelled to leave without anything."[46] While many were encouraged to partake of such meat substitutes as oysters, in season, and save the meat for the fighting men, oysters, too, were scarce. In Wilmington they were two dollars "a fry" when available,[47] while in Charleston an editor missed them to the extent that he wrote an editorial on the subject. In the course of the article he said: "One of the charmed months, bearing the mystic 'R' has passed away another is ½ spent and our eyes have not been gladdened nor our palates excited by so much as even 1 specimen of our old molluscuous favorites."[48] A poor substitute for oysters was offered. This was made of green corn, egg, flour, butter, salt, and pepper mixed together in a batter and fried.[49] This, of course, could be used only when the ingredients were available, and some of these items proved to be scarce. In an effort to get fish, those who could turned to fishing. One Louisiana father would awaken his children early every morning with the call, "Get up girls, fish or no breakfast."[50] That more fish were not used as meat substitutes was due to the lack of the essentials for catching them. There was a shortage of hooks, lines, seines, and traps, and there was difficulty fishing off the coast during the war.[51]

In addition to fish, there were other substitutes both palatable and nourishing. Among these were eggs. One contemporary remarked that the "hundred ways of cooking an egg became well-known in the Confederacy."[52] Fowl and wild game were used when obtainable, but these were not often to be had at any price. Hunting became more than a sport, for in this way the "meat" was often supplied those living in rural areas. One editor ran this in his paper: "We want to buy a coon and 'possum dog, [with which] to hunt our meat during the coming year. . . . A dog that will hunt coon, possum and kill sheep occasionally will command a good price at these 'headquarters'."[53] But hunters who had fine dogs with which to hunt were often stymied by the lack of ammunition, for most of this found its way into the Army.[54]

With meat practically nonexistent, fishing tackle scarce, and ammunition for hunting purposes hard to obtain, other substitutes had to be found. By the fall of 1864 things had come to such a pass that one editor suggested his readers resort to eating rats, frogs, fried snails, young crow, snakes, locusts, earthworms, birds' nests, cats, and dogs; he added that "a word to the wise is sufficient."[55] By this time, however, many Confederates had already been eating these things. Rats had become an item in the diet of many. President Davis was quoted as saying that he saw no reason for not eating them, for he thought they would be "as good as squirrels."[56] They were eaten in quantity by the besieged citizens of Vicksburg. On the eve of the capitulation of that city, a lady noted that rats were "hanging dressed in the market for sale . . . there is nothing else."[57] They sometimes brought as much as $2.50 each.[58] In Richmond, too, they found their way to the tables, while recipes for cooking them were circulated among the women.[59] Rats, however, never became the item of diet that mule-meat did. In Vicksburg, mules were slaughtered daily and sold to those who wanted fresh meat.[60] But this meat was expensive. A lady said that she sent "five dollars to market each morning, and it buys a small piece of mule meat."[61] Mrs. Roger A. Pryor, who spent a part of the war in Petersburg, Virginia, wrote that one morning she saw a dead mule "lying on the common, and out of its side had been cut a very neat, square chunk of flesh."[62] Some people, in their hunger for meat, ate their pets. A resident of one of the caves in Vicksburg had her daughter's pet jay-bird killed and made into soup;[63] and considerable controversy arose in Savannah when a group of men were accused of rounding up dogs, slaughtering them, and selling them as lamb.[64] During the war, the lowly peanut came into general use as a food, and, specifically, as a substitute for meat.

The meat shortage probably would never have been so serious had it not been for a shortage of salt. This was needed as a preservative, yet it was almost totally lacking in most sections of the Confederacy. Of all shortages, salt received more attention from the Confederate Congress and state legislatures than any other. This commodity was desperately needed, and the lack of it caused many thousands of pounds of meat to spoil. It had been produced in the South prior to the war, but most of these sources were soon captured, and, in some instances, the salt mines were flooded by the Federals. The blockade made it increasingly difficult to bring this item into the Confederacy through the ports. And no satisfactory substitute was found. Saltpetre was sometimes used, but it, too, was always scarce, and the manufacturers of ammunition had first call on it. Wood ashes sometimes served as a substitute, but this proved unsatisfactory. In the search for salt, many people scraped the dirt from the smoke house floors, but this source was soon exhausted. Others tried boiling brine until the salt could be extracted, but, although this was urged upon the people by the newspapers, it was a slow and expensive method, and the results were negligible. Always a part of the saline story was the shortage of kettles, barrels, and sacks, needed in the making and shipping of the commodity. The congested and inadequate transportation facilities also made it difficult to distribute equally the available salt, as well as the basic essentials necessary to its manufacture. The authority on the salt problem in the Confederacy wrote that "despite the most persistent search . . . [and] enthusiastic boring to locate subterranean brines, despite scientific testing of weak brines, no important new sources of salines were discovered, with one exception of the mine of rock salt at New Iberia [Louisiana]."[65] With only one new brine discovered, and with only one major salt producing area in the Confederacy, that of the Saltville, Virginia, there was need of a substitute, but an adequate substitute was never discovered.

Among the many food shortages were fats of all kinds, butter, oils, lard, and mayonnaise. Of these, the shortage of butter seemed to be the most serious. Prior to the war, a large amount of butter had been shipped into southern cities from the North. This was said to be preferred because it was neatly packaged and "more satisfactory than that of domestic production."[66] With the coming of the war, it became necessary for the South to produce its own butter. In an effort to stimulate production, newspapers and farm journals presented the problem to their readers. In one such article, the editor of the *Southern Cultivator* stressed the point that the reliance on nothern butter was great, and that so far as he knew "there is not a dairy farm in the State of Georgia." Yet he insisted that southern farmers must supply the demands of the Confederacy.[67] Despite the effort to stimulate its production, there never was enough during the war. The words "No Butter" or "scant supply of butter" were constantly seen in the market reports of the southern papers. Early in the war, a Texas newspaper bragged that Texas could supply the whole Confederacy with the product. She failed to do so, however.[68] Not to be outdone, the wife of a South Carolina minister found a way to produce a small amount of butter for her household. She saved whatever cream she could skim from the milk and placed it in a glass jar. Then with a spool on the end of a stick serving as a dasher, she churned the cream and made enough butter to give her husband a taste of this rare commodity.[69] Since all housewives were not this resourceful and many lacked the cream to churn, the scarcity continued during the entire four years of the war. When a housewife did succeed in finding a little butter, it was often rancid, but it was too precious to throw away. She, therefore, resorted to current recipes that told her how she might restore the sweetness to it.[70] Lard and cooking oils, like butter, were hard to obtain. About the only substitute for such items, but one that was given widespread publicity, was oil made from the seeds of sunflowers. It was described as an admirable substitute for olive oil. Mayonnaise, too, was an almost forgotten luxury in most homes. Because of the shortage of oils which form a base for this dressing, recipes were concocted that produced a substitute called mayonnaise only by courtesy. Even the simple ingredients needed were often lacking.[71]

With the possible exception of meat and salt, the food shortage most complained of was sugar. That part of the Confederacy lying east of the Mississippi River was almost entirely dependent on the sugar produced in Louisiana. When the Federals took control of the area around New Orleans in 1862, the supply of the Confederacy became less and less. When the Confederacy was bisected and the Mississippi River lost, the sugar supply from Mississippi to Virginia almost entirely disappeared. Only that hoarded by housewives, that arriving spasmodically by blockade-runners, and the little cultivated in the area of Florida and Georgia was to be had. The shortage affected all people. As early as the summer of 1862, Mrs. Kirby Smith wrote her husband apologizing because she could not find any white sugar for him in Lynchburg.[72] W. W. Renwick, a South Carolina merchant, received a communication that not only indicates the sugar shortage but reflects a sense of humor on the part of a customer as well. The communicant was writing on behalf of his wife who had heard that Mr. Renwick had a quantity of sugar at his store, and it was her understanding that it was reserved for his neighbors only. The husband assured the merchant that his wife considered herself a neighbor of his "especially now when she can see the bottom of the barrel." She wanted an entire hogshead of sugar.[73] There seems to be no record as to whether or not she was neighborly enough to have had the request granted. Whenever a little "real" sugar made its appearance on the table during the war, it received considerable comment, for it was among the scarcest of articles.[74]

Because of its scant supply, fairly satisfactory substitutes were found for the genuine article. Of all these substitutes, sorghum was most often used. It became familiar throughout the Confederacy. One lady said that "a history of the 'Southern Confederacy' would be incomplete without . . . mention of sorghum."[75] Another contemporary wrote that "the land was submerged in sorghum."[76] Mills for its production sprang up like mushrooms over the South; they were, as a rule, primitive and inexpensive. They usually consisted of "three upright cylinders, of which the center one, turned by horse-power, moved the other two by means of cog-wheels. A tub set underneath the machine caught the juice," and this juice was boiled down and clarified.[77] In fact, this sorghum boiling "added another to the great Southern festivals of corn shucking and hog-killing." The result of each boiling was different. No two kettles were alike "in color, taste or consistency."[78] Much interest was stimulated in the results, however, and the makers carried around samples to compare with those made by their friends.[79] Whenever the planter found himself unsure of some step in the procedure of making sorghum, he would ask the advice of someone who did know. So it was that Robert F. W. Allston wrote to James Henry Hammond in the summer of 1862: "My sorgo is not yet ripe, when it is I desire to know how to proceed forewith, so as to lose neither time nor material in experimenting. With this in view, I beg you to give me benefit of your experience."[80] "Universal sweetner" that it was, sorghum was used whenever sugar was called for. It found its way into cakes, cookies, and pies, but one of the most unusual uses was in jellies and preserves.[81] Sorghum jelly was fairly common,[82] but this, as well as preserves that contained sorghum, "always had a twang."[83]

There were other sugar substitutes but they never became as widely used as sorghum. Among these was honey. The people were encouraged to substitute this for sugar, but the production of honey fell off during the war, and it was never sufficient to meet the demand.[84] Maple sugar was used whenever it was obtainable. This sugar, and maple syrup, as well, was said by some to be "as good as that produced in the North."[85] Most of that used during the war came from the mountain areas, but it never reached the markets in sufficient quantities to supply the demand.[86]   Persimmons were also used to make sugar, and both watermelons and figs were made into syrup and used as sweetening.

Because of the shortages of sugar and syrup, desserts practically disappeared from southern tables. Usually on such important occasions as Christmas, the housewives would ingeniously concoct some dessert that would be acceptable, despite the sugar shortage. But even then, many felt that apologies were in order, for to indulge in such luxuries was thought by many to be unpatriotic. Edmund Ruffin's granddaughter wrote him on Christmas Day, 1862, that her family was "so unfashionable as to have a dessert."[87] And, when Henry William Ravenel's wife made him a cake on his forty-ninth birthday, May 19, 1863, he apologized in his diary for such extravagance, adding that she "insists upon keeping up the usual custom of cake and wine, even at the cost of some little self-denial afterwards."[88] Molasses pie, made with sorghum, flour, and walnuts was a fairly common dessert.[89] There were Confederate "ginger snaps" that contained no ginger or sugar and, from descriptions, very little "snap."[90] There were "plum puddings" without plums,[91] but fruit cakes contained all sorts of fruit. One recipe called for dried apples, peaches, figs, walnuts, and hickory nuts, and flavored with what few spices could be begged, borrowed, or stolen and with corn whiskey "made by the government."[92] Another fruit cake contained "dried cherries, dried whortleberries, candied watermelon rind and molasses."[93] Among the simplest of desserts was that made from crushed peanuts sweetened with whatever happened to be on hand.[94] Many a party was given during the war "with a gallon of sorghum and some goobers."[95]

The shortage of white sugar and syrup prevented the making of dainty desserts and pastries, but the scarcity of flour also contributed to the lack of these delicacies. A high grade of white flour was practically unobtainable during most of the war. A favorite receipt for pie crust called for white potatoes in the absence of flour;[96] and corn meal was often used in the making of pastries, cakes, and waffles.[97] If there had been a lack of flour for dessert only, there would have been no great problem, but wheat bread became so scarce and expensive as to prevent its use by the rank and file. Early attempts of newspapers to get the southern people to grow wheat met with little success. With outside sources closed and with the lack of proper machinery, soil, weather, and experience to grow it at home, the supply of wheat dwindled.[98] The little flour that was milled was darker than the prewar flour and much coarser. When one woman found some "Number One" flour hidden away in a relative's home, she was so elated that she recalled it in later life.[99] Both dark and light flour continued scarce during the war. Whenever anyone was so fortunate as to receive any as a gift, friends were called in to share the wonderful delicacy. These "biscuit parties" were always a success; one woman declared that some of those eaten at such an event "were more delicious than any eaten before or since."[100] Because of the scarcity of bread, housewives very often had to resort to a sort of rationing with their families. One remarked that it "was almost ludicrous to see with what painful solicitude . . . [she] would count rolls" or measure the bread with a string, so that no one would get more than another.[101] By the spring of 1865, the price of flour had risen to $1,200 a barrel; and at this price it was rarely obtainable. Professional bakers continued to raise prices. In Richmond the bakers produced three sizes of loaves "which sold at one, two and three dollars." The first was described as visible only with microscopic aid, "the second can be discerned with the naked eye, and the third can be seen with outline and shape distinct."[102] Because of the shortage of breadstuffs, soldiers threatened to go home and help their hungry families obtain bread.[103]

Substitutes had to be found for flour from which nourishing breadstuffs could be made. Apparently the most ingenious were unable to find a tasty substitute. One physician who studied the problem of shortages and the indigenous plants that might relieve these shortages, concluded that "any substance that contains starch . . . may furnish materials for bread."[104] And, in truth it did. Rice flour became very common in those areas where rice was grown. In one recipe book, published midway in the war, there were eleven recipes calling for the use of rice flour. Rice bread frequently bore the name "Secession Bread"[105] but, for all its merits as described by the Confederate press, one daring housewife who attempted to make it said that it resulted "only in brick-bats or sticky paste."[106] A majority of the southerners resorted to the use of cornmeal, already a common food before the war. Many who ate it during the war, however, would have preferred wheat bread had they been able to get it. When the cornmeal was bolted and sifted through a fine sifter or muslin cloth,

it made a passable substitute for flour.[107]   The editor of the
Houston *Telegraph* urged his readers to use cornmeal, by telling
them that it was more patriotic to eat the domestic product.[108]
Before the war was over, even this item became scarce, and those
who had earlier scorned it were happy to get it.   In 1862 a North
Carolina farmer wrote to his son: "the corn crop is wretched . . .
the prospect is far worse than it's been since Columbus discovered
America."[109] With bread so difficult to obtain, it was natural that
the distillers should become a target for criticism.   Just how much
corn went into distilled spirits is not known, but it became so
scarce in certain areas that the people went along the roads and
picked up stray kernels that had fallen from the wagons.   The
children of Charles Campbell, the historian, picked up grains from
the feeding troughs of the army horses.   These they "washed,
dried and pounded" for food.[110]   After cornmeal became difficult
to obtain, hominy was suggested in its place but hominy, too, was
scarce.   Rice flour, cornmeal, and hominy were delicious by comparison with some of the flour substitutes.   Pea-meal came into
fairly general use, when nothing else could be had.   It was described as having a peculiar and disagreeable taste, and on the
whole "very unpalatable."[111]   There was, also, sorghum flour that
produced a pinkish bread comparable to buckwheat.[112]   Pumpkin bread was made by boiling a pumpkin in water until a thick
substance was obtained, running this through a sieve, and then
adding a little flour or meal.   The result was "excellent bread,"
according to the *Confederate Receipt Book*.[113]   Acorns, persimmons, clover, and lilies were also used in making bread.

There was also a shortage of fresh fruits, vegetables, and condiments in many parts of the Confederacy.   Even in sections where
fruits and vegetables were plentiful, the distance to the needy
areas, the poor transportation facilities, and the lack of refrig-
eration prevented proper distribution.   Most noticeable of the
scarce fruits were those produced in tropical or semitropical
climates, and formerly imported into the South.   These consisted of citrus fruits, pineapples, and dates.   Shut off from the
oranges, lemons, and limes of the West Indies, the southern
people began to look toward Florida for these fruits.   Although
Florida fruits were marketed before the war in smaller quantities, the blockade furnished a stimulation to fruit growing in this
southernmost state that was amazing.   The newspaper frequently

commented upon the deliciousness of the Florida fruit, and one young lady from Georgia pronounced the oranges "very good."[114] Pineapples were not grown in any abundance in the South, and there seemed to be no substitute for them. But dried persimmons were substitutes for dates.[115] When lemons were unobtainable, even from Florida, citric acid was used instead.[116] Common fruits, apples, peaches, and plums, were also scarce. Pumpkins, cut into pieces and dried in the sun, were suggested as substitutes for dried apples;[117] and one recipe for apple pie "without apples" was circulated.[118] One paper published a recipe for fruit preserves "without fruit"; it was made from molasses, nutmeg, and eggs.[119] The fruit shortage continued throughout the war, some areas being totally without this desired article of diet.

To a lesser extent than fruit, fresh vegetables were lacking. These could be grown in one season, whereas it would take an orchard several years to mature. But vegetables were by no means plentiful. The seed shortage prevented many from raising the desired quantity; and lack of experience and preoccupation with other things were contributing factors to the small yield. Very few vegetables were for sale in the markets. At one time in 1865, only watercress was to be found in the Richmond markets.[120] Irish potatoes were generally scarce in most of the Confederacy, but sweet potatoes seem to have been more plentiful.[121] In an effort to get some green foods in their diets, herbs and flowers were eaten.[122] On the whole, however, the shortage of fresh vegetables was less frequently mentioned in contemporary accounts than that of meat, bread, and sweets.

Spices, pepper, flavorings, vinegar, and baking soda were scarce during the war. Although some spices and pepper were brought through the blockade and some housewives had a quantity on hand when the war began, these seasonings were among those items which generally disappeared early in the war and few substitutes were found. Those who had a sufficient supply of pepper sometimes used it instead of spice, but this was not very satisfactory.[123] The majority "long contented themselves" without these things.[124] Flavoring for desserts was also scarce, but the cooks of the Confederacy found substitutes in the leaves of trees, especially of fruit trees. Peach leaves were substituted for vanilla;[125] peach and cherry leaves combined made almond flavoring, and the rose taste could be derived from rose leaves.[126] Vinegar, too, was to be had only in small quantities, if at all. Recipes for making vinegar were among those most frequently seen in the newspapers of the period. Some are interesting because of the ingredients recommended. One called for molasses and water mixed and permitted to stand for two months; another, in the same paper, suggested that "excellent vinegar" might be made from blackberries, water, and molasses mixed and put in the sun for two weeks.[127] Beets were sometimes used as a source of vinegar. A number of factories were established for the purpose of manufacturing vinegar in the South. Bicarbonate of soda, used as a leavening agent in bread, was decidedly scarce and difficult to get. Ashes left after burning corncobs became widely known as a successful substitute. Red cobs were thought to contain more alkali than white. The ashes were gathered, water was added, and put into jars ready for use. The ashes of hickory logs were used in a similar manner, and the results were described as "quite good."[128]

The food shortage affected the farm animals, for there was a continuous shortage of fodder. Work animals, cattle, sheep, hogs being fattened for slaughter, and dairy cattle all suffered. In an effort to alleviate the shortage of forage and grains, various grasses were grown in the hope of finding a substitute for northern hay, and chinaberries were found to be a substitute for the decreasing corn supply.[129] Peas and peanuts were widely cultivated and used as feed for swine and cattle, but there was never enough food for the animals. Those who owned livery stables and boarded horses were forced to raise their prices as feed became scarce and more costly.[130] In Richmond, in March, 1863, it cost $300 a month to board a horse. A single feeding was $5,[131] and prices rose as feed became more difficult to obtain. Many owners were forced to close their stables and sell their animals. Those kept as pets were at starvation's door, and their owners were distressed over their inability to secure food for them. One diarist observed that his daughter's cat had been staggering from hunger for several days; when it finally died several months later, all was grief in the household. Yet the owner admitted that its going was probably for the best since it had cost $200 a year to feed the cat. Rats and mice began to disappear, both from hunger and from being killed for food.[132] A nurse in a Richmond hospital told of rats so hungry that they would drag poultices off the patients and eat them.[133]

Beverages also were scarce in the Confederacy and coffee was the most sorely missed of them all. Certainly the shortage of no other beverage was responsible for such frequent complaint by contemporaries. One wrote that "The coffee shortage caused more actual discomfort among the people at large" than did any other.[134] This commodity began to disappear before the summer of 1861 had passed, and it was rarely seen after the fall of the same year. When one woman had to give it up, she wrote that she lost her "elasticity of spirit."[135] Another cried "Sour Grapes" to those who vowed that they did not miss the universal brew.[136] But as one saw apple pies without apples, one also found "coffee" houses where no coffee was served.[137] So dear did coffee become that the jewelers of Atlanta were reported to have bought all the coffee available "for sets in breast pins instead of diamonds."[138]

There were those, however, who managed to have a little coffee from time to time. Some had hoarded a supply, and a small quantity continued to come through the blockade. Those who had coffee usually brewed a weak beverage and added other ingredients to make it go further. These blends might include parched corn, rye, wheat, okra seed, or chicory,[139] and the results were not always satisfactory. One diarist declared that such adulterated coffee was delicious,[140] another thought it nauseating.[141] Whenever the real product made its appearance, it was the signal for unrepressed glee. Sometimes it was referred to as "true-true" coffee,[142] and one young lady, in recording the day's menu in her diary, underlined "real coffee" twice.[143] When a train carrying "blockade" coffee was wrecked near Sumter, South Carolina, the eager, and thirsty, inhabitants of the area rushed to the scene of the wreck and took home sacks of the real bean. One editor wrote that "more real coffee has been drunk in that neighborhood within a few days than for a long time."[144]

The civilian population attacked the problem of substitutes for coffee with a determination and energy unlike that exhibited in the search for other expedients. No other single item had more substitutes. The people worked at the project unceasingly, with the result that "few were the substances which did not . . . find their way into the coffee pot."[145] Boundless was the pride of the housewife who discovered and put into use a substitute that would deceive her guests into thinking that they were drinking the real thing.[146] Nearly all women had their own combinations, but usually they shared the secret with those who were interested. Among the most popular, and apparently most successful, of the substitutes was rye. This was boiled, dried, then ground like coffee.[147] A mild debate was carried on through the newspapers as to whether or not rye thus used was harmful to the body; regardless of the points made, people continued to use it.

Another substitute frequently used was okra seed. More expensive and troublesome than rye, it was nevertheless popular. Its proponents were convinced that it was by far the best substitute.[148] The okra seeds were dried and parched in a similar manner to rye. Corn, too, was used and prepared in a like manner, and there were those who preferred corn "coffee" to any other.[149] The dashing General J. E. B. Stuart was reported to be of this group.[150] Sweet potato "coffee" was another of the more popular wartime expedients.[151] Potatoes were peeled and cut into "chunks" about the size of coffee berries. The pieces were spread out in the sun to dry, then parched until brown, after which they were ground. The grounds were mixed with a little water until a paste resulted, after which hot water was added. When the grounds settled to the bottom of the coffee pot, the beverage could be poured and drunk. The sediment was said to be among the best cleaning agents for carpets, curtains, and similar household accessories.[152] Other coffee substitutes were acorns, dandelion roots, sugar cane, parched rice, cotton seed, sorghum molasses, English peas, peanuts, wheat, and beans.

In practically every town of any size there were those who chose to sell coffee mixtures and blends. The newspapers were filled with advertisements of these products. The following advertisement, published in an Alabama paper, was typical of hundreds of others. It ran as follows:

My Coffee Substitute

has been successfully introduced to the citizens of Mobile, Atlanta, Macon and Columbus. It is a wholesome, palatable, and nutritious drink, more nearly approaching genuine coffee flavor than any discovered.[153]

Free samples were usually given away to interested persons, and the cost of the substitute was reasonable. But housewives generally seemed to prefer their own mixtures.

To a lesser extent than coffee, tea was missed during the war. It was never as popular as coffee, yet there were those who wanted it sufficiently to search for substitutes. Most common of the expedients was sassafras tea, a beverage long familiar to many, especially Negroes.[154] The leaves of blackberries, raspberries, huckleberries, currants, willow, sage, various vegetables, and the leaves of the holly tree were used as tea substitutes. One of the most famous substitutes was "yaupon" tea. Long in use by many, it became popular in coastal regions where the yaupon grows in abundance. To make this tea, one used the leaves and twigs, usually boiling them in water and adding molasses and milk. Fortunately for the times, it "was considered vulgar to use sugar for sweetening Yopon." The story is told that this same lady who refused to use sugar, remarked that yaupon tea was so healthful that it had kept her "out of heaven" for years.[155]

Next to coffee, the beverages most often mentioned among the shortages were alcoholic stimulants. Foreign sources of supply were only slightly tapped during the war, but when choice wines, brandies, and whiskies were brought through the blockade, they met with immediate sale despite their tremendous cost. This scarcity forced people to seek substitutes. Practically everything was used to produce the distilled beverage. One editor facetiously gave this recipe for lager beer, so sure was he, after tasting some of local make, that these ingredients must have been compounded:

> Take an old bootleg, and an old cast-off red flannel shirt, and put in five gallons of rainwater. Let it stand for two weeks and ferment well. Then put it into a ten gallon keg, adding two quarts of chinaberries, three gallons of water from a tub used by shoemakers to soak leather in (three months old) . . . and one pound of assafoedita. Let it stand for one week and add a couple of Florida beans.[156]

Brandy made during the war was so dangerous to drink that it was reported the insurance companies refused to insure the life of any individual who was in the habit of taking occasional drinks.[157] It was said that the whiskey "cauterizes the mucous membrane of the windpipe; sets the brain on fire, and sends a cold tremor through the system. The soldier who indulges in half a dozen nips is likely to stay drunk for a week; and the second or third application drives the breath out of the body."[158]

It is interesting to learn just what did go into these beverages. Whiskey, one of the most popular of the alcoholic drinks, and one of the most profitable to make, was distilled from anything and everything. Regardless of the content, all of it found immediate sale. The Richmond *Examiner* said that of the enterprises stimulated by the war, "the manufacture and sale of whiskey" took the lead. It was "sold in the back rooms of family grocers and confectionary shops . . . and in the more reputable establishments of trade."[159] "Moonshiners" did a good business, "running day and night, . . . finding ready sale for all they produced."[160] Despite rigid state legislation against the use of grain, a great amount went into whiskey. Most of this was made from corn or other grains, but it was also distilled from sweet potatoes, rice, sorghum seed, and persimmons. The descriptions given most of these whiskies ran from a mere "unpalatable" to "vile," but they all agreed on the effect. One person summed up the matter as follows: "They seemed to fly through the system with alacrity."[161] Beer, too, was made from various and strange substitutes. Frequently molasses and water with a little ginger, plus yeast, when it could be found, were brewed together and called "Confederate Beer." Corn and persimmons were also used, the latter being referred to as "possum beer."[162] For hops, which were very scarce, peach leaves were used extensively.[163] But the beer that resulted caused one editor to scream, " 'Mein Got,' our German friends must raise the blockade."[164] Since palatable wines and brandies could be made from fruits, the results were much more satisfactory than in the case of whiskey and beer. Brandies, liqueurs, and wines were made from blackberries, apples, peaches, plums, watermelon juice, elderberries, and carrots. In Alabama, brandy was made from the sweet potato; the product was described as the worst of all "liquified lightning."[165] Apparently only the most brazen attempted to call any of the wartime brews "champagne." But one amateur distiller made what he called champagne from three parts water and one part corn, with enough molasses added to sweeten it properly. It was totally without effervescence, the name being the only thing that bore a resemblance to the real champagne.[166] In Savannah, Georgia, juniper berries and whiskey blended together was sold for "imported Holland gin."[167] William Gilmore Simms found his brew of persimmon beer "equalled to the best sparkling

'Jersey champagne,' "[168] but most people failed to find such satisfaction in the domestic products.

Milk, too, was scarce in many parts of the Confederacy. One prominent lady recorded in her diary that her household "had not had milk more than twice in eighteen months, and then it was sent by a . . . friend."[169] When milk could be obtained, it was usually adulterated so that a little might go farther. It was sometimes mixed with water,[170] and at other times with ground corn.[171] When cream was not available to use in coffee or tea, beaten egg whites were sometimes substituted.[172]

Even water of a drinkable quality was not always available in the Confederacy. One of the chief complaints of the people of besieged Vicksburg was that they had only the muddy water of the Mississippi River to drink.[173] The best hostesses of Richmond were sometimes forced to offer their guests water from the James River, "which was often thick enough and red enough" to pass as "something more nourishing."[174] Recognizing that such situations existed in the South, the *Confederate Receipt Book* published a formula for purifying muddy water.[175]

The severity of the food and beverage shortage caused institutions responsible for feeding large groups of people untold confusion. Practically all colleges and boarding schools left the board charges unannounced until the opening date. Some imposed penalties on all who left any food on their plates,[176] while from Porcher's School in South Carolina, the son of former Governor Allston wrote that nothing but squash and hominy was to be had for months at a time.[177] Elizabeth Allston, daughter of the former governor of South Carolina, wrote that the fare went from bad to worse at Madame Togno's School in Columbia. For tea the students had only corn dodgers and water, and they finally ceased going to supper. Boarding houses, too, found the going difficult. They rationed their food among the boarders so that all might be assured of a fair portion of the scanty fair. Hotels found it necessary to go on the European plan because of food shortages.[178] In crowded houses, where one cook might serve several families, there was a constant difficulty in keeping provisions separate. Coffee proved the easiest to isolate for "each housewife had her own particular concoction."[179]

Despite grave shortages of food, people could still make light of their hardships. Some reported that they ate green persimmons to shrink their stomachs;[180] a newspaper editor wrote that the people of the Confederacy should laugh, for laughter would make them fat. He added: "With the prevailing scarcity of provisions— 'laugh' is about the cheapest thing they can fatten on this spring, and we would not be surprised if they did not raise the price of that."[181] No group in the Confederacy suffered from the lack of food more than did the inhabitants of Vicksburg during the siege. Yet they could laugh at their troubles. When the Federal army took the town, a soldier found the following menu:

Hotel de Vicksburg, Jeff Davis Co., proprietors—

Soup: mule tail

Boiled: Mule Bacon with Polk Greens

Roast: Saddle of Mule a la teamster

Entrees: Mule head stuffed, Reb fashion; Mule Beef, jerk a la Yankee; Mule liver, hashed a la explosion.

Dessert: Cotton berry pie, en Ironclad, Chinaberry tart.

Liquors: Mississippi Water, vintage 1492, very inferior, $3. Limestone water, late importation, very fine. Extra (black seal) Vicksburg bottled-up—$4. Meals at Few Hours, Gentlemen to wait on themselves. Any inattention in service to be reported at the office.

Jeff. Davis and Comp., Props.[182]

Because of the scarcity of food and drink, refreshments at social gatherings were very simple. "Starvation parties" were popular during the war. These were simple affairs where good fellowship and water were the only things to be had. Occasionally all would contribute money and hire a fiddler so that there might be dancing; but refreshments were "strictly forbidden."[183] Often in the family circle, after a scant evening meal, conversation would turn toward the tasty dishes enjoyed in bygone days.[184] One lady tells how she always kept a recipe book on her mantel, and when such conversation started, she read a recipe for a rich pudding or cream. She admitted that it failed to satisfy the appetite, but it was "as good for the digestion."[185]

Of all the shortages on the Confederate homefront, that of food was the most pressing. It was a daily problem and when solved for one day, there was no assurance that it would be solved for the next. This meant that housewives had to be on a constant lookout for new foods to prepare and new ways to prepare them.

V

CLOTHING

A SHORTAGE IN CLOTHING WAS MUCH SLOWER TO DEVELOP THAN the food shortage, yet it became serious before the end of the war. The editor of the Charleston *Mercury* told his readers that he was confident that two years of war would "result in the manufacture of all our clothing. There shall be Southern chintzes and calicoes in 2 years of blockade."[1] His opinion was typical of the general attitude during the first year of the war; but his predictions failed to become reality. During the first eighteen months of the conflict the majority of the civilian population faced no grave clothing scarcity, but as the months rolled into years, old clothing wore out and there was little new to replace it. Then it was that the Confederate homefolks were faced with the necessity of finding and utilizing substitutes. Southern ingenuity produced many unusual and interesting articles of clothing. While the people never found it necessary to use the primitive mode of dress, or undress, all sorts of odd materials were converted into wearing apparel.

The South had been accustomed to receive a major portion of its clothing materials and shoes from Europe and the North. The cotton mills in the South had produced a coarse grade of material used most often for the slaves. And, even had they produced a better quality of cloth, they were not sufficiently numerous to supply all the people of the Confederacy. The same situation existed in the manufacture of shoes. There were a few cobblers scattered over the South, but they could not supply the Confederacy. There was a general pathetic ignorance of tanning methods and of even the rudimentary essentials of making shoes. Many clothing factories, along with the services of the shoemakers, were taken over during the war by the Confederate and state governments for the purpose of supplying needed clothing for the armed

forces. Since little clothing was produced in the South by manufacturing concerns and since the usual importations were cut in
quantity by the blockade, the southern people found it necessary
to solve the problem through production and renovation of old
garments and shoes, or to do without. Dry goods stores were
forced to close, so scarce did merchandise become,[2] and before
the war was half over, people found that their rag-bags "proved
a magical repository of boundless possibilities."[3] Some items of
clothing were brought through the blockade, but these were most
often luxurious articles or army clothing and shoes. Such articles
even when made available to the average citizen were often so
expensive as to be prohibitive. The women who ran the land
blockade brought shoes, materials, and accessories whenever they
could, but these were, as a rule, for themselves, their families, or intimate friends. Miss Constance Cary, with her cousin, the lovely
Hetty Cary, made a trip to Washington in the spring of 1863 and
were elated to find well-stocked stores displaying articles that had
been nearly forgotten in the Confederacy. While there, these
young ladies went on a buying spree, which Constance chose to
call "A nine day wonder." Laden with the latest creations "snatched
from the protecting clutches of Uncle Sam," they made their way
back into the Confederacy; when once again safe in Richmond,
they became arbiters of fashion, a position they enjoyed for several months, and their "imported" garments were copied by those
who could get the essentials to do so.[4] Despite these and similar
importations, clothing was so scarce and in such demand that
men with only a little surplus money felt it wise to invest in "cotton yarn, cloth and leather."[5] So ill-clad were many people during
the last two years of the war that it became a problem for them
to keep warm. Some used quantities of paper, when this could
be had, as a protector "against cold and exposure." It was found
that two folds of newspaper in shoes were "equal to a good card-
board sole," while a sheet of paper between the chest and under
garments helped to prevent chest colds. Paper leggings were also
recommended to keep the ankles warm.[6] Most people did not
have to resort to such extremes, but the South that surrendered
in April, 1865, was inhabited largely by poorly clad people.

Of all the problems of dress, none was so serious as that of
shoes. Among the soldiers, this caused grave concern and was
responsible for both Confederate and state legislation. The prob-

lem among civilians never had such repercussions, although it was serious. Much interest was aroused in the need for tan-yards and shoe factories, and many amateurs studied the problems of treating leather; patents issued for various formulas showed this widespread interest in the processes. Editorials called attention to the need for shoes and urged their manufacture. Despite this interest in and attempts to produce them, the shortage remained one of the most serious homefront problems from Virginia to Texas. Just as Mrs. James Chesnut[7] and Miss Constance Cary[8] had the greatest difficulty in procuring shoes in Virginia, so a young refugee in West Texas was forced to go twenty miles before finding a pair in a country store.[9] Hearing a rumor that Charleston harbor was cleared of all blockading vessels, the granddaughter of Edmund Ruffin wrote to her grandfather that she was elated to hear the news, adding "I hope now we will be able to get shoes."[10] There were those who felt the shortage so keenly that they refused to go walking "for fear of wearing out their shoes."[11] Certainly the problem was universal and serious from the first year of the war through the last.

As the prewar shoes wore out, civilians assumed the problem of providing themselves with this necessary article of dress. Like most other solutions for shortages, that of obtaining shoes fell largely upon the women. During the war it was a common sight "to come suddenly upon a bevy of pretty girls sitting tailor fashion making and mending shoes."[12] They tanned skins as well as converted them into shoes,[13] being always interested in the newest and best methods of tanning. They found and utilized new hides for shoes, many of which in ordinary times would never have been considered. No animal was safe from the amateur cobbler once the value of his skin was established. There was always hesitancy in killing cows for their hides, but when cows were killed for meat their hides were used for shoes. Calves were rarely slaughtered. Horsehide was commonly used in making leather; large numbers of horses were killed in battle, and it was a common sight to see agents of the War Department, as well as civilians, collecting these bodies for the sole purpose of obtaining the skins for shoes.[14] Shoes made from dogskins became a fad during the war, and advertisements were frequently run in the newspapers requesting that such skins be brought to local shoemakers. The price of these skins varied, depending upon the time and place, but one dollar for a medium-sized skin was the average price.[15] It was said that once their value was determined, the dogs in the Confederacy "shook in their skins."[16] The skins of deer, sheep and goats, squirrels, and pigs were used for shoes during the war. Pigskin was generally conceded to be unsatisfactory, for the finished shoe made from this leather stretched out of shape after being worn only a few days.[17]

When hides were collected, the next problem was soaking and treating them. Some people used untreated skins for moccasins,[18] but most shoemakers found it more advantageous to tan the leather as well as they could. The shoes so treated had greater longevity. Small tanneries were established in every state. These were usually cooperative affairs, although some were individually owned. When small groups or an individual financed the building of the bark mills and vats, they charged a fee to tan hides for others. The usual charge was one-half of the hides tanned. Unfortunately for the barefooted Confederacy, the process of properly tanning the skins was a long and intricate one,[19] and success by the inexperienced was usually obtained only after several failures. During the war, those interested in leather tanning found fairly successful tanning agents in the indigenous plants. Among those most commonly used were the leaves and bark of the oak, myrtle, dog-fennel, sweet-gum, and the roots of the palmetto. Isaac Bierfield of Newberry, South Carolina, received a patent for the process using dog-fennel; he charged from $300 to $10,000 for the privilege of using his formula.[20] Some discovered the essentials of the process and used them for their own tanning without paying Bierfield.

Shoes were made from old leather articles as well as from newly tanned material. In fact the old was often preferred to the new because prewar leather was better and longer wearing than that processed during the war. Consequently, anything containing suitable material for a pair of shoes might find itself so converted. Leather furniture, trunks, belts, gin-bands, and saddles were used in the manufacture of shoes.[21] It was said that no sensible man would leave a saddled horse outside "a church, store or post office after dark," for fear that he would find that "some one had appropriated . . . [the] saddle skirts for sole leather."[22] Whenever cavalry boots were discarded because of worn-out soles and feet, the ingenious women would appropriate the tops for shoes for themselves and the children. Shoes for children could be more easily made from old leather objects, for less of the precious commodity was needed. Fine, dainty shoes were made for children from the excellent morocco bindings found on books and in pocketbooks.[23]

When it was impossible to obtain leather, either old or new, substitutes were found. Among these, the most widely used was wood. When sole leather was not obtainable, wooden bottoms were often tacked to the uppers. Factories, too, made similar shoes for sale. Such a manufacturing concern in Raleigh, North Carolina, produced an average of one hundred pairs daily with leather tops and wooden soles, when materials could be had. These soles were described as so durable that they "will last until the next war."[24] There were variations of this type. Some had strips of leather or cloth across the foot, producing a sandal effect. Others were all wood, hollowed out in such a way as to resemble Dutch footwear.[25] The material used for these was usually light, such as from the ash, poplar, willow, and roots of the blackgum tree. The first wooden soles to be made were so thick that it was said they added greatly "to the stature of the community," but as the process was perfected they were made thinner and often reinforced with bits of iron. These shoes were very noisy and were so destructive to the floors and carpets that they were often left in entrance halls.[26] Nevertheless citizens were encouraged to wear them. They were described as durable, easily made, healthful, and cheap—the average cost being about thirty cents a pair.[27] They often created much amusement, for they were so hollowed out as to resemble rockers, and the sight of stolid citizens rocking along and sometimes gaining such momentum that they could not be easily checked was ludicrous in the extreme.[28]

There were substitutes for leather shoes, among them various kinds of cloth. Such sturdy materials as canvas, duck, and Osnaburg were used when available, for they proved more durable than most other fabrics. But none was so durable as wood. Judith Brockenbrough McGuire told of making shoes from a part of canvas sails taken from a vessel wrecked on the James River;[29] Mrs. Roger A. Pryor made shoes for her children from an old carpet, lining them with flannel.[30] The cloth shoes were frequently colorful if not durable, for they were often dyed brilliant colors by the use of berries. More unusual were those made from old felt hats. Such material might be used for soles as well as tops when given a coating of wax, rosin, or tallow.[31] Footwear was also knitted,[32] made of fibers plaited and coated with varnish,[33] and made from layers of pasteboard glued together with meal paste.[34] Wrapping one's feet in the oriental fashion was not unknown, although a person who was forced to resort to this practice was the object of special pity. When a lady office worker, who had fainted at her desk in the Treasury Department, was taken up, "her feet were found wrapped in large pieces of lint." One diarist said this was so inadequate a covering for her feet that it could not have prevented "her blood from freezing."[35] The first person to resort to cloth foot covering in a community was frequently the object of much attention. A reputable farmer, from the Cape Fear region, wore a pair of these shoes into Fayetteville, North Carolina. He wrote his son that "the little boys pointed at them and laughed heartily, and every man and some women made some remark about them—one fellow even borrowed a pair of spectacles to see whether . . . [I] had on shoes or stockings and after examining them minutely, he swore they were neither."[36] The editor of a Virginia paper made a ridiculous suggestion which shows not only the shortage of shoes, but at the same time a shortage of baking ingredients. He facetiously suggested the use of some pie crust, which he had recently tested as a substitute for leather.[37]

There were other shortages that affected, in turn, the supply of shoes. India rubber was entirely lacking because of the blockade, therefore one did without overshoes or attempted to discover a substitute. The one recommended was a waterproof mixture made of turpentine and rosin and used as a coating on leather or cloth.[38] In an effort to conserve the soles of shoes, iron reinforcements were added when iron could be found.[39] Shoemakers, both professional and amateur, found the shortage of tacks and nails an insurmountable difficulty, especially in the making or mending of tough leather or wooden shoes, while the shortage of strong needles made stitching impossible.[40] Wooden pegs were used when tacks could not be had. Shoe polish and blacking were also scarce during the war. Berries and plants were used most frequently for making polish. A polish made from chinaberries and water boiled together and added to vinegar, egg, and lampblack was widely used.[41] Pokeberries, too, were used, the results being gaily colored shoes. A favorite blacking agent, which omitted the use of chinaberries, consisted of soot or lampblack mixed with molasses, eggwhites, and vinegar; oils and sometimes whiskey were added to this recipe.[42]   Admitting both the shortage of shoes and blacking, a farmer wrote his son that although the shoe situation seemed hopeless, if he had blacking, he would black his feet, thus deceiving people into thinking he owned shoes.[43]   With the struggles involved in getting shoes, it is little wonder that many people reverted to going barefooted[44] while others were delighted to be able to purchase even secondhand, misfitted shoes.[45]   It was generally conceded that among the most fortunate people in the Confederacy were those who received a pair of shoes as a gift.[46]

The shortage of textiles was never as critical as that of shoes, but it was a sizable problem.   Women who had done little sewing, except fancy work, were faced with reconverting and renovating old garments.   Old clothes were usually made over several times during the war until they finally fell into shreds.   These were turned inside out, and upside down, and they were darned and patched until the original cut and color were scarcely distinguishable.   Trimmings were ripped off old dresses and used on others—usually to hide worn spots or to lengthen the dress of some growing young lady.   Such cleverness had its rewards, especially when the effect was pleasing, for even the most intimate friends sometimes credited the wearer with a new dress.   One young lady who appeared at a party in a dress made from a combination of two old dresses was the object of much envy when her friends thought her gown to be new.   In order that her secret might be kept, she stayed in the darker parts of the drawing room "not daring to stand anywhere near the central chandeliers."[47]   These made-over clothes were objects of much comment.   While some were lovely tributes to the ingenuity of the women, others were described as disgraceful or humorous.   Children, as well as adults, had scant wardrobes, usually wearing clothes made from those of their parents and relatives.   Even the children of Jefferson Davis wore "cut-down" garments,[48] for the clothing scarcity affected all people.

In an effort to relieve the scarcity of clothing, women of the Confederacy turned to knitting, carding, spinning, and weaving. These arts were not entirely forgotten in the Confederacy, for there were those in remote areas who still relied upon them for their clothing.   And the poorer people over the South practiced them to a varying degree. Many women knew little or nothing about these essential steps in the production of material, but the war brought the necessity of learning them to their very doors. In this time of need there were professional teachers who traveled over the Confederacy teaching the womanly arts to the eager, threadbare ladies,[49] but it was the local Negro "Mammy" who most often taught her "Mistis."[50] Before the second winter of war had passed, the homes of the Confederacy became small domestic factories. Encouraged by newspaper editorials,[51] the women began to lay aside the dainty embroidery and crocheting, the piano and guitar, and to take up knitting needles and hand-cards.[52] They knitted as they "walked about in performance of household or plantation duties,"[53] on their front porches, and in their carriages. They not only knitted stockings, gloves, and caps, but also jackets, shirts, skirts, and even bed covering, and many became very proficient. One woman declared that the women of the Confederacy could knit as well as those of Germany.[54] While knitting was by far the most common art used to produce clothing in the home, spinning and weaving also increased during the war. Homemade looms were set up and spinning wheels brought down from the attic and dusted off. A girl living on a North Carolina farm wrote to her brother of many things, but in one concise statement she told him much: "Pa has made a loom and we are weaving."[55] The essence of this statement was repeated many times as the homefolk of the Confederacy wrote to their sons in service and their friends far away. Those who spun and wove developed a friendly rivalry that made pleasant recreation from what might have been sheer drudgery. They exchanged samples of their materials and often sent samples to the local editor, who in turn expressed his gratitude in the columns of his paper. An Alabama lady told of "spinning bees" that became common in her neighborhood. Spinning wheels, cards, and cotton were hauled by wagon to the house of some neighbor, who acted as the hostess. Any number of spinning wheels might arrive for one of these "bees," "sometimes as many as six or eight were whirring at the same time." While some women spun, others carded, cut out finished materials, or sewed. Children were sometimes included in such gatherings for they, as well as women, learned to spin and weave, thus adding to the resources of the family.[56]

The chief concern of those who suddenly chose to industrialize their homes was the shortage of the necessary tools and machinery. Cards were the most needed as well as the scarcest. These were placed on the approved contraband list by the government of the United States, and they became so greatly needed that they proved to be among the most valuable cargoes that a blockade-runner could carry. State legislation was enacted authorizing governors to import or manufacture, and distribute these necessary items to the needy. As they were scarce, they also became prohibitive in price. Before the war was half over they had increased in price from forty cents to thirty dollars a pair.[57] So critical was the situation that it caused real anxiety among those who had to produce their cloth or do without, for the poorer people, unlike the leaders of society, had no clothing stock from which to draw. Theirs was not a problem of renovation, but of production. If a family had any cards, the chances were they possessed not more than one pair, and only the most trusted hands on the place were allowed to touch them.[58] Card factories were established in every state, and several states put their prisoners to work manufacturing them. The Georgia penitentiary had one of the best records of production, averaging a pair an hour when the necessary material was available for the making of the cards.[59] The materials needed were leather and steel wire. Dogskins were used often during the war, and anyone who obtained these might exchange them for cards at the factories. They were always in demand.[60] The wire was not so easily obtained, although some was manufactured for the use in cards. Even though card factories sprang up like mushrooms and made commendable contributions to alleviating the shortage, there remained a scarcity that was alarming. Attempts were therefore made to spin uncarded cotton, but this was never wholly satisfactory. General Duff Green was interested in this problem, and the uncarded cotton he had spun on his plantation was woven into a very coarse material.[61] Despite the glowing predictions of southern editors that the Confederacy would soon find cards unnecessary, they continued in great demand during the entire conflict.

Looms, too, were scarce at the outbreak of the war. Those used in former days had been destroyed or had fallen apart, and new ones were too bulky to be brought through the blockade. Most of the looms used during the war were primitive, homemade affairs. There were those who had several looms installed in loom houses,[62] but most of the people placed theirs in the kitchen or in some unused room. These homemade looms were apparently quite satisfactory for they banged along day after day. An Arkansas lady who had made her loom, unaided by anyone, wove an average of eight yards of cloth a day on it.[63] Although there were a few factories which manufactured looms, they were not responsible for the majority of those found in Confederate homes, nor were they usually as satisfactory as the homemade ones.[64]

Spinning wheels were more plentiful in the South. It seemed that every attic harbored at least one, for they were brought forth suddenly and with great rapidity in the hour of need. A few factories in the Confederacy manufactured these, too. Sewing machines, like spinning wheels, seemed more plentiful, although new ones were not imported through the blockade because of their size and weight. Some were manufactured in the South early in the war, but the shortage of parts and necessary materials made the total production negligible. Even those who owned sewing machines were forced to let them lie idle during the war because of the lack of proper thread. The homemade thread was unsuitable for the machines, and that usually imported was very scarce.[65]

The result of this intense interest and concentrated effort in spinning and weaving was the famous Confederate homespun. Made in every state of the Confederacy, that produced in North Carolina and Georgia gained widespread fame for its beauty and durability. The wearing of homespun became fairly universal. Such men as Governor Joseph E. Brown[66] and Alexander H. Stephens, both of Georgia, wore it with pride. The latter was inaugurated Vice-President of the Confederacy in a homespun suit made by two ladies of Taliaferro County, Georgia.[67] Edmund Ruffin[68] wore homespun, as did several members of Congress, and the custom was even more widespread among the lesser-known folk of the Confederacy. These suits became so common among the men that it was an unusual sight late in the war to see men clad in broadcloth. Not only was the latter scarce, but it was considered unpatriotic to wear anything shipped through the blockade. As a diarist recorded, "nothing but homespun was respectable."[69]

Homespun made for dresses was frequently very pretty, being woven into checks, stripes, plaids, or plain. Women took great pride in the quality and beauty of their material, gladly exchanging samples with their friends. It was a common occurrence during the war to receive a letter from some female relative and find enclosed several samples of the latest products of her loom.[70] Some of the material was nearly as fine as muslin, while some was so coarse that straws might be shot through it without injuring it in any way. Women founded societies whose purpose was to wear nothing but homespun; they tried to make this as beautiful as possible. Men throughout the length and breadth of the Confederacy recorded their thoughts of women so attired, and the majority thought them lovely. While in Virginia, Heros Von Borcke exclaimed of a bride wearing homespun, "Ach, she was most beautiful in von spunhome dress";[71] in South Carolina Joseph Le Conte declared that he had "never seen more becoming gowns" than those of homespun;[72] and, in Texas, a farmer remarked that when his wife came into church in her homemade dress, he thought "she looked sweeter than any woman ever did."[73] Brides in homespun became the usual thing, especially in rural areas, but one saw far less of such fabric in towns and cities.

The homespun dress was memorialized in song. In 1862 a patriotic young lady wrote "Homespun Dress" to the tune of the popular "Bonnie Blue Flag." It became popular and for many years was sung as one of the songs coming out of the war. There were six stanzas and a chorus, part of which went as follows:

My homespun dress is plain, I know;
My hat's palmetto, too.
But then it shows what Southern girls
For Southern rights will do.
We send the bravest of our land
To battle with the foe;
And we will lend a helping hand
We love the South, you know.

Chorus
Hurrah! Hurrah!
For the sunny South so dear.
Three cheers for the homespun dress
That Southern ladies wear.[74]

All did not agree on the beauty and patriotism of wearing homespun. In the columns of the *Southern Illustrated News*, a popular newspaper-magazine of the war years, heated debate was carried on over the wearing of this domestic product. It started with a letter to the editors from a young lady in Virginia. She wrote that because she had worn a homespun dress to church the women of the congregation had smiled, sneered, "whispered and nudged each other." She asked the editors whether or not she should wear such fabric again. They assured her she should continue to do so, and when her dress was worn out, she should send them a scrap that they might "put it away with other prized mementos of . . . [the] year."[75] A month later, far-reaching effects of this controversy became evident when a correspondent from Mississippi wrote that the ladies of that state had "been wearing them [homespun], not from necessity but from choice,"[76] to which a Richmond reader responded that "not five out of five hundred ladies" in Richmond would "be caught in the street with a home-spun dress."[77] This was the last of this particular feud, but it shows the attitude toward the homemade dress during the war.

When there were no more old clothes to mend, and when homespun could not or would not be worn, substitutes were found and converted into articles of wearing apparel. In doing this, both imagination and ingenuity were needed, but the Southern women of the sixties apparently had both. Any piece of material large enough for a garment, and found in the home, was in danger of being converted. Draperies and curtains were most frequently used. Damasks, nets, laces, velvets, and, in truth, any material suitable for draping windows were found equally well-suited for draping the feminine frame. Brides wore wedding dresses of curtain materials; and some of the loveliest frocks in the Confederacy were made of materials once used in curtains.[78] So popular was this source of dress material that a verse of the day ran:

> Let me whisper: this dress I now wear for thee,
> Was a curtain of old in Philadelphee.[79]

Carpets, too, were cut up, but these were usually used for shoes; some, however, found their way into suits and coats. Sheets and pillow cases were converted into clothing to such an extent that an Alabama lady asserted that she doubted if there was a fine sheet in any house in the South when the war ended.[80] Blankets were sometimes used to make shirts, but so scant was the supply of blankets that this was the exception rather than the rule.[81] Mattresses were sacrificed on the altar of fashion, the cotton or wool stuffing being carded and spun, and the ticking made into shirts and dresses. Materials bought before the war to be used in the clothing of slaves were taken by the masters and mistresses for their use when nothing else could be bought. When this was done, discontent among the Negroes was often the result. Such was the case on the plantations of R. F. W. Allston of South Carolina, where there were complaints and work stoppage because of the lack of clothing for the Negroes.[82]

Because of the shortage of wool, new combinations of material were ingeniously worked out by the southern women. Among the most common of these combinations was that of cotton and rabbit, or raccoon, fur. This produced a soft flexible fabric that was described as "handsome . . . and . . . durable."[83] It was much warmer than pure cotton. Whenever wool could be had, it was combined with the fur; thus, a little wool would go much farther. Cow hair and dog hair too, were combined with cotton, producing a wool-like material. For those who could not obtain materials to combine or could not spin and weave, it was suggested that the furs of animals be used as cloaks or coats, or that skins be used for clothing.[84] Various species of nettle were said to produce a beautiful "linen-like cloth,"[85] and linen was one of the scarcest of materials in the Confederacy, for it was an imported fabric and much of it went for bandages. These various expedients were widely worn and frequently mentioned in the contemporary writings. Apparently they were not as pleasing or as satisfactory as the materials of other days, but they were made to do. One lady wrote that the southern people were fairly well satisfied with these substitute clothes, until someone came along in clothing imported through the blockade. Then, the wearer of this home-made material would become dissatisfied.[86]

Among those articles of clothing most frequently described by the women were hats. The struggle to obtain stylish head coverings was a constant one, and the results obtained were both lovely and ludicrous. While all women in the Confederacy did not spin or weave, practically all did make hats. Few were imported during the war, but when one did manage to get through the blockade, its wearer received an unusual amount of attention from others of her sex. A South Carolina lady received a bonnet in this manner; the first time that she wore it to church "there was not a woman in the congregation . . . who heard one word of the sermon; and the following week that bonnet had more visitors than any ten of the most fashionable women in the city."[87] But for such rare exceptions, headgear was made of nearly anything at hand. Many were constructed from old dresses, scraps of material, or from other hats. Those produced were often cooperative affairs. Neighbors and friends frequently pooled their resources including bits of ribbons, lace, and velvet, and from this pool would emerge hats for all the group. There were those who would "go quite a distance for only enough to trim a hat."[88] Such reconverted headgear often included paper brims, but they were nevertheless worn with pride by the designers, for few could afford to patronize millinery shops or to buy new trimmings, even when these were available. To charge $500 for a new ladies' hat or bonnet made in the Confederacy was the rule rather than the exception among milliners,[89] and imported bonnet ribbon was so expensive as to be prohibitive to most.[90]

Headdress made of grasses, leaves, and straw came into widespread use during the war. Straw hats were made from wheat, oats, and rye. The straw was gathered as nearly uniform in size as possible. It was then soaked overnight in boiling water, after which it was dried and plaited. If the natural yellow tint was not liked, the finished product was bleached by holding it over fumes of sulphur. Hats were also made from the needles of the long-leaf pine, from various species of wire grass, and even from corn shucks. But perhaps the most commonly known head coverings woven in the Confederacy were those made from palmetto. The South Carolina girls prided themselves on these creations, and some were conceded to be lovely. So popular did these homemade straw creations become that an old verse, first sung in the early part of the century, was revised to fit the occasion:

> Who now of threatening famine dare complain
>   When every female forehead teams with grain?—
> See how the wheat sheaves nod amid the plumes,
>   Our barns are now transferred to drawing rooms,
> And husbands who indulge in active lives
>   To fill their granaries may thresh their wives.[91]

Bonnets were the most widely worn of all styles. While some were simple "Quaker" or "Shaker" types, others were the ever-present sunbonnets. But the most unusual of all were the "skyscraper" bonnets. These were huge affairs, made of any light, thin material available and standing four or five inches above the forehead.[92] Of these, one lady said:

> As the hopes of the Confederacy declined, the bonnet reared it-self more aloft. . . . It was much easier to put on an addition to a bonnet beginning quite small, as they were worn in '61, than to take it off from the same. . . . As our bonnets rose with their ample scoop, the material declined in quality . . . until . . . almost anything was considered suitable to make a bonnet of; that is, to cover the pasteboard and wire additions, which were added from time to time . . . a bonnet of novel shape . . . [had] a sort of front portico or balustrade addition . . . I learned, upon inquiry that word had come through the blockade that bonnets were worn larger in front, next came a whisper that bonnets were worn larger behind. In an incredible short time . . . there appeared . . . sheds as it were, built upon the original body of the bonnets.[93]

To trim the headgear anything available was used. Old ribbons and bits of lace most often were resorted to, but feathers of all kinds were used also. Necessity compelled that these most often should be chicken feathers.[94] Delighted was the girl, however, who had a whole bird to perch on her hat or bonnet. A Georgia girl received one from a beau, and she was so delighted that she profusely recorded it in her diary.[95] More unusual were those hats trimmed with shavings from cow horns. These bits of horn were pasted or sewn on a pasteboard brim and trimmed with odd bits of ribbon, producing what was known as "cows' horn turbans."[96] Reminiscent of the French Revolution were the gay cockades worn on hats during the Civil War. The emblems might denote the city or state of the wearer, or they might be merely a colorful little rosette or a small Confederate flag. Whatever they were, they were extremely popular and were worn all during the war. Flowers, too, were widely used for trimming. Artificial flowers were used most often, but real ones in season were sometimes worn. In winter, when fresh flowers could not be found, holly berries and ivy served as trimming.[97]

Men wore homemade headgear. The tall silk hats disappeared almost entirely during the war, and those that were seen were usually well-worn, with the nap lying in all directions or entirely worn off.[98] Men's hats were often made of straw or pine needles. Betty Herndon Maury was very proud of the head covering she plaited for her husband from wheat straw.[99] As a substitute for felt, a material was woven from a little wool or cotton combined with animal hair, and it was suggested that the men of the Confederacy adopt the coonskin cap of the frontiersmen. Knitted caps were widely worn by the men, especially in the winter. Even President Davis wore one to church in the latter part of the war.[100] Many men, dominated not so much by fashion as women, tried to make old hats do for the duration of the war, but when this was impossible, they used these various substitutes or went bareheaded.

So expert did women become at the milliners' trade that they built up a regular business of making and selling hats. While many chose to keep their art amateur, those who became professional represented every rank of society.[101] In Fayetteville, North Carolina, palmetto hats were brought to markets from rural areas by the cart-load.[102] Hat factories sprang into existence all over the South, and millinery shops continued in business, although prices were high. The advertisements of the factories and millinery shops stressed the point that hats made in the South were as stylish and durable as any made in Europe or the North.

Shortages appeared in various miscellaneous and necessary items of clothing. As in the case of other items, substitutes were used when the genuine article was not available. Of all such items, undergarments are mentioned most frequently, for the substitute materials were most unsuited for these items. Prior to the war, underwear had been most commonly made from linen, fine cotton material, or silk. These were unobtainable by most people during the war, and a coarse homespun was all the new material that was generally available. None complained more bitterly of undergarments of this fabric than Emma LeConte. She especially dreaded wearing such a hot, coarse material in summer.[103] But its use was a last resort. Usually every sheet and pillowcase as well as every old garment of suitable material would be used before using homespun. J. B. Jones was elated when he received an undershirt made from a "dilapidated petticoat" that had belonged to his wife. He even resorted to buying secondhand underwear, so desperate did he become.[104]

A subject of vital importance to the women of the Confederacy centered around the problem of where they were to get corset stays and hoopskirts. This concerned many of them quite as much as the war issues for it was said that "women must lace, while men will fight."[105]   Corset stays were among the most lucrative items brought through the blockade. A man who captained a blockade-runner tells of how he surprised a meek young salesman in a Glasgow, Scotland, store by asking him for one thousand pairs of stays. "Such an unusual request sent him off like a rocket to a higher authority," and, upon obtaining permission from a superior, he permitted the customer to have the stays. When these were sold in Wilmington, North Carolina, the captain made a profit of 1100%.[106] If there was a reluctance to discuss the critical situation of corset stays between men and women, it was not evident. One young Confederate soldier, who had been with General Lee's army when it invaded Maryland, brought back to Virginia a pair of corset stays for his fiancee.[107]   Most women, however, found it necessary to substitute wooden splits for the usual stays; most often the splits were made from white oak, but hickory was sometimes used. Stays were removed from old corsets, and with these an entirely new garment was made from homespun. Those who stood in favor with the local blacksmith might get him to make stays. Mrs. Roger A. Pryor succeeded in so doing, the result being the best she ever had.[108]   There was less said, generally, about the hoopskirt situation, but hoops were scarce during the war for they were too bulky to import with great profit. Many women were forced to forsake the style of hoops, others followed the tendency to reduce their size.[109]   Both alternatives emphasized the necessity for corsets. Those who were determined to have hoops might piece together old ones or make them from grapevines. Both became common during the war.

Miscellaneous items demanding substitutes were numerous, and some are worthy of special mention. Raincoats were made from oilcloth, or even from rubberized piano covers. Handkerchiefs were made from nearly any material available, for this necessary item was scarce and expensive. When General Kirby Smith asked his wife to buy him some, she could find only three in Lynchburg.[110]   Before the cessation of hostilities, handkerchiefs cost as much as $20 each.[111]   One man was seen to tear a page from a book every time he felt the need of a handkerchief. Shortages forced women to knit socks and stockings as well as gloves, ties, and suspenders. Although not absolute necessities, both fans and parasols were greatly desired by some women. These, too, were made in the homes. Feather fans were easily made and were frequently sold, even, it is recorded, by the ladies of one of the oldest and most famous families of Virginia.[112] Patchwork parasols and umbrellas became the vogue through necessity. These were made on old frames from stray bits of material too small to be of any other use, but some of the finished products were very attractive.[113]

Women's fondness for fashionable clothes was never absent from the South during the war. As one woman said, her love for new fashions and pretty clothes was merely "scotched, . . . not killed."[114] Of course there were those who maintained that fashion concerned them not a bit,[115] yet they generally expended considerable effort to find the latest styles. The cut of the cloth was usually regulated not so much by what the future wearer wanted as by what he could get, and there was quite a diversity of styles because of the shortages. After mid-1863 nearly anything could be expected. It became a common sight to find large women squeezed into small garments, and small women floating around in large ones, while tall women seemed to wear short dresses, and short women "trailed about in fathoms of useless material."[116] Despite force of circumstance, interest in foreign styles was to be found in the South. When a Miss Perdue opened her ladies' shop in Memphis in the fall of 1861, she advertised the latest Southern styles, and appealed to women to come in and judge for themselves whether or not these clothes did not outdo "anything New York could present to the South."[117] And one of the most popular and oft-quoted columns was that written by Constance Cary for the *Southern Illustrated News*. This was a correspondence passing between two mythical personalities, "Secessia" in Baltimore and "Refugitta" in Richmond. "Secessia" wrote of the fashions and hair styles to be found beyond the blockade, while "Refugitta" told of the difficulties of obtaining anything in the South. The women were particularly anxious to see "Secessia's" column, for here they read of the latest fashions: "Refugitta's" letters were helpful, for from these they received valuable ideas.[118] Newspapers passed on to lady readers any fashion news coming into their offices. Wilmington remained the last source for such news, and until the fall of Fort Fisher, mention was made in the Wilmington *Journal* of the latest styles abroad. Whenever a dress or bonnet would get through the blockade, it would have many and varied reproductions, limited only by the scarcity of materials.

Patterns coming through were handed about among the women; originality of these was totally lacking in many communities save for the diversity of interpretations.[119] A fashion magazine was a choice gift. Soldiers sent them to friends and relatives when they were fortunate enough to obtain them.[120]

The problem of dyes for homespun and home-knit articles was not vital but was aggravating. The search for dyestuffs forced the people into the woods. This treasure chest for coloring had long been known to the people in remote areas and to many of the poorer people and Negroes, but when the war brought about a diminution of commercial dyes, all women were forced to use the primitive methods of dyeing cloth. The first problem was that of finding which plants produced which colors. Indigo was among the more familiar of these plants, and a few women grew this for the purpose of obtaining its purplish-blue dye.[121] The bark of swamp maple produced a clear purple, while the famous Confederate gray came from the myrtle bush, or a combination of pine and sweet gum bark. The hulls of black walnut, sumac berries, red oak bark and roots, sorghum seed, and plum roots, produced varying shades of brown, while the sumac berries also dyed some articles black. Yellow was obtained from cocklebur leaves and stalks, red from pokeberries, and green from hickory and alum. Orange was derived from sassafras bark and roots, and pink was obtained from a combination of pumpkin and pokeberries. While it is impossible to catalog all the plants used for coloring, it is known that the women turned into amateur chemists. They were aided by directions and hints published in the newspapers and magazines, and by the exchange of information with their friends. One lady admitted that she and her friends "were more anxious to learn a new process of dyeing" than they were of learning "a new stitch in crochet or worsted work."[122] A favorite riddle of the day ran like this: Question—"Why am I like Saint Paul?" Answer—"Because I dye daily."[123] Women banded together in groups and went deep into the woods for their bark, berries, and leaves;[124] when they returned they faced the struggle of suitable agents to "get" the colors. Copperas, produced by soaking a piece of rusty nail or iron in water, was resorted to most frequently.[125] It was also made of buckeye, alum, oxgall, sugar of lead, lye and lime water. Different materials accepted dyes with different results, and there was always much interest in a new experiment.

At a time when every piece of clothing was especially precious, proper cleaning was of great importance. Hints about the removing of spots and cleaning of materials were found in the newspapers and magazines. Such simple recipes as the use of Irish potatoes to clean silk or of tomato juice to remove rust stains were seen frequently.[126] A decoction of the leaves of the Virginia creeper was guaranteed to restore lustre and freshness to silk,[127] while wheat bran boiled with water and used for washing dresses restored "body" to lawn and muslin and also prevented fading.[128] There were a few cleaning establishments in the South, but these were found only in the larger towns, and they were not present in all the towns. One lady bemoaned the fact that there were no French cleaners in Richmond. She conceded that this was "a minor tragedy, but one that sank deep in . . . her soul."[129] Throughout the war professional cleaners advertised in the local papers, but there is virtually no evidence of the effect of their methods.

The clothing situation was critical in the Confederacy by the fall of 1863, and it became increasingly so with each passing month. But the people went about the solution of the problem with good humor and with generosity. They laughed, borrowed, and exchanged. Necessity, in truth, became the "mother of invention" for all of the people, and the citizens proved that they could manage, even though the blockade and the invading armies squeezed them like an anaconda.

HOUSING AND HOUSEHOLD GOODS

S HELTER, LIKE FOOD AND CLOTHING, CREATED PROBLEMS DURING
the Civil War and, while the housing shortage did not affect
all people, many suffered acutely. Some areas were more crowded
than others, but in practically every community there were houses
containing more people than their builders had planned. Refugees,
fleeing from the enemy, flocked into safe sections and created
grave housing problems. Towns and rural regions near camps
were filled to overflowing with families of soldiers, with camp fol-
lowers, and with speculators. Those who lived in out-of-the-way
areas, but were self-sustaining, were obliged to play host to hungry
city cousins; while those living in crowded towns found themselves expanding their households, filling them with country
cousins who had to come into town. This migration continued
for four years, varying but never ceasing. The almost total lack
of building during the war coupled with abnormal destruction
of property magnified the overcrowded situation.

Of all the congested areas in the Confederacy, none could compare with Richmond. The housing shortage was the first serious
one to be felt in the Confederate capital.[1] Into Richmond swarmed
government leaders and workers, military and naval officials, speculators, soldiers on furlough, foreign visitors and reporters, seekers
of privilege and commissions, mere onlookers, and their dependent families. The influx of people, plus the demand for government offices, resulted in bedlam of the worst sort. Never before
had such chaos on such a wide scale been witnessed in the South.
During the first year of the war, one observer declared that Richmond's Main Street was more crowded than New York's Broad-
way;[2] and in the crucial July of 1863 an English traveler said,
"Richmond was never intended to hold so many inhabitants as
it does now."[3] Private homes were opened with varying degrees

99

of cordiality to those who sought shelter, but few "guests" could hope to have more than one room made available to them. In this one room a family might sleep, cook, eat, and entertain. One diarist wrote that her room in Richmond accommodated "three people, all cooking needs, a ton of coal, woodpile [hidden under the bed], foods, trunks, clothes hanging around, [and] laundering needs."[4] Mrs. Virginia Clay-Clopton, one of the more prominent social leaders in the Confederacy, had no parlor at her disposal in Richmond in 1862. She was embarrassed at having to entertain an Alabama friend, William Lowndes Yancey, in her bedroom.[5] Constance Cary was fortunate enough to have a parlor as well as a bedroom, but they were some distance apart. Her parlor was a doctor's office, while her bedroom was in a nearby hotel. This arrangement was far from convenient, but it was made to do.[6]

Hotels, as well as private residences, had capacity crowds under their roofs. Rooms were filled to overflowing, and beds were set up in the "parlors, halls and even on the billiard tables."[7] So crowded and inconvenient were the facilities of even the best hotels in Richmond, that an Alabama soldier wrote his fiancee that life in camp was "almost preferable" to living in a Richmond hotel.[8] It was nearly impossible to get a room in a hotel, unless one had influence. The editor of a Houston, Texas, paper arrived in Richmond in the summer of 1862 and immediately went to a hotel. It was sometime before he could get within speaking distance of the clerk, and when he did get close enough to request a room, the clerk, seeing that he had no "gilt buttons, epaulets or any mark of military distinction, . . . cooly replied that if . . . [he] could get a bed with a friend, . . . [he] would be fortunate."[9] Faced with so many customers, the problem of food was a major one with hotel management. Late in the war many hotels stopped serving meals altogether,[10] while during the entire four years, they were forced to forego serving meals table d'hôte.[11] Because of the shortage of help and food, the hotel dining rooms were forced to limit service to a few hours each day, and long before the time for the doors to open, crowds "stood hungrily around"; and when the doors were opened they rushed in "scrambling for seats."[12]

Boarding houses practically ceased to exist in Richmond during the war. It was found to be more profitable and far less worrisome merely to rent rooms. Permission was usually given to cook in the rooms, and most roomers resorted to this practice. When all the conventional places were filled to capacity, the unconventional were sought out as places of abode, and even these became scarce. "Empty factories, schoolhouses and abandoned cabins" were converted into places of shelter.[13] Basements and attics were homes to hundreds. With such conditions, it is little wonder that those searching for a place to live walked for hours, day after day, following every possible clue, and when no clues were to be had, they resorted to knocking on door after door. Judith Brockenbrough McGuire, a middle-aged refugee from Alexandria and a woman of high social standing, walked the streets of Richmond every day for two weeks before finding a miserable hovel of a room.[14]

So crowded was Richmond that its population overflowed into nearby areas. Ashland, fifteen miles to the north, housed many who worked in the capital and were forced to commute, even in that age of uncertain transportation facilities. The hotel there made use of every available room, utilizing both the billiard room and the ballroom as places of abode.[15] Houses, too, expanded to take in Richmond's overflow. In one eight room house in Ashland six families lived for two and one-half years while the men commuted to the capital to work.[16] No other area was so crowded for such a long period as was Richmond and the surrounding countryside.

The housing shortage was felt to a lesser degree in other cities, but wherever there were homeless people, they suffered as acutely as those in Richmond, and crowded households on Atlanta's Peachtree Street were just as uncomfortable as those on Cary Street in the Virginia capital. Everywhere houses were stretched to "india-rubber capacity,"[17] and the households were "very heterogeneous."[18] Mrs. McGuire found that, as a rule, those living in the country would stretch the capacity of their homes to accommodate more of the homeless, while those in the towns of the Confederacy were far less cordial.[19] Despite the lack of cordiality in the towns, people continued to crowd in. Petersburg, Charlottesville, and Lynchburg, Virginia, were crowded beyond anything ever before experienced. Raleigh and Charlotte, North Carolina; Columbia and Greenville, South Carolina; Atlanta and Augusta, Georgia; Mobile and Selma, Alabama; Jackson, Mississippi; Little Rock and Arkadelphia, Arkansas; Shreveport, Louisiana; and Houston,

Texas, were all packed to capacity with their own citizens and with people who had resided elsewhere before the war. From picturesque Winchester, high in the Shenendoah Valley, to tiny Laredo, on the Mexican border, there was a housing shortage. Midway in the war no room was available in Winchester, and travelers were forced to journey on in search of a room.[20] In Laredo, a refugee family from Louisiana, finding no hotel, was forced to rent an adobe house. As this adobe had only a dirt floor, bunks for beds, and no toilet facilities, except a public fountain on the patio, the inhabitants were far from comfortable.[21] Advertisements for houses, appearing in Confederate newspapers, were frequently run for weeks; then they would suddenly no longer be in their customary corner. Whether such houses were found or the advertiser gave up in despair is not recorded. An example of this sort of advertising was in the *Southern Confederacy* for several weeks in the fall of 1861:

> The advertiser wishes to rent a neat cottage house with 6 or 8 rooms, having garden, lot and stable, and good water.[22]

It is not known whether he got his desired home, but the long drawn out effort to secure a house indicates an already crowded Atlanta. Few people, however, aspired to a whole house. The "one-room-rule" became nearly as universal in other parts of the Confederacy as in Richmond. A common answer when asked if one was "housekeeping" was "No, I room-keep."[23] In many towns people walked for days in search of lodging of some sort. Mrs. Cornelia McDonald walked through the little town of Lexington, Virginia, for three days. She found only one set of rooms and the owner refused to rent her these because she had children. Finally she was forced to resort to a very unsatisfactory arrangement of a boarding house.[24] But even boarding houses decreased in number as food and help became scarce and mere rooms became dear. The boarding houses in rural areas fared fairly well during the war but, unfortunately, were not in such great demand as those in the towns.

Hotel rooms were scarce in all parts of the Confederacy. Montgomery was the first city to feel the impact of greater numbers than could be accommodated by local hostelries. As the provisional capital during the early months of the war, it saw a sudden and overwhelming influx of people. Every available space in the hotels was utilized and beds were added in all of the rooms; the occupants were many and varied and usually unknown to each other. When the English journalist, W. H. Russell, visited Montgomery in May, 1861, he found that his room contained "four large four-post beds, a rickety table and some chairs of infirm purpose and fundamental unsoundness. The floor was carpetless, covered with the litter of paper and ends of cigars, and stained with tobacco juice. The broken glass of the window afforded no ungrateful means of ventilation." Three mattresses were placed on the floor to accommodate late comers.[25] Such congestion and unattractive surroundings became general as the war continued. Inland towns and port towns, Virginia towns and Texas towns, all faced the problem of too many travelers and too few hotel accommodations. The editor of the Wilmington *Journal* voiced his disgust at the situation by writing, "The want of Hotel accommodations, always a hard case in Wilmington, has now become a crying yea, a roaring and bellowing evil, . . . one that is . . . not to be endured."[26] A Houston editor, in a quieter but more facetious tone, wrote: "The number of travelers who daily arrive in this city is astonishing. Our hotels are mighty crowded from garret to basement. Texas may be sparsely populated, but we have seen people enough during the last few weeks to whip any Yankee force that may be sent here."[27] There were those who found cozy, comfortable hotel rooms, Mrs. James Chesnut, Jr., being an example,[28] but they were the exception rather than the rule. Eliza Frances Andrews found what must have been the worst among the dirty, poorly furnished accommodations in a Milledgeville, Georgia, hotel. When Miss Andrews and her friends entered, their "hearts sank," so inadequately was it furnished and so filthy was it kept. There was "no . . . wash basin, pitcher, nor towels, and the walls on each side of the bed were black with tobacco spit. The fireplace was a dump heap that was enough to turn the stomach of a pig, and over the mantle some former occupant had inscribed this caution: 'One bed has lice in it, the other fleas and both bugs; chimney smokes, better change.' "[29]

Because of the lack of hotel accommodations, travelers were frequently uncomfortable and even inadequately cared for. To aid as best they could hotels permitted travelers to sit in the lobbies, and railroad waiting rooms were usually filled both day and night. Louise, daughter of Senator Louis T. Wigfall of Texas, was forced to spend a night in an unidentified Georgia town sitting on her baggage on a train platform because no space was available in any house.[30] Only a short time before the collapse of the Confederacy, already overcrowded Charlotte, North Carolina, witnessed the influx of hundreds of refugees fleeing before General Sherman's army. One cold February night three hundred women and children descended upon the town at one time and none could find rooms. Mrs. Joseph E. Johnston, wife of the Confederate General, described this situation as "lamentable."[31] Fortunate, indeed, were wartime travelers who could find accommodations, but rare to the point of being practically nonexistent was he who had a hotel room to himself. Fitzgerald Ross, an English traveler, was elated to find such single accommodations in a Staunton, Virginia, hotel.[32]

Lack of houses forced the people of the Confederacy to devise substitutes for customary places of abode. In originating and locating such substitute dwellings, the imagination and ingenuity of the Confederate people kept pace with that exhibited in finding substitutes for food and clothing. Those who could afford to do so, their number was limited, bought or rented entire hotels for their families to live in when they were forced to leave their homes.[33] More common were the less pretentious substitute homes. Public buildings were simply taken over by the homeless. Colleges, schools, churches, eleemosynary institutions, and factories were made into temporary homes when circumstances so directed.[34] Drawing rooms, dining rooms, and halls were converted into bedrooms;[35] servants' houses and even stables[36] furnished welcome shelter for some. Boxcars, always scarce, were sometimes turned into homes, and boats, too, were used when available. Both of these last mentioned alternatives were considered luxurious for the times. Attics were swept out and furnished with odds and ends, "contributed by anyone who had a superabundance,"[37] while cellars were inhabited by many. These were damp but nevertheless welcome to the homeless.[38] Tents were used by some, although they were never considered very desirable.[39] Of all the housing expedients resorted to by the Confederate civilians, none was more colorful and ingenious than the caves. They were extensively used in Vicksburg, and in many other areas where the terrain made them possible. In besieged Vicksburg, however, it was said that they became "the fashion," and those who understood the job of digging caves were well paid. These cost "from thirty to fifty dollars"; many were large, fairly comfortable affairs, usually dug in the shape of a "T", providing three nooks that might be made private by hanging curtains.[40] Caves were frequently used in North Carolina and Georgia. The universal complaint voiced by the dwellers, wherever they were found, was that of constant dampness. In rainy weather the walls frequently oozed water, and there was constant darkness mingled with the damp, chill air.

The price of houses and rooms kept pace with the inflationary trends of the times. Rents were tremendously high. In Richmond small rooms rented for $60 per month, plus part of the heating bill in 1861; similar rooms rented for $100 per month in 1865.[41] J. B. Jones rented a four room house for his family in 1862, paying $1,200 per year for its use, but he consoled himself with the hope that he and a friend might jointly rent a twelve room house for a mere $1,800.[42] By 1864 he recorded that the rent on a modest dwelling near his was $6,000 per year.[43] Prices were in proportion elsewhere in the Confederacy, and they rose as the Confederate currency depreciated. Real estate sometimes demanded fabulous prices. A Charleston gentleman wrote his wife, then in France, that he was amazed at a friend's house being sold for $90,000.[44] The great scarcity played a part in forcing prices skyward.

While adequate housing was always a problem during the war, obtaining a roof over one's head did not give assurance that worries were ended. There was a pathetic shortage of many household effects. This was felt by those who managed to live in the most spacious surroundings, as well as those who existed in makeshift homes. Lighting, heating, furnishings, utensils, linens, laundry needs, and many lesser household items were scarce, and their absence created daily problems for housewives.

The problem of adequate lighting for the homes was never completely solved, and few things were as vexing to the civilian population as this insufficiency. A fundamental shortage that tended to affect all people was that of matches. Some of the well-known and much sought after "lucifer" matches were brought through the blockade, but the quantity was inadequate to supply the needs of the Confederacy. Factories were established in the South, but "Confederate" matches were not satisfactory.[45] They usually came in tiny blocks from which a match was broken when needed. The manufacturers sold them in blocks because there was a shortage of boxes.[46] Newspapers published instructions for making matches at home,[47] but because of the complicated process and the difficult-to-procure and unfamiliar ingredients, the process did little to relieve the shortage. Housewives devised several ways of saving them. Fires were carefully banked at night and "great was the consternation if the coals died out."[48] In those towns where gas was used for illumination, at least one burner was kept on all day so that the others might be lighted from this one at nightfall. Ingenious as this may have been from the standpoint of saving or doing without matches, it defeated its purpose by creating a shortage of gas.[49]

Candles, normally imported from New England, were scarce in the Confederacy. Substitutes devised by the southern people were known as "Confederate" candles, and were frequent subjects of discussion during the war. So varied were the designs of these that all cannot be described. Basically, they were made of strips of rags sewn together, twisted, and then dipped time and time again into liquid wax. The candle made by this process was about the size of one's small finger and at least two yards in length, often longer. It was wrapped around a bottle or corn cob, for it was incapable of standing alone. Sometimes it was wrapped in ornate designs. As the candle was used, it was unwound several inches at a time and bent in an upright position.[50] The wax utilized might vary in formula, but it generally consisted of beeswax, rosin, and turpentine.[51] When beeswax could not be obtained, various substitutes were used, among them wax made from myrtle berries boiled in water, or that made from the leaves of the prickly pear boiled with tallow. No one was completely satisfied with the "Confederate" candles. One lady described them as "miserable";[52] another said they burned so fast that even "during family prayers" someone had to watch them.[53] They were, however, given as Christmas gifts and were recognized as "a labor of love."[54] Although most of the tallow molds used in former times were lost or destroyed by 1861, some existed and were put into use. Some housewives tried to make candles without molds, but they were not very successful. The candles had a way of "falling over like the Tower of Pisa as soon as the wick was ignited."[55] Regardless of what kind of candle one used, all agreed that thrift must be practiced in their use. To use more than one candle was thought to be "reckless and foolish extravagance."[56]

Those who used oil lamps also ran into difficulties. The oil customarily used was kerosene, of which little was available during the war. The people of the Confederacy were forced to devise substitutes. One of these, manufactured commercially, was terebene oil, a preparation made from redistilled turpentine. Many objected to this oil because it produced a great quantity of smoke.[57] Other substitutes were made from peas, sunflowers, cotton seed, and corn. Another shortage that affected lamp lighting was that of wicks. Instructions for making these were published in several papers but the improvised wicks did not suffice, and many were forced to use "Confederate" candles or other means of lighting.[58]

Various expedients were found and utilized by those who found it impossible to use either candles or lamps. Pine torches were among the more simple of these expedients. These had always been used by the rural folks of the South; they were now widely used by urban dwellers and referred to as "Confederate gas."[59] They were highly praised for the quality of light they shed. Another simple method of lighting was the placing of sycamore balls or sweet gum globes in a shallow bowl filled with some sort of oil or grease, usually lard. The results were interpreted differently by various users. A young girl declared that they produced a "fairylike light";[60] a gentleman thought they made a "sickly glare."[61] But one thing was certain, they failed to give sufficient light for an entire room. Another substitute was paper twisted into a wick and placed in a saucer of grease. This method was widely used, but produced only a faint glow.[62]

In some few cities and larger towns of the Confederacy, gaslight was used for street, office, and home illumination. But the consumers had their troubles, and the battle to maintain constant service caused the officials of the gas companies to have many headaches. The shortage and inferior quality of coal, rosin, lime, and even of wood used for making and purifying gas, together with worn-out machinery and poor transportation facilities, affected the output and quality of gas. The gas jet that was often kept burning all day in home and office naturally wasted an abnormal amount in a time when production of even the normal amount was impossible.[63] Because of the shortage, gas was sometimes cut off in the daytime and street lights were seldom on at

night.[64] Even with these precautions, the problem of supplying
it for all was never solved. A Richmond paper declared that the
spasmodic appearance of gas gave the citizens of that town "more
concern and trouble than . . . [did] the presence of Grant."[65] That
produced had such an unpleasant odor that people constantly complained; and some believed the gas was responsible for several
deaths in Richmond.[66] Its price, $80 per thousand feet, was so
high that it was an unobtainable luxury to many.[67] But a Charles-
tonian, writing to his wife who was then visiting in France, declared that Greenville, South Carolina, was an excellent town to
reside in during the war because it had "a constant supply" of
gas.[68]

Heating, like lighting, homes created serious problems. Old
stoves were made to last whenever possible, for new ones were
seldom available. Little iron was to be had for manufacturing
stoves, and their weight and bulkiness prevented blockade-runners
from carrying them.[69] Those who used wood-burning fireplaces
were most fortunate, but the problem of getting wood proved very
troublesome. Some coal-burning grates were manufactured for
use in fireplaces, but people who used them were often handicapped
by a lack of coal.[70] Some people, living in makeshift homes, had
neither stove nor fireplace; they had to resort to cooking outside,
while they lived in frigid quarters.[71] The lack of fuel, both coal
and wood, contributed to the problem of heating. There was
sufficient wood in the forests, but the inadequacy of labor and
transportation made its cutting and hauling impossible. The
wood shortage was widespread, appearing in the first winter of
the war and continuing throughout the conflict.[72] Even when
dealers managed to get it from rural areas, they faced the insurmountable difficulty of delivering it to their customers because
of the lack of wagons and teams. Prices of wood rose sharply as the
shortage became more acute. A South Carolina family paid $100
a cord for it in January, 1865.[73] The shortage, coupled with the
high price, forced many to cut their own timber when it was at all
possible; some even burned up fence rails.[74]

Little coal was obtainable during the war. Richmond seems
to have felt its lack more seriously than any other area. As early
as October, 1861, the supply in this city had dwindled until it was
wholly inadequate to meet the demand,[75] and it soon became necessary to put one's name on a coal list far in advance of the date

of delivery. J. B. Jones was depressed by the fact that Richmond was cold because of a lack of coal while there were "millions of tons . . . almost under the . . . city."[76] As in the case of wood and other commodities, the shortage of labor coupled with inadequate transportation facilities made it impossible to obtain coal. During the winter of 1864, there was real suffering because of both the wood and coal shortage. Even green pine was sold at exorbitant prices, but it was not a good fuel. It was said that the chief value one derived from buying and using green pine for fuel was the warmth he got from the constant labor it took to make the wood burn.[77] Fireballs were suggested as a substitute for both wood and coal. These were made by mixing small pieces of coal and sawdust with sand, clay, and water, and rolling the mixture into balls, and allowing them to become hard. These could not be used to start a fire, but they maintained a "strong heat" once the fire was started.[78] At best Confederate homes were dimly lighted and poorly heated.

It was a difficult task to furnish the makeshift homes in which so many people lived during the war. Much furniture was destroyed by the enemy as he advanced into the South, and that not actually destroyed could not be removed by refugees fleeing for their safety. Beds were especially scarce; old ones stored away in attics were brought down to take care of the overflow of guests whose extended visits were made necessary by the vicissitudes of war. When there were no more beds, various substitutes were found. Some made bedsteads from rough boards, but pallets were more generally used. Springs were made from strips of rope, or material, and poles were sometimes used. Mattresses and pillows were stuffed with many different articles: seed cotton, straw, leaves, black moss, and palmetto. Dr. F. P. Porcher says that cotton was first used for stuffing mattresses during the Civil War. He thought it the best substance because

> vermin will not abide in it; there is no grease in it, as in hair or wool; it does not get stale or acquire an unpleasant odor as feathers often do; moths do not infest it as they do wool; it does not pack or become hard as moss does; nor does it become dry, brittle or dusty as do straw, hay, or shucks. It is the cheapest, most comfortable, and most healthy material for bedding.[79]

Quite often mattresses were used on the floor without the benefit of bedstead. Baby beds were unobtainable in sufficient quantity;

at least one baby slept in a cradle made from a coffin.[80] Chairs
and tables were also scarce. In overcrowded Houston, Texas, hotels lacked sufficient chairs to accommodate their guests;[81] and all
over the Confederacy boxes, when they could be found, were used
in place of chairs. The furniture made during the war was usually
plain and some of it quite rough. Homespun was used for uphol-
stery and straw for stuffing. Wicker furniture became popular
during the war, because it was simple to make. Grapevines were
said to make a pretty and not uncomfortable chair or sofa.[82] Furniture was scarce enough to command fabulous prices. Secondhand furniture was so expensive that some found it profitable to sell
whatever unnecessary pieces they might own,[83] and they found
a ready market for it.

Housekeepers found it difficult to secure bedding. They had
donated so much for bandages and cover early in the war that
before 1865 many faced real shortages. The natural process of
wearing-out, coupled with destruction and loss, contributed to the
shortage. It was the usual thing to find ragged sheets and pillow
cases in many of the finest homes. A Georgia girl found only one
sheet on a bed in the room of a friend;[84] this practice was one way
of making a limited supply go a long way. Many were forced to
use homespun sheets, cases, and towels just as they were forced
to wear homespun garments. These were coarse and unsatisfactory,
but they did suffice, nevertheless.[85] Those living in sections infested with mosquitoes faced the problem of obtaining mosquito
netting with which to cover their beds. There seems to have been
no substitute for this article, and one had to do without once the
netting wore out.[86]

Blankets, given so generously early in the war, became precious
articles after 1862. The simplest way to remedy the blanket shortage was to cut up carpets, and this practice became almost universal. Brussels carpets were sacrificed for this purpose as readily
as the rag rugs.[87] On the coast, in the area around Wilmington
and Charleston, moss blankets were woven and used. They were
described as "thick and warm."[88] Another substitute was a comfort
made from two homespun sheets lined with layers of newspapers.
This, although warm, was noisy and so stiff as to be uncomfortable.[89]

Dishes, cooking utensils and silverware can be added to the
list of scarce items. These articles had been imported before the

war and few new ones could be obtained, for it was almost impossible to manufacture them in the South during the conflict. The only cooking utensil left in many households by the end of the war was a skillet, although some also had a coffee pot. A lady in Virginia managed to rent a skillet from a servant. The charge for this was one dollar per month.[90] Another Virginia lady had no utensil but a giant coffee pot discarded by a hotel. Her neighbor was highly amused to see her using it as a container for dough.[91] China and glass when broken were practically irreplaceable. These items were among the first sought at auctions, but few came through the blockade because of their fragility. In place of Haviland, Spode, or Wedgwood, tin plates and cups came into widespread use. Even social leaders were forced to use tin,[92] and some were obliged to eat from discarded tin cans.[93] Gourds came to be highly prized as cups in all parts of the Confederacy. Domestic pottery was used when it could be obtained. That made in the Valley of Virginia gained renown, although it was coarse, rough, and of a dirty-brown color. Virginia pottery plates, cups, saucers, washbowls, pitchers, and milk crocks, although unattractive, were "convenient and useful."[94] Bottles served as tumblers after their tops had been cut off by means of a hot wire, but the edges were sharp and often cut the user.[95] In an effort to restore broken china, pottery, and glass to a usable state, various mending agents were made, and much publicity was given those that were successful. Among substitutes for regular mending cement, which was no longer obtainable, were baked potato combined with flour, and lime combined with eggwhite. Much silver was taken by the Federals, lost, or buried during the war. Refugees were seldom able to carry silver with them, and forks, knives, and spoons were at a premium. Stirring sugar or cream into a beverage became nearly as much a ritual as pouring it at parties; one person with a single spoon would stir each cup before it was served to the guests.[96] Wooden spoons, forks, and knives were used extensively. Some were plain, others ornate.[97] A lady wrote that a man with extremely long fingernails informed her that, since he had no spoon, he used his nails instead.[98] Ornaments that help to beautify a table were almost totally lacking toward the end of the war. Salt and pepper containers were made from paper, and old bottles served as candleholders and vases. The lowly bucket became an item to cherish. A mother, living on a farm, sent her son a bucket of butter, but she asked him to be sure and return the bucket.[99]

Practically all cleaning articles were unobtainable before the war ended. Soap was one of the scarcest commodities, and the inability to get it caused much concern. Much effort was expended in trying to relieve this shortage, but little was accomplished. Lack of fats and potash prevented the making of an adequate supply. Drives to collect grease and fats were made in some of the larger towns. In New Orleans the housewives might obtain one pound of soap in exchange for two pounds of grease.[100]   A substitute made from rosin instead of grease was used.[101]   Various oils, heretofore unused, were tried; among these was the oil from cotton seed, corn shucks, and chinaberries. When made from the latter, it was called "Poor Man's Soap."[102]   Potash, obtained from burning wood, was marketed for use in its manufacture. The Medical Department of the Confederate government recommended the use of wheat straw ashes as ideal for this purpose.[103] Ladies who missed the delicately scented imported soaps used rose leaves to perfume the harsh homemade product;[104] perfumes or colognes that had come into milady's possession before the war were used in a similar manner.[105]   Newspapers encouraged women to turn to soap making. Many made it for the use of their families only; others eked out a living from its sale.[106]   It was made in great quantities by factories established for that purpose. Advertisements of such factory-made soap appeared in many newspapers at various times during the war; and one soldier advertised recipes at $5 each. He assured his readers that his recipes did not call for grease, yet the product washed clothes "with less rubbing than ordinary soap, and . . . [made] them much whiter."[107]   Despite these wartime expedients, soap remained among the rarest, most precious commodities. Hotels ceased to furnish it, and homes used it sparingly. Commercial starch was also lacking. While not an absolute necessity, it was desired by those who wanted their wearing apparel kept fresh and neat. Hence "each household made its own starch" from bran of wheat flour, green corn, sweet potatoes,[108] or Irish potatoes.[109]

Keeping the family's clothes and bodies clean without soap was indeed difficult, but keeping the house clean was also a problem. Soap was needed in washing dishes, woodwork, and floors, as well as in washing clothes and bodies. There was also a scarcity of brooms. Newspapers frequently mentioned this scarcity. Brooms made of corn and broomsedge came into general use. An editor, pleased with the one made and presented to him by an Atlanta belle, promised to send her a beau when they became more plentiful after the war.[110] Broom factories were established in Georgia, and broom corn was raised in considerable quantity, in an effort to alleviate the shortage of this household necessity. Mops were scarce, and newspapers published instructions on how to make them. But less attention was paid to mops than to brooms.

Most people found that wartime accommodations were less comfortable than those to which they were accustomed. If they remained at home, their once spacious houses were usually crowded with homeless relatives and friends. If they left home, they were almost sure to find themselves in congested, uncomfortable surroundings.

VII

DRUGS AND MEDICINE

O F ALL THE MAJOR SHORTAGES APPEARING DURING THE CIVIL WAR that of medicine received greater study and more widespread concentrated effort designed to remedy the situation than did any other. Individuals, prominent and little-known, and the government, worked to find the answer to the shortage of medicine. Substitutes were discovered, but these were not generally effective; the use of them would have been amusing had it not been for the suffering resulting from lack of more efficacious means. The army and navy were in need of great quantities of medicine and anaesthetics, always dire necessities in time of war. The people at home required their usual quantity, and when this was not forthcoming they were forced to do without or to concoct their own from the medicinal plants at hand.

The South had been dependent upon the outside world for medicine of all kinds, except "home remedies" used by many of its people. Of all imported, none was so necessary in the South as quinine, since malaria was prevalent over most of the region. As if striking at the most vulnerable spot in the Confederacy, the United States, immediately upon the outbreak of war, placed medicine on the contraband list. Few war measures caused feeling to run so high in both the North and the South, for many felt this to be an inhuman, barbarous act. When the American Medical Association met in New York in 1864, some doctors decided that they would try to get the restrictions regarding medicine going into the Confederacy lifted in the name of humanity, but their motion to that effect was tabled "indefinitely."[1] And the restrictions were not removed for the duration of the war. A poem urging the continuance of the contraband principle was widely circulated in the Northern newspapers as follows:

115

No more quinine—let 'em shake
No more Spaldings pills—let their heads ache;
No morphine—let 'em lie awake:
No mercury for the rebels take
Though fever all their vitals bake;
No nitre drops, their heat to slake;
No splinters though their necks they break,
And, above all, no Southern rake
Shall have his 'wine for stomacks sake,'
Till full apology they make.[2]

From the adoption of Federal restrictions, there was never sufficient medicine to relieve the sickness and suffering in the Confederacy.

The people of the South had three possible sources of supply.
They might capture enemy medical stores and surgical equipment,
run the blockade, or manufacture medicines from ingredients at
hand. Before the war ended, they did all three. Of these, the
first netted the least for the homefront. Medicines and surgical
equipment were captured from time to time, but this became increasingly rare as the course of the war turned against the Confederates. And when such supplies were captured, they were diverted to military channels and had no effect on the supply of
medicines for civilians.

The second source of supply, through running the blockade,
proved far more successful. Small in bulk and high in price, medicine became a part of the cargo of nearly every blockade-runner.
These cargoes destined for civilian use were usually sold at auction
at the port where the ship docked. They went to the highest bid-
der, and by the time they had seeped down to the people in remote areas, they were exorbitant in price. Auctions of imported
medicines were regular occurrences until the ports were captured
by Union forces. They were announced through the local papers
in advance of the sale.[3] Land blockade-running was more interesting than running of the water blockade. Some made a profession of this with medicines. Drugs could be easily concealed on
one's person and were highly remunerative. This trade took place
in all sections where North met South. "A large contraband drug
trade was carried on by an almost continuous line of houseboats
floating on the Mississippi River." Drugs were sent down the
river originally from Paducah, Kentucky, or Cairo, Illinois, by

Northern speculators or traders and were sent ashore into the Confederacy at night.[4] During the late winter and early spring of 1862, a story was widely circulated that some of the quinine sent into Tennessee and Arkansas in this manner was poisoned; heated editorials and warnings followed. The quinine was believed to have contained strychnine, and the people were cautioned against its use.[5] An Alabamian, who several times succeeded in getting through the Federal lines around Memphis, carried medicine in an old hospital wagon marked with a yellow flag and the word "Small-pox."[6] No one dared interfere. Women, too, brought medicines through the lines, some making regular expeditions, others occasional. The Cary cousins brought medicine,[7] and so frequently did other ladies of prominence run the blockade with drugs that one author assured his readers that "nice" women were engaged in the practice.[8] Those who tried to bring medicines into the South were not always successful. The story is told of one lady who made four successful trips before an accident overtook her. Apparently she had her "cargo" of drugs tied under her hoop skirts, but a string broke at an inopportune moment and "the walking drugstore was brought to 'dire combustion.' "[9] Even children took part in the smuggling of drugs into the South. There is one instance of quinine being hidden in a doll's head and thus brought through the lines.[10]

The rank and file of the people, especially those in the remote areas of the Confederacy, attempted to manufacture their own medicines. The interior towns suffered most from the lack, for those nearer the lines or on the coast managed to get some drugs through the blockade. Doctors and druggists made medicinal remedies of whatever drugs were available. These were sometimes made in quantity and advertised for sale. Usually such advertisements contained a statement that the advertiser had been urged, begged, or induced to put his knowledge into practice so that the people might benefit.[11] Next in importance to the hundreds of druggists and doctors who made medicine from stocks on hand and from plants were Negroes, who had, in many instances, long been accustomed to using various indigenous plants as medicine. They were "versed in all the science of herbs and barks for teas and lotions," and they frequently improvised practical prescriptions.[12] Often without the aid of local druggists, physicians, or Negroes, women recalled the favorite remedies used by their grandmothers. They found their medicine in the forests and fields; said one: "The woods . . . were . . . our drug store."[13] Even in a town the size of Richmond herbs were often used instead of licensed medicines,[14] and the lack of drugs sometimes forced drugstores to close their doors.[15]

The war increased interest in the dissemination of medical knowledge, for necessity forced the people to find their remedies close at hand. Druggists held conventions to discuss the problem of how to secure medicines. One, meeting in Augusta, Georgia, in the spring of 1863, adopted a resolution to appoint a committee of three to accept samples of medicines and chemicals manufactured from the natural resources, and to examine these products. This committee was also to have charge of distributing scientific apparatus that might be donated to the cause of furthering research.[16] The short-lived monthly magazine, the *Confederate States Medical and Surgical Journal*, January, 1864, to February, 1865, was, by its own confession, established "not only as an organ of the Southern medical profession, but as a means of imparting information to those who have been debarred from any intercourse with the scientific world."[17] This publication was favorably received and distributed as far as the bounds of the Confederacy would permit. It was largely devoted to medical problems of the military camp, but it published some helpful articles pertaining to the utilization and manufacture of plants at hand. It constantly sought such information from its readers.

Of all the agencies interested in finding and spreading information of medical value, none was so energetic and productive as the Confederate government. Knowledge of medicine that would help the sick and wounded soldiers was of paramount importance, but findings of the Medical Department of the Confederate Army were broadcast over the South for the benefit of the civilians. The government issued pamphlets containing instructions for preserving health and avoiding illnesses,[18] and lists of plants having medicinal value.[19] It interested itself in securing medical supplies from abroad, establishing agents in Europe for this purpose; but after 1863 they were not too successful. These agents were interested primarily in obtaining medical supplies for use of the armed forces. The effect of such purchases on the homefront was slight.[20] By far the most ambitious and far-reaching program of the Medical Department was the establishing of medical and chemical laboratories and the carrying on of research in indigenous plants. Laboratories were established in nearly every southern state. They were located in Richmond, Virginia; Charlotte and Lincolnton, North Carolina; Columbia, South Carolina; Augusta, Macon, Atlanta, and Milledgeville, Georgia; Montgomery and Mobile, Alabama; Knoxville, Tennessee; Arkadelphia, Arkansas; and Tyler, Texas.[21] Each laboratory was severely handicapped by lack of proper equipment. One of the lesser tragedies of the war was the case of a blockade-runner, bringing much needed apparatus from Europe, which successfully ran the blockade into Wilmington, only to see the city fall before the equipment could be distributed and put into use.[22]

While lacking sufficient medical apparatus, these southern laboratories called into the service some of the best-known scientists in the South. Among these were John and Joseph LeConte, James Woodrow, W. R. Johnston, D. D. Curtman, Julian Chisholm, and William H. Prioleau. None were better trained and more successful in the production of medicines than James Woodrow and the LeConte brothers. These three worked in the laboratory at Columbia, South Carolina, during the entire war.[23] Although not associated with any one laboratory, Samuel Preston Moore, Surgeon-General of the Confederacy, was in a great degree responsible for the research in indigenous plants. He was intensely interested in the subject, and realized the absolute necessity of falling back on native drugs. In the spring of 1862, he stressed the necessity of developing internal resources and using such resources in the manufacture of medicine. He sent pamphlets over the South, describing "indigenous, medicinal substances of the vegetable kingdom," and urging their use. He asked that any information found regarding these plants be sent to his office in Richmond.[24] But his greatest contribution to the dissemination of medical knowledge on the homefront came when he detailed the Charleston physician, Francis Peyre Porcher, to collect and publish a study of the indigenous plants, their medicinal and chemical value. After a year of concentrated study and collecting, Dr. Porcher published in 1863 the first edition of *Resources of Southern Fields and Forests, Medical, Economical, and Agricultural.* In this study are listed the various plants, their properties, and methods of making use of them. It was widely distributed during the war, and was a great help to the folks at home. After the war, a larger, more detailed edition was published, based on much scientific data discovered during the war.

Quinine, morphine, and chloroform were the most critically needed of all drugs. On the homefront, the shortage of quinine was more noticeable than either morphine or chloroform, but all three were needed in the army. So necessary was quinine that one diarist declared that "Next to munitions of war, few things seemed more important than quinine."[25] Malaria was widespread in the Confederacy, and it not only took lives but reduced the efficiency and productiveness of the people. A shortage of quinine became apparent during the first summer of the war,[26] and it became more acute as the war continued. After 1863 this vital drug sold for $400 to $600 an ounce when it could be had at all.[27] It became necessary to try to find substitutes for it. No other medicine was the object of such study. Many substitutes were discovered and eight or nine were frequently used. The most common was a decoction made from the bark of dogwood, cherry, or willow trees, considered the best substitutes for Peruvian bark. Sometimes the bark of all three was boiled together, at other times separately. Often they were combined with whiskey.[28] So familiar did this simple remedy become that it was given the nickname of "Old Indig."[29] A mixture of red pepper, tea, and table salt was frequently used as a substitute for quinine. It was said that this never failed "to keep off a chill."[30] Another favorite of the day was cottonseed tea, made by boiling cotton seed in water; it was enthusiastically described by one user as "better than quinine."[31] Other commonly used substitutes for quinine were horehound tea, herbs and whiskey combined, dog fennel, and a decoction of water and parsley. These were to be taken internally. Turpentine rubbed over the body in quantity was believed to check the recurrence of chills.[32] But nothing could take the place of genuine quinine. The Richmond Enquirer told its readers that no shortage caused the North to chuckle like that of quinine; but, said the editor, the South need not worry for it had "a dozen substitutes."[33] Three years later it was conceded that the "efforts to procure a reliable substitute for quinine . . . [had] proved a failure."[34]

Morphine and chloroform had no trustworthy substitutes. They were especially needed in the surgical cases resulting from war injuries, but they were also needed whenever surgery was attempted among the civilians. Practically all the morphine and chloroform used in the Confederacy was brought through the blockade, and there was never enough to supply the demand.[35] It was hoped that opium would serve as a substitute; and Surgeon-General Moore tried to get the cultivation of poppies, the source of opium, underway in the Confederacy. In the late spring of 1862, he asked Francis Peyre Porcher to do research in obtaining opium from the poppy. Dr. Porcher proved that this could be done and that the opium thus collected was of "excellent quality."[36] So confident was General Moore that opium could be gathered in quantity, and so pressing was the need for the drug, that he issued a circular in March, 1863, instructing medical purveyors over the South to publish in local papers the need for growing poppies and producing opium. In the same circular, Moore instructed the purveyors to furnish women with poppy seeds, and to instruct them in the gathering of juice from the tiny green capsules within the poppies. The women were asked to send the gum-like substance to the nearest purveying depot.[37] Such notices appeared in the newspapers throughout the South, and there is considerable evidence that the response to appeal was general. Men, women, and children, planted poppies with a great burst of patriotic fervor; and newspapers spurred them on in these efforts.[38] Some proudly recorded such cultivation in their diaries.[39] When the time came to gather the gum and send it to the nearest purveyor's office, enthusiasm lagged. "Large quantities of poppies were raised, but very little opium was gathered";[40] and the movement as a whole was only "relatively unsuccessful."[41]

In treating practically every ailment known to medical science, the southern people substituted homemade mixtures for the usual medicines. It is exceedingly interesting to note that the exponents of each guaranteed satisfactory results, even when the strangest cures were recommended. There were many recipes for tonics, but a few merit special mention. One such, guaranteed to be a "cure-all," consisted of "vinegar with nails or iron filings held in it. No second dose was ever needed . . . it was enough to show the patient the bottle."[42] Another tonic was made from a decoction of hops and watermelon juice.[43] Diarrhea was said to be cured by drinking a tea-like substance made from water and raspberry or whortleberry leaves,[44] while dysentery might be cured by either blackberry roots, persimmons and water brewed together,[45] or salt,

vinegar and water combined.[46]   Ice,[47] which was always among
the scarce items, or tea made from peach leaves and water,[48] was
recommended to relieve nausea, while a teaspoonful of charcoal
and one-third teaspoon of soda mixed in hot water was a common
remedy for headaches.[49]   Itch remedies were many and varied.
Among them were ointment made from elder-bark, water, lard,
sweetgum, olive oil, and sulphur flour,[50] and a simpler remedy of
poke root rubbed over the body.[51]   Aperients were widely used.
Castor oil, the old faithful, was most commonly used.   The cultivation of the castor-oil plant (palma Christi) was encouraged because of the scarcity and the unreasonably high price of castor oil
imported through the blockade.   A factory for the manufacture of
this medicine was projected.[52]   Many families manufactured castor
oil on a small scale, sometimes for their own use and sometimes
for the purpose of selling it;[53] and other laxatives used were made
from the leaves or roots of the butternut, peach, or May apple
trees, boiled in water.[54]   Since these were considered too strong
for children, lard and syrup heated together were suggested for
their use.[55] A medicine made from tulip and poplar trees was supposed to cure gout and rheumatism;[56] and tinctures of the jimson
weed and Mayhaw roots were employed for the relief of pain.[57]
In place of common disinfectants, a decoction of elder leaves[58]
or red oak bark[59] was used, and an alcohol made from chinaberries
was widely employed.[60]   A "soothing, agreeable 'eye-wash'" was
made from young elm or sassafras branches;[61] and a fairly efficient
gargle was obtained from a mixture of milk, charcoal, and turpentine.[62]   Scurvy, more prevalent in the armed forces than on the
homefront, was treated by dietary methods.   Fresh green vegetables were used, and in order to insure them in sufficient quantity, Surgeon-General Moore instructed medical purveyors to
gather them.[63]   Publicity was given this order, so that any cases
among civilians might be similarly treated.

All sorts of surgical implements and medical equipment became
scarce during the war.   Many were lost in battle, others were worn
out; and contributions of such items to the army and navy decreased the quantity on the homefront.   Some few of the instruments were brought through the blockade and fewer were manufactured in Richmond;[64] these were diverted into military channels and brought practically no relief to the doctors serving the
homefront.   The South had neither the materials nor the skilled

workers necessary for the manufacturing of delicate surgical instruments.[65] Substitutes were devised whenever possible. A fork was used instead of a surgical hook in a delicate skull operation;[66]; a strip of bark served as a tourniquet; a knitting needle took the place of a tenaculum; a penknife was used for a scalpel; and splints were fashioned from fence rails.[67] Bandages and sponges were scarce. Old sheets, pillow cases, and linen garments were made to serve as bandages, and homespun sometimes had to be used because of lack of softer, more absorbent materials.[68] Bottles and corks were unobtainable in sufficient quantity. The former were manufactured in Louisiana, Alabama, and South Carolina, but substitutes for cork had to be devised. They were made from pieces of old life preservers, cloth pressed together, and corncobs.[69] Heated gun shells took the place of hot water bottles.[70] Medical books became scarce, for many were destroyed during the war. "Books were far more scarce than instruments, [and] many civilian doctors gave, loaned, and exchanged books with Army doctors."[71]

Because of the call to duty, the number of physicians and surgeons left at home soon became insufficient to meet the demands. Often only one doctor was left to serve an entire county, and in some cases he was superannuated.[72] It was said that if "one was taken ill, there was no doctor to drive up in his family gig to bring hope and comfort."[73] The cost of a visit was unusually high; a single visit often cost $30. Few doctors were trained in the Confederacy during the war, for most of the young men followed the colors into battle, and educational plans were disrupted. And nurses "were not always available."[74]

No shortage existing on the homefront received so much attention and concerted effort, from both men and women, as did that of medicine and medical supplies. But these efforts usually resulted in frustration and failure, for few shortages were so incapable of substitution. Imaginary ills were about all that could have been cured with Confederate medicines.

In this section are the photographs provided for the first edition of *Ersatz in the Confederacy* by the Confederate Museum, Richmond, Virginia.

Homefront and battlefront shortages meet in these makeshifts. The homespun dress and straw hat were made in Virginia, the homespun coat and cowhair pants in Georgia, the hospital nurse's apron in Tennessee, and the canvas shoe with wooden sole in South Carolina.

The costume (left) was a Virginia product, and the patchwork bag was carried by Mrs. Jefferson Davis, wife of the President of the Confederacy. The dress (right), a Mississippi product, was of calico. It was worn by Mrs. Davis who paid $1,000 in Confederate money for it. The silk parasol was made of thirty-six pieces which were originally the ruffle of a child's dress. The hat was made of Louisiana palmetto and the handkerchief, hand embroidered, came from Texas.

The sugar ration from Maryland and the coffee ration from North Carolina (upper left) served nine portions each. The battle flag (upper right) was made from the wedding dress of Mrs. A. P. Hill, wife of the Confederate general. The green water glass (lower picture) was made in Virginia and sold for $60 a dozen. The myrtle berry candles came from Georgia. The medicine case, the tablet on which pills were made, and the china "nourisher," called "the little goose" by patients, were used in a military hospital.

These slippers were made for President Jefferson Davis from a couch cover in Mississippi. The two tapers (left) were made in Virginia; the tallest is wrapped around a corn cob. The taper twisted in the metal saucer was made in North Carolina, and the grease lamp (right) came from Arkansas.

The books in this picture were made in South Carolina. *Mother Goose* was commercially printed, and the cook book was put together in a private home. The "Secession Apron" is a North Carolina item.

This elaborate straw hat was a household product of North Carolina, and the straw splitter was a South Carolina domestic invention which made straw more pliable in the manufacture of hats and other articles.

The palmetto sunbonnet came from South Carolina, the fan and child's homespun dress from Virginia, the homemade stockings from Alabama, and the cornshuck hat from Missouri.

The playing cards, a blockade runner's importation, were contributed by Louisiana and carry pictures of Confederate military leaders. The envelope, made of wallpaper, and the homemade soap, which originally concealed a secret message, came from Florida. The child's straw hat, decorated with chicken feathers dyed blue, was an Alabama item.

VIII

TRANSPORTATION, INDUSTRY, & AGRICULTURE

T RANSPORTATION FACILITIES AND INDUSTRIAL AND AGRICULTURAL equipment were of paramount importance during the war. But, at the time when transportation, industry, and agriculture should have been accelerated as never before, grave shortages appeared and greatly restricted the output of field and factory. Shortages in these three fields of endeavor, in turn, produced shortages along other lines, both in the army and on the home-front. It is the latter, however, which interests us here.

The problem of transportation was one of the most serious facing the Confederate government, and of all branches, railroads caused gravest concern. Shortages within the railroad system were present when the opening shots were fired over Charleston harbor. Many parts of the South lacked facilities, while the varied gauges made rapid transit impossible. The railroads were inadequate to meet the heavy duty suddenly thrust upon them in 1861, and during the four years of war they were gradually weakened by lack of replacements for worn-out parts and by destruction.

A major weakness of the system was the lack of iron foundries and machine shops. The papers warned the people of this shortage, but little attention was paid to such warnings. Food, clothing, and medicine were immediate and very personal problems, but to the average citizen a collapse of the railroads seemed remote, even if possible. There was a pathetic faith on the part of most people, even the leaders, that the war would be short and that the railroads were adequate to carry the extra burdens of a short war. The Tredegar Iron Works completed a few locomotives already begun and then, like smaller iron factories, turned to the production of arms. Soon all foundries were under government contract, and arms were their chief products.[1]

125

Southern railroads had depended largely on the products of Northern foundries, and war cut this source of supply; but government leaders seemed little concerned about it until 1863. The lethargic attitude toward the railroads during the first twenty-four months of the war was painful. When those in charge of the railroad system finally awakened to the situation, they found the blockade so effective that they were unable to get more than a "trifling" bit of relief through it.[2] The situation, therefore, went from bad to worse.

A shortage of rolling stock began to appear early in the war. Cars were needed to transport food and troops, but the supply was never adequate, and it became a greater worry as the war stretched on. A few cars were manufactured in Savannah, but the production of one plant could never adequately supply the needs.[3] Locomotives, too, were scarce, and the extra burden placed upon them during the war caused many to wear out earlier than they ordinarily would have. In April, 1863, Assistant Adjutant-General William M. Wadley wrote to Secretary of War Seddon that the railroad system of the South needed "31 engines and 930 cars"; Wadley warned Seddon that deterioration had been 25% since the outbreak of the war and that the war might last for another two years.[4] Apparently the War Department was not yet ready to concern itself with the problem. Meanwhile, rails were becoming hazardous because of the unusually heavy loads constantly carried over them. Those of the main-traveled lines were being completely worn-out. The presidents of the major railroads met in Richmond in 1863 and estimated that 49,000 tons of rails must be manufactured every year if the railroads were to maintain service for the military alone; they estimated that if the iron foundries of the Confederacy, including the Tredegar Iron Works, manufactured rails alone, they could produce only 20,000 tons per year. But these works were under government contract for weapons of war. The presidents warned the Government that it must turn toward the manufacturing of iron for the railroads or they would fail.[5] Cars, engines, and rails were sadly needed; and the shortage of these reflected a shortage of iron. Secretary of War Seddon wrote President Davis in April, 1864, that additional skilled labor was needed to manufacture railroad equipment.[6] Evidence points to the fact that there was also a shortage of the unskilled labor needed to keep the roadbeds in good repair.[7] And the laborers lacked the necessary tools with which to maintain the roads. William Goodman, president of the Mississippi Central Railroad Company, bombarded the office of the Secretary of War with letters in which he described the situation of his railroad. There were shortages of axes, shovels, files, framing tools, food for workers, and equipment of all sorts.[8] There is no record that anything was done to aid this road. Another shortage, minor but important in the running of the railroads, was lubricating oil. Unable to obtain this from without the Confederacy, the people were able to find in lard oil a substitute for this item. Lard oil was manufactured commercially in the South, but the quantity manufactured was inadequate.[9] Other substitutes suggested, and used to a lesser extent, were castor oil, described as "the best lubricator known,"[10] and peanut oil.[11] Advertisements in newspapers continually begged for lubricating oils for the use of railroads. The following is typical:

> The Montgomery and West Point Rail Road, requires a large quantity of Lard for greasing Cars and Machinery, and will pay the highest market price for large or small lots delivered at their Depot in Montgomery.[12]

Realizing the value of the railroads to the war effort, railroad men held conventions annually, and tried to devise some means of maintaining and improving facilities. The first such convention met in Richmond in December, 1861. The body resolved to establish foundries to manufacture iron rails and other equipment, if the government would promise to purchase from such establishments. Nothing was done to put this plan into general execution.[13] In April, 1862, a committee of railroad men made a report to Secretary of War Seddon in which they outlined a policy which, if it had been followed, would have greatly simplified the problem of transportation. The report proposed that canals and waterways be used as often as possible to relieve the loads on railroads; that government warehouses should be constructed at convenient points, and that these be well guarded; that the railroads be paid per diem rates for cars and other equipment when used on another railroad; that the government carry on a scrap drive for the railroads; and that skilled mechanics and artisans be imported to be used in manufacturing railroad equipment.[14] This plan as a whole was received indifferently by the War Department and other government agencies, although there were scattered scrap drives. In April, 1863, the presidents of the southern railroads again convened in Richmond and again addressed Secretary Seddon on the condition of the railroads and appealed to Congress for remedial legislation. They urged the following legislation: that a railroad bureau be established within the War Department to take charge of railroads used by the government; that a per diem payment on borrowed equipment be guaranteed and that government transportation be given preference; and that the government furnish tools and iron, subsidize plants established to manufacture railroad equipment, and detail mechanics to work in these plants rather than serve in the army.[15] The convention adopted and addressed another set of resolutions to the "War Department." These reiterated the program set forth in April, 1862, covering greater use of water transportation, more convenient storage places along railroads, importation of European artisans, and regulations to prevent interference with schedules by military officers.[16] No record is available which shows that these recommendations were acted upon by the Confederate government.

In March, 1864, William M. Burwell, chairman of the Committee on Roads and Interior Navigation of the Virginia legislature, wrote Secretary Seddon that, in the opinion of the Committee, the lack of certain railroad extensions and connections, a deficiency of rolling stock, especially locomotives (the Virginia railroads had one-fourth to one-eighth of the necessary "motive power"), poor rails, and "a refusal of roads of the same gauge to allow freighters of other roads to run over their rails, thereby involving unnecessary transshipments," constituted obstacles to the internal commerce of the state and nation. The committee suggested the following remedies: military control of the railroads, the organization of locomotive factories with a detail of skilled workmen, and the importation or manufacture of needed repair parts.[17] No action was taken on the recommendation.

Governmental action to alleviate transportation difficulties was slow in coming. During the first two years of the war, appropriations were made by Congress to build and aid in various ways a few railroad lines needed for military purposes, but it was mid-1863 before an overall policy was inaugurated. From 1863 until the end of the war, the governmental policy was so designed as to aid in the war effort, but the welfare of the civilian population was completely ignored.   In secret session, on May 1, 1863, Congress passed a law authorizing the Secretary of War to investigate conditions of the railroads, and to ask them to devote their energies to the transporting of freight, supplies, material, and men for the government, excepting one passenger train every twenty-four hours.   They were to run trains according to a schedule set up by the Quartermaster-General.   If the railroads refused to do as requested, the Secretary of War might seize them and force them into government service.   Provision was also made in this law for the removal of property from one railroad to another.[18] So began what one student described as a "hand-to-mouth" policy.[19]   When the rolling stock of one railroad wore out, that of another less used road was impressed and substituted on the more traveled roads.   Agents of the Confederate government were sent out over the South to look into the situation and to impress and redistribute rolling stock and rails.   Smaller lines gave way to more important ones, leaving many sections untouched by any railroad and making a few roads all-important.[20]   Naturally, such a policy reduced the area tapped for food, clothing, and other essentials, and, at the same time, removed large areas from any contact with the center of government.   In March, 1864, Assistant Adjutant General John Withers authorized the Quartermaster-General to order all passenger trains to give governmental trains the right of way.[21]   By mid-1864, passenger travel, especially in Virginia, came practically to a standstill.   The government suddenly determined to move only the necessities of war, and many communities, accustomed to import food, suffered thereby.[22]   The Quartermaster-General, at last recognizing the lamentable conditions of the railroads, recommended that no furloughs be given to soldiers for fear it would further complicate the movement of food near the battlefronts.[23]   Finally, and ironically, the Confederate government realized too late the lack of essentials which were necessary to improve the railroads.   Less than sixty days before the surrender at Appomattox, a joint resolution was passed authorizing President Davis to institute an inquiry

> to ascertain whether, by liberal [aid and encouragement] from the Government, the manufacture [of railroad] iron can be stimulated within the Confederate States to such an extent as will materially assist the Government in maintaining lines of communica-

tion necessary to the public defense; and if so, whether it would be practicable to have some built and equipped by similar aid and encouragement from the government. . . .[24]

But this step was taken too late. The Confederacy fell before anything could be done to carry out these provisions.

As a result of the "too little and too late" policy the Confederate government was severely criticized. One contemporary declared that "No department was worse neglected and mismanaged" than the transportation department;[25] another especially condemned the mismanagement of railroads.[26] Although it might have acted sooner, the government, too, had problems that were difficult to solve. There was constant friction between the government and the railroads. The latter often flatly refused to permit their rolling stock to be used on another road. This attitude is reflected in a letter written by Lieutenant-Colonel F. W. Sims to Brigadier-General Alexander Robert Lawton on March 31, 1864. Colonel Sims wrote that, in order to insure better transportation between Richmond and Wilmington, consolidation of three railroads would be necessary. His plan failed because the railroads would not give their consent.[27] The Confederate government also collided with state laws that either ran counter to the policy of the central government or confused the general enforcement of Confederate laws. In Virginia, for instance, priority of transportation was given to food intended for consumers, both civilian and military,[28] and in Georgia the railroads were forced to ship articles of prime necessity, penalties being attached to those railroads refusing or purposely delaying shipments.[29] Disagreements between the agents of the Confederate and State governments over the use of railroads were frequent.

The problem of railroads was the most serious, but there were other transportation shortages that had far-reaching effects. Among these was the shortage of horses and mules. This affected both transportation and agriculture and became a point of grave concern and widespread discontent. The shortage on the homefront was mainly the result of the impressment policy of the Confederate government, a policy which became more rigid as more horses were killed in cavalry battles. By 1863 the problem of horses was becoming acute. In March of that year Quartermaster-General Abraham Charles Myers wrote to President Davis that there were between six hundred and seven hundred mules, recently bought in Texas, being wintered in Louisiana because of the quantity of forage there; and that when they were brought across the river they would relieve the scarcity of horses in the eastern area. At the same time General Myers suggested that the shortage of horses and mules be relieved by regularly obtaining them from Mexico, Texas, California, and New Mexico.[30] Ironically on July 4, 1863, General Myers wrote to Major A. H. Cole, Inspector-General of Field Transportation, that many horses and mules had "been for months on the borders of the Mississippi River" and they had not yet been brought across.[31] The very day this letter was written, Vicksburg fell, and the Trans-Mississippi division became practically useless as a source of supply. In this same letter, General Myers instructed Major Cole to capture horses and mules in the area around Gettysburg, but the Confederates began their retreat in Pennsylvania before the letter was delivered. Impressment became more severe and, after practically all horses had been taken, General Samuel Cooper ordered that mules should be impressed.[32] Especially acute was the shortage of horses and mules near the battlefront, for the animals were quickly transferred from the farm to war service. As a result of this policy the homefolk were forced into the use of varied makeshifts. Sometimes a single animal was used to draw a large conveyance accustomed to be drawn by two or four animals, and the single beast was often a pitiful specimen of horseflesh. When a Richmond teamster changed horses he merely "changed one skelelton for another."[33] Nearly all horses were impressed but "mules [were] . . . rare in [the] draft,"[34] and mules replaced horses at home.[35] Occasionally, one would see a combination team of horse and mule pulling a lady's carriage.[36] Joseph LeConte was delighted to ride along on "an old broken down horse" abandoned by General Sherman's men.[37] In the Confederacy primitive oxen were frequently used as beasts of burden.[38]

All sorts of substitutes were relied upon for the customary carriages, wagons, and boats, which began to disappear during the war. Carriages and wagons were particularly scarce in Virginia, for they, too, were impressed for the army. Carriages, useless for ordinary service in war, were often used as ambulances.[39] A critical situation, created by the shortage, appeared early in the war. When Jefferson Davis was inaugurated President of the permanent government in February, 1862, "carriages were engaged a week beforehand to convey persons to the Capitol Square." These were hired "at the most extraordinary prices."[40] When Miss Hetty Cary, generally conceded to be among the loveliest of the Confederate belles, married dashing, debonair Brigadier-General John Pegram, the wedding was a great social event. Yet this prominent couple was forced to ride to the church in a "shabby old Richmond hack."[41] By 1864 carriages had become so scarce and so precious that the general charge for rental was $25 an hour.[42] Broken-down wagons and carts replaced good ones of better days, and makeshifts constructed from poles and wheels were used by even the most prominent families.[43] One lady declared that a cart made from rough, unplaned boards on wheels was "a 'Godsend'."[44] Even these crude conveyances were not always available and many people were forced to walk long distances. Frequently ladies, once accustomed to carriages and coachmen in livery, walked home from evening parties during the war. The walk completed an evening of wartime social events, where women wore made over garments, had no refreshments and few escorts. Frequently men and women walked from one town to another because horses, mules, wagons, and carts were nonexistent, and the chances of a "lift" were slight. One gentleman walked from Fredericksburg to Richmond in the summer of 1864, and declared that he saw not a single horse, mule, or cow along the route.[45] Perhaps one of the greatest nuisances, particularly to women, was the lack of transportation to and from the railroad stations. Frequently there was no conveyance of any kind in which to move bags and trunks, and in many cases masculine help could not be had. In Richmond, as early as 1862, both carriages and porters were absent from the railroad station, and in Culpeper, Virginia, a lady traveler paid to have her trunks dragged to the depot.[46] Because of the lack of private carriages, many who were unaccustomed to public conveyances found themselves crowded into a packed stagecoach. When the foreign traveler, Fitzgerald Ross, visited the Confederacy, he found it necessary to telegraph ahead in order to get reservations in stagecoaches that traveled along the main lines; and he then found the coaches crowded both "inside and out, and many who wanted to go were left behind." He had to ride "squeezed up on the top of the coach."[47]

Railroad men continually encouraged the use of water transportation to relieve the crowded railroads, but the boats of the Confederacy, like the land conveyances were in a sad state, especially during the last years of the war. The overseer at Chicora Wood, a South Carolina plantation belonging to the Allstons, wrote Adele Petigru Allston, wife of the former South Carolina governor: "I will have to work on the Boat before she can be loaded with Rice. She leaks very bad in the Bottom."[48]   Similar complaints were frequent during the war. When it became necessary for Senator Wigfall and his family to cross the Mississippi River, no boat was available. Not to be defeated, the Senator put the ambulance, in which he and his family were riding, into the hollowed-out trunks of trees. The mules, which were pulling the ambulance on land, swam the river pulling the aqua-ambulance behind them.[49] A Louisiana lady, forced to flee before the invading enemy, went by boat from one of the bayous into the Mississippi River. She found "a seething mass of craft of all kinds and descriptions that could be made into possible conveyances to carry away the terror-stricken people . . . all making a mad rush for the Red River."[50]

It is little wonder that so many people detested the press and the crowded conditions of travel. Civilians were urged to stay at home, but this encouragement seemed to net little results. Mothers, sisters, and sweethearts were determined to visit the men in camps, and refugees from war-torn areas added to the general congestion. Trains accommodated their human cargo within and without the cars. The experience of a Houston, Texas, editor traveling through East Tennessee was typical. He wrote that "the seats, aisles, platforms, baggage cars, aye, and the tops of the cars were covered with passengers and troops, and 1000's were left at the depot begging to come."[51] Those who got a place within the cars found conditions exasperating, to say the least. Seats were sometimes "without backs and some without bottoms";[52] and frequently there were no windows, fire, or lamps in the cars even in winter.[53] In the hottest part of summer there might be no water coolers in the cars. Water containers were often casks with open tops into which went dippers, glasses, canteens, and hands; when empty they were inverted and used for seats.[54] Delays in schedule, sometimes involving days, became the rule rather than the exception. One traveler told of having three detentions during the eighty mile stretch between Augusta, Georgia, and Columbia,

South Carolina. Each lasted from nine to thirteen hours.[55] It is little wonder that the dispositions of Confederate travelers were none too pleasant. An editorial in the Wilmington *Journal* summed up the situation very neatly:

> Although traveling may be sometimes recommended as good for the health, it is highly injurious to the temper and manners . . . that small portion of humanity known as the 'traveling public,' is the most selfish, discontented, cross-grained section to be found on the top of the earth . . . the 'traveling public,' whose motto is 'Look out for number one,' upon which, as all act simultaneously, there is bound to be a rush, a struggle and a worry.[56]

The lack of adequate transportation facilities made travel unpleasant and at times hazardous, but its effect on the distribution of essentials of life was of greater concern. Frequently food decayed in one part of the Confederacy, while actual want existed in another.[57] As early as the fall of 1861, the sugar growers of Louisiana became concerned over the inability to ship their crops into the east of the Mississippi.[58] Sugar was abundant in Louisiana, but in other states of the Confederacy people counted the grains of the precious commodity; and while the Trans-Mississippi region, for the most part, had sufficient fare during the war, the region east of the Mississippi often went hungry. The inadequate transportation system prevented a "share-alike" plan.[59] A girl in Farmville, Virginia, wrote to her father, who was sixty miles away in Richmond, that "the cornucopia of plenty is ready to be emptied into the lap of Richmond so soon as the government is willing to take the necessary steps to procure transportation to the city."[60] It became more and more difficult to transport private supplies, and the people on the homefront often went cold and hungry, for wood and coal, like food, could not be properly distributed.[61]

It became increasingly difficult to obtain and even to keep beasts of burden late in the war because of impressment, capture, and natural causes. The reason for their loss was really of little concern to the farmers, the important point was that they were gone and could not be used in making the crop.[62] Things had come to such a state by the spring of 1864 that General Henry Lewis Benning, speaking in Columbus, Georgia, urged the use of cows as a substitute for horses and mules in the cultivation of crops.[63] This suggestion was put into practice in far-flung areas of the Confederacy.[64] Some farmers were forced to pay to have their impressed grain hauled to a government warehouse because their own dray animals had been seized earlier.[65] Wagons, also scarce, were needed to get crops to market, but many farmers had no vehicles of any kind toward the end of the war. Some of the more ingenious managed to construct something resembling a wagon from odds and ends, which was so unusual that it was said to "baffle description."[66]

Some shortages were acutely felt in transportation, agriculture, and industry. Fundamental in each of the three fields was a shortage of iron. Lack of iron prevented a greater output of locomotives and rails, and also the production of farm tools and industrial equipment. Newspapers and farm publications warned of an iron famine unless greater effort was turned toward its manufacture.[67] The iron which was produced was converted into arms to such an extent that little was left with which to manufacture new farm implements. Concerned over this, Governor Thomas Hill Watts of Alabama wrote to Secretary of War Seddon in early 1864 that, unless iron was obtained for agricultural implements, planting interests could not be carried on. He pointed out that iron was being produced in Alabama, but those producing it were under contract to sell to the Confederate government, and farmers even in the "best iron region of the State" could not get enough to make and repair their agricultural implements. He urged that the Confederate government permit manufacturers to produce and sell farm implements.[68] Secretary Seddon replied that some cast iron and a little rolled iron might be diverted to civilian use.[69] Those areas of the Confederacy far removed from iron deposits felt the shortage more keenly than did Alabama. Industry experienced great impetus during the war, but the increase was in the field of domestic industry capable of producing with the barest essentials. The machinery produced between 1861 and 1865 was taken under government contract to supply the armed forces. Civilians interested in either agricultural or industrial equipment "had to depend almost entirely on the reworking of old iron." An unremitting search was carried on "for every superfluous or cast-away scrap."[70] Like iron, the shortage of lubricating oil affected transportation, agriculture, and industry. While the machine age in agriculture had not become a reality in the South prior to the war, there was need for lubricants in agricultural machinery and in wheel axles. Sperm oil, so often used for lubricating purposes, was exhausted in most of the Confederacy by the fall of 1861, and it became

necessary to find a substitute.[71]   Castor oil, peanut oil, and cotton
seed oil were suggested as substitutes.   The shortage of workers
affected the output of agriculture and industry just as did that of
transportation.   Women and children tilled the fields and harvested
the crops, and unskilled labor was frequently used where skilled
labor was needed in industry.[72]

Practically every conceivable implement used on the farm became scarce during the war.   Farmers reclaimed implements that
had been thrown aside as unfit for use.   Consequently, farm work
took longer and produced less than would have been possible with
better implements.   Realizing the necessity of taking care of what
tools were available, newspapers encouraged farmers to repair
their old tools.   One paper urged that three days each season be
spent in repairing "ploughs, harness, harrows, hoe handles, and
other such things.[73]   During the second summer of the war, a well-
to-do-planter near Gloucester, Virginia, wrote his son that there
was not a single hoe on his place fit for use in the cornfield.[74]
Ploughs, scythes, rakes, and similar tools were lacking on hundreds
of farms.   Barrels, tubs, and kettles were scarce; this shortage was
particularly disastrous in a region where syrup making was prevalent.   A vat made of wood and reinforced on the bottom and half
way up the sides with iron, was substituted for the kettle used in
boiling sorghum.   Although not as satisfactory as a solid iron
kettle, such containers were used on many plantations.   Barrels,
used in storing and shipping molasses were so scarce that "barrel-
making was . . . forced upon the South."[75]   Made by amateurs,
the barrels would not "hold molasses."[76]   Baskets, used by many
cotton pickers before the war, became so scarce that sacks came
into general use;[77] but these became a rarity before the end of the
war.   Frequently made of old material, they were often incapable
of carrying the weight thrust upon them and the contents were
sometimes lost.   An Atlanta merchant was pleased to announce
the receipt of forty bushels of seed peas at his place of business,
but he warned customers that they must "furnish sacks to put
them in."[78]   The "old oaken bucket" began to disappear from
Southern farms during the war.   Some cypress buckets were manufactured in the South, but, more often than not, they were manufactured for the government.[79]   Such common and simple farm
necessities as troughs used for the feeding of animals rotted away
or were destroyed by invading armies and could not be replaced.

Bureau, wardrobe, and washstand drawers were used as substitutes near Decatur, Georgia, in 1864.[80] Because of the dearth of leather, saddles and harness were scarce, but farmers early discovered that oak or hickory splits could replace leather, and that, if necessary, ropes could be substituted for leather bridles. The latter was not resorted to often, however, for a rope shortage was most aggravating to farmers. There were hundreds of uses for good rope on every farm, but hemp rope, commonly used before the war, became an item seldom seen after the blockade became effective. Substitutes were found, however. Among them were moss, grasses of various kinds,[81] okra stalks,[82] and cotton. Frequent mention was made of the scarcity of iron ties used on cotton bales, but wooden hoops came into general use and were generally satisfactory.[83]

The task of keeping one's property in good condition and of replacing buildings that were destroyed became nearly impossible for Southern farmers. Nails were so dear that one gentleman declared they were worth "their weight in silver."[84] They were so precious that they were usually exchanged for other rare articles rather than sold for depreciating Confederate money.[85] Lumber, too, was scarce. Advertisements appeared day after day in the newspapers asking for lumber for certain specific uses. Also lacking were paint, bolts, locks, and screws.[86] Encouraged to grow grains, farmers often found themselves without threshing and milling facilities and, because of the various basic shortages, it was impossible to manufacture threshers or to erect mills. Such primitive methods as beating the grain over barrels or boxes were frequently resorted to; those who could do so attached "threshers and fans to their gin houses."[87] The many shortages of farm supplies caused farmers constant worry. Their lot was not an enviable one.

Industrial shortages were serious, too. Because of weight and cumbersome size of most industrial equipment, very little was brought through the blockade. That already in the Confederacy had to suffice, and the owners trusted to luck that it would last for the duration of the war. Parts needed for repair could only rarely be obtained from without the Confederacy and the lack of experienced workers, coupled with the scarcity of raw materials, made their manufacture within a major difficulty. Scarcity of coal and wood prevented a greater industrial output. The smaller industries established during the war utilized simple, easily constructed equipment, some of it made from wood.[88]

Bound together by common problems and greatly restricted in their efforts by many shortages, transportation, agriculture, and industry failed to meet the demands for wartime production and distribution and thus contributed not only to the problem of shortages but eventually to the collapse of the Confederacy.

IX

THE LITTLE THINGS OF LIFE

MANY EVERYDAY ITEMS, TAKEN FOR GRANTED BY THE MAJOR-ity of people, disappeared during the war or became so scarce that they were rarely in evidence. Included among them were articles ranging from coffin screws to china-headed dolls, from postage stamps to Christmas tree decorations. Any one of the many such items in itself seemed to be of little importance; but when combined they greatly changed the overall picture of life on the Confederate homefront. Successful substitutes were found for some articles, but for others nothing was available, although people taxed their brains almost beyond endurance in an effort to invent a usable expedient.

Paper was among the many "little things" of which there was a shortage. This was one of the most severe and far-reaching scarcities that appeared during the war. The most noticeable lack of paper was evidenced in the newspaper of the day. Dependent, to a great degree, for outside production of paper, the South, nevertheless had several sizeable paper factories in 1861. But the necessary rags, chemicals, machines, and type could not be obtained in sufficient quantities during the war to maintain ordinary production. The Richmond *Whig*, one of the more foresighted of the Southern papers, warned the people of the necessity of saving rags as early as June, 1861. It cautioned that without thriftiness in collecting lowly rags, newspapers would have to curtail their size and some would have to discontinue publication.[1] But the *Whig* was like "a voice crying in the Wilderness," for in that first summer, few bothered with such petty details. Papers continued to plead in a similar vein throughout the war, but little resulted from such efforts. Consequently, they were "curtailed in size," and, as a rule, were dingy and cramped in appearance, yet their publishers carried on as best they could, rendering service to the young nation.[2] Early in the war, newspapers were being printed on the cheapest and commonest of paper with the very worst kind of ink. These made an impression on the hands as well as on the mind of the reader.[3] With the pride of accomplishment, *The Record*, a weekly publication in Richmond boasted "the whitest paper and the neatest printing of any journal issued in the South."[4] An editorial convention met in Atlanta in the spring of 1862 to discuss the shortage of paper, but did nothing to alleviate it;[5] and its lack continued to harass editors, publishers, printers, writers, and people generally, for newspapers were especially desired in time of war.

In an effort to find substitutes with which to make paper, experiments were carried on in various sections of the Confederacy. Most paper made in the South continued to be made of rags, but several new sources were found. Next to rags, straw was generally used in making paper. Such things as corn husks, the root and stalk of the cotton plant, sunflower stalks, and cotton were used in limited quantity. The advantage of the last article was that no bleaching chemicals were needed.[6] Despite these experimentations, newspapers could not get either the prewar quality or quantity of paper. The shortage became evident very early in the war, and, since worn-out machinery could not be replaced, since sufficient manpower to run the presses and put out the paper was lacking, and since transportation facilities were restricted, the publication and distribution of newspapers were more and more curtailed.

One of the very first concessions to the paper shortage was the reduction of the size of papers. This practice was universal. One day a newspaper might be of fair size, the next day one-half the usual size, and the third day it might be several inches in length and only two columns in width. Extra editions, carrying the latest news from the front, were usually "mere slips of paper" sometimes having only one column.[7] In October of 1861, the *Southern Confederacy*, published in Atlanta, was reduced to one-half size and was printed on brown paper, and to make matters worse the editor had no idea whether or not they "could publish the next day."[8] About eight weeks later the editor of this newspaper wrote that the public had an issue that day only because he had "seized" some paper as well as "raked up all odds and ends" in the office. Even after this exertion, the issue was only half a sheet.[9] By 1862 the shortage of paper had been felt in every section of the South, and by June, 1862, all four Richmond newspapers, the *Whig, Enquirer, Examiner,* and *Dispatch,* had been reduced to half a sheet. The same was true of the Mobile, Memphis, Vicksburg, and New Orleans newspapers, as well as those of smaller towns and cities.[10]

One concession made to the paper shortage was at least colorful. When white, gray, or brown paper was unobtainable, the undaunted southern editors resorted to the use of bright colored paper and the results were most effective. General use of the latter came late in the war, but as early as January, 1862, the Charleston *Mercury* appeared on a lovely fuschia paper;[11] later the color was toned down to a dusty salmon.[12] A Georgia editor reported that a certain Mississippi newspaper arrived in his office in five colors.[13] The files of the Houston *Tri-Weekly Telegraph* resemble a rainbow. From October, 1862 through November, 1863, this paper was printed on seven different colors and shades including brown, shell pink, orange, moss green, kelley green, blue, and yellow. Few newspapers managed to have such an assortment of colors. Of equal interest to the many-hued papers were those printed on the blank side of wall paper. Probably the most famous of these was the Vicksburg *Daily Citizen,* published in that city on the eve of its surrender. The last issue of this paper was nine and one-half inches wide and sixteen and seven-eighths long. Because a number of different kinds of wallpaper were used, the result makes a varied and interesting file. The last editorial printed before the city's surrender to General Grant declared: "The 'Citizen' lives to see it [the surrender]. For the last time it appears on 'Wallpaper'. No more will it imagine the luxury of mule meat and fricassed kitten. . . . This is the last wallpaper edition . . . it will be valuable hereafter as a curiosity."[14] Other newspapers that resorted to the use of wallpaper were the *Pictorial Democrat,* of Alexandria, Louisiana,[15] and the *Weekly Junior Register,* of Franklin, Louisiana.[16]

Newspaper editors resorted to several expedients to save paper. They adopted the general custom of cutting the size of advertisements or eliminating them altogether. The editor of the Charleston *Courier* approached the problem in an unique manner by asking his correspondents to refrain from sending long communications and long articles to the paper.[17] For most small town papers and county weeklies, there was only one solution to the problem—suspension of publication. This they reluctantly did. Mississippi witnessed the suspension of a majority of its papers. Of the seventy-five papers published in the state before the war, only nine continued publication to the end of the war. In neighboring Alabama twenty-six per cent of the periodicals suspended publication.[18]   As early as January, 1862, seventeen of the twenty-six Florida newspapers were forced to suspend activities.[19]   When the editor of the West Baton Rouge *Sugar Planter* faced the suspension of his paper because of various shortages, he took the event good-naturedly, and wrote in the last issue:

> The editor of this paper being now out of employment, owing to a temporary suspension of the same, is anxious and willing to do something for a livelihood.   He is' desirous of accepting any small job, such as sawing wood, sweeping chimneys, nursing a baby, milking ducks, watering turkeys, 'toting' bundles, grinding an organ with monkey accompaniment, running for Congress, speculating in shinplasters, selling wood or charcoal, or in any capacity his valuable services might be required . . . [he] has no objection to serving as a deck hand on a flat boat, selling ice-cream, or acting as paymaster to the militia.[20]

City newspapers, having morning and evening editions, generally eliminated one and struggled to maintain the other.   At a time when so much was happening, the anxious civilians were more poorly served by the newspapers than in less trying times.

Various journals and magazines were forced to curtail publication for the same reasons that compelled the newspapers to do so.   The influential *DeBow's Review*, fleeing New Orleans in 1862, was faced with suspension.   Although finally establishing temporary offices in Columbia, South Carolina, only one issue came off the press in the last year of the war.   The *Southern Literary Messenger* had to cease publication in 1864, long after many of its competitors had given up the struggle.[21]   *Southern Field and Fireside* appeared spasmodically because of paper shortage brought on by the burning of the Bath Paper Mills which supplied it with paper.[22]   The *Southern Cultivator*, dependent, too, upon the Bath Mills, managed to publish issues with varying frequency; it became necessary to combine two months into one before the war was over, and to publish only bimonthly.   There were very few journals established during the war.   Among these was the *Southern Illustrated News*, published in Richmond.   Its first issue was in September, 1862, but it succumbed to the shortages in November, 1864. Another short-lived magazine was the *Confederate States Surgical and Medical Journal,* which ambitiously began publication in January, 1864, only to fold up in February, 1865. The people of the Confederacy were forced to forego in a large measure their newspapers, their literary magazines, and their agricultural journals.

Books were more scarce than either newspapers or magazines. Prior to 1861 books were brought into the South in quantity from the North and from England, for the works of the English authors were greatly admired by the Southern reading public. The blockade practically halted this importation, although a few books did come through.[23] Whenever a new book made its appearance, it was received with much applause and passed around among many.[24] The publishing houses in Richmond, Mobile, Macon, Atlanta, Greensboro, and other towns were handicapped by lack of paper, manpower, good ink, and by old worn-out, irreplaceable machinery. They published a fair number of new novels, histories, military works, textbooks, song books, and music, and reprinted older classics, but they could not possibly keep up with the demand.[25] Books produced in the Confederacy were ordinarily brown paper editions, bound in any available material, usually wallpaper. The firm of Sterling, Campbell, and Albright of Greensboro, North Carolina, was one of the more prolific southern publishing houses. The organization was established in 1861 and continued to publish mainly textbooks until April 26, 1865. Handicapped by the same shortages that plagued other houses, this company ingeniously solved many of its problems. Most of its paper was made in plants in Wake Forest and Salem, North Carolina, both utilizing raw cotton. Additional paper, as well as ink and machinery, were obtained by searching the South for these items. In February, 1862, James W. Albright, one of the partners of this firm, visited Columbia, Charleston, Savannah, Mobile, and New Orleans in an effort to obtain needed materials. Unable to obtain stereotypes at home, the firm commissioned Professor J. J. Ayers of Greensboro to go to Liverpool, England, for them. He did so and succeeded in bringing them back on the blockade-runner *Ad-Vance.*[26] Many publishers were not so fortunate, and books remained on the list of scarce items. J. B. Jones had frequent lengthy delays in publishing the southern edition of his book, *Wild Western Scenes.* It had been published first in Philadelphia in

1860. In June, 1863, a Georgian, M. A. Malsby, after considerable delay, succeeded in obtaining sufficient paper to publish the first half, but the cost was exorbitant.[27] Book dealers were faced with bookless shops or with such a diminished stock that they could not supply the demand. An English traveler went into an Augusta, Georgia, bookstore in the late summer of 1863 and asked for a book which he saw on the shelf, only to have the dealer reply that he could not sell his "last copy."[28] During the siege of Vicksburg, one of the ladies of the town went into a local bookstore to purchase something to read. The solitary book found resting on the once-filled shelves was Harriet Beecher Stowe's *Sunny Memories of Foreign Lands.* The salesman sold it to the lady "cheap" for he said he had difficulty selling Mrs. Stowe's books, even in a time of scarcity.[29]

Writing paper, envelopes, account books, and wrapping paper were all scarce during the war. Letters were written on the poorest quality paper that blotted and splotched until the writing was hardly legible. Much of the paper produced in the South was soft and hard to manage. When it became impossible to obtain regular writing paper, even of the poorest quality, Southerners turned to substitutes. Wrapping paper, blank pages of books, scraps of old letters, and even prescription blanks were used to write the tenderest billet-doux or the most business-like letter.[30] Envelopes were as hard to obtain as writing paper, but the people managed to make their own. They were made of brown wrapping paper, while old letters, wallpaper, once used envelopes, and even pictures were turned so that the blank side remained on the outside.[31] It became a favorite evening pastime to make envelopes from the various bits of paper. Women used these expedients for their private correspondence and men for their business correspondence. Whenever envelopes could not be obtained, letters were folded and made to serve as their own envelopes. So scarce were writing paper and envelopes that they were considered to be among the most precious gifts. Jefferson Davis' handsome young secretary, Burton Harrison, presented Miss Constance Cary with a box of cream-colored imported stationery when he was trying to win her favor.[32] When General W. D. Pender, stationed at Camp Gregg, Virginia, was fortunate enough to obtain such scarce articles as sugar, note paper, and envelopes, he sent them to his wife in North Carolina, asking her to say nothing about receiving them from him.[33]   The Confederate forces, retreating after the battle of Gettysburg, brought back as booty "a number of boxes of fine stationery . . . from Carlisle, Chambersburg, etc."[34] But the shortage continued to irk the people until "one dreaded the task of an epistle, however short."[35]

In an effort to stretch the paper supply, cross writing became prevalent. Regardless of the kind of paper used for correspondence, the thrifty wrote in customary fashion from left to right and then turned the paper and wrote from bottom to top. The result was a letter difficult to read and unique in appearance. It gave the over-all effect of square designs formed by the lines crossing each other at right angles.

Those who kept diaries did so only with the greatest of trouble and effort. Mrs. Judith McGuire wrote a major part of hers on brown wrapping paper;[36] Eliza Frances Andrews kept hers in old day-books, and was careful to conserve even this paper by writing very small and between the lines.[37] The original diary of Mary Boykin Chesnut was kept on the inferior domestic product known as "Confederate Paper."[38] Others were kept on various kinds of old notebooks, and on all sorts of paper; some few managed to use leather-bound notebooks. For note-taking, old shingles were often used. An Alabama editor used one for several months, writing an editorial on it and erasing it for another. A slate served the purpose for another editor.[39]

The poor quality and shortage of paper were evident in government publications. Pamphlets, circulars, and instructions sent from the Richmond offices were usually on rough, absorbent paper of the poorest quality. Early in the war passports were printed on brown paper; throughout the South generally, official blanks and forms were difficult to obtain. Even marriage licenses were exhausted in some areas.[40] Not as necessary, but always in demand, was sheet music. This was also difficult to obtain because of the dearth of paper. That published was on a very poor grade.[41] Since little classical music could be published, it gave way to the patriotic war tunes such as "Beauregard's March" and "Jeff Davis' Waltz."[42] But popular patriotic numbers were scarce, too. En route from Alabama to Virginia, a soldier stopped in Augusta, Columbia, Charlotte, and Raleigh trying to find a copy of the popular song "My Maryland," to send to his fiancee. He finally found one in Richmond "after visiting all the music and book stores in the city."[43] Such items of luxury as debut cards were impossible to obtain. Miss Isabel Maury of Richmond wrote to her cousin Miss Mollie Maury of Birkenhead, England, that invitations to the few war debuts made in Richmond were verbal.[44] Wedding and reception invitations were tendered in a similar manner.

Although a number of paper mills were in operation and new ones were established, none worked at full capacity during all four years of war. Some were destroyed by fire or war; others were unable to replace worn-out machinery and parts; all were handicapped by the lack of raw materials from which paper was made. Small domestic plants, specializing only in the making of envelopes from any available paper, sprang into existence. Practically all Southern newspapers carried advertisements for these local firms at one time or another. Naturally, newspapers were always interested in production of and products of paper and they did much to encourage such production. Yet paper continued to be both scarce and high. Newspapers and journals were forced to raise their subscription rates. During the one year the *Confederate States Medical and Surgical Journal* was published, the editor found it necessary to double its rates from $10 to $20.[45] After inflation set in, "no newspaper received subscriptions for more than six months," these being payable in advance.[46] Midway in the war, poor paper was selling for $40 per ream,[47] while subscriptions to daily papers averaged about $8 to $10 a month.[48]

Like paper, commercially made, imported ink became scarce; but, unlike paper, it was capable of fairly successful substitution. Practically every household had its recipe for ink; some produced a dark, clear ink, and others a pale, illegible ink. Extract of logwood, the bark of magnolia, dogwood, red or white oak, the rind of pomegranate, elderberries, green persimmons, were all used to produce ink of sorts. Each had its exponents who fought tenaciously for its good points. Edmund Ruffin, arch-patriot of the Confederacy, had a complicated recipe which apparently produced an ink of fine quality. He combined maple bark and pine leaves, cut less than one-half an inch long, and boiled them in water in an iron vessel; when the fluid was three-fourths evaporated, he removed the vessel from the fire, and added one teaspoonful of copperas, one teaspoonful of sugar, and a tablespoonful of vinegar to each pint of fluid. He strained and bottled the product which he thought was very satisfactory.[49] Some manufactured and sold ink on a small scale. The Wilmington *Journal* advertised a recipe for a new "Portable Ink" designed for the soldier's use. The recipe cost one dollar. Readers were assured that anyone could manufacture the ink; no pen was needed, for one could write with this marvelous substance with a pointed stick. It was available in three colors, blue, red, and green.[50] Many people complained that "Confederate" ink was too light,[51] or had an "unpleasant odor."[52] But some insisted that it was very effective. One point in its favor, according to a New Orleans editor, was that it "neither moulded nor carroded" steel writing pens.[53] The ink was satisfactory for letter writing, but was no good for printers. The *Southern Confederacy* ran the following plea from May 28 to 31, 1862:

> Printers News Ink
> Who has any for sale?
> Where is it?
> What is the price?
> Why don't somebody make it?
> Nothing would pay better.
> Where is ink made?
> Address us immediately.

On May 31, the editor received a recipe for ink from a reader, but it was apparently unsatisfactory, for he ran the questionnaire again from June 3 through 13.[54] The print in the newspapers grew dimmer and dimmer as the war continued.

The lack of sufficient and proper paper and ink were obstacles enough to throw in the path of Confederate correspondents, but there was also a lack of steel writing pens, to which the people were accustomed. When they could not obtain steel pens, they reverted to the goose quill of former days,[55] and the man who had mastered the art of trimming such quills to a fine point was extremely popular. In order to preserve the few steel pens available, people were urged to put nails or pins in the ink wells. It was supposed that any corrosive action in the ink would be expended on these bits of iron or steel, thus protecting the writing pen from rust.[56] Pencils, too, were hard to obtain, and there seemed to be little interest in manufacturing them. Some used coal as a substitute for graphite, while the more patient and painstaking were known to melt stray bullets and pour the "molten lead into the cavity of small reeds from the cane brakes." When hard, these were "trimmed to a point" and used. They left only a faint mark, but "served the purpose."[57]

Minor though it was, the problem of sealing envelopes was something with which the people had to contend. Glue, like many other commodities, was scarce, and substitutes were devised. The gum exuding from peach, plum, or cherry trees was often used, and old sealing wax wafers were melted and reused. A favorite paste was made from flour and water, but the glue manufactured in the Confederacy was inferior. That used on stamps was so poor that they often had to be stuck with some homemade mixture if they were to adhere to the envelope.[58]

The quality of glue used was not the only problem relating to stamps. These small bits of paper were in themselves one of the most aggravating shortages of the war. In the early months of the conflict there were no Confederate stamps, and throughout the war they continued scarce in many sections of the warring South. Some of the Confederate stamps were produced in the Confederacy; others were manufactured in England and imported into the South. Newspapers were always quick to criticize the shortage or lack of stamps in the community, but when some did finally arrive at the local post office, the same newspapers printed the good word to be broadcast through the community. During the winter of 1861-62 Confederate stamps were first distributed to the larger towns and there were seldom enough to last from one shipment to another. It was December, 1861, before either Charleston or Savannah secured their first stamps,[59] but the more remote areas did not get any until the summer of 1862. The lack of organization as well as the lack of dyes, steel plates, and experience, impeded efforts to manufacture stamps. Green dyes were so difficult to obtain that stamps in lower denominations were usually printed in some shade of blue.[60] In 1864 a North Carolina farmer wrote his son that he was unable to obtain any more stamps.[61] Another father, writing his son, enclosed a letter to a cousin and instructed him to "put a postage stamp on it and forward it—we have no stamps—could you send us a few?"[62] Two alternatives were open to those having no official stamps. Some postmasters issued stamps, good only in the local community, but adequately serving the immediate area.[63] A second alternative, and the one more widely used, was to pay the postmaster the price of the letter and have him mark it "paid";[64] herein lay a major grievance of the people. This practice drained from the civilian population the already rare small coins and, as a result, became a target for some of the most severely critical editorials of the war, ranking with those aimed at speculation and inadequate transportation. On November 19, 1861, the editor of the *Mercury* wrote that the complaints about the lack of stamps had grown "louder and louder and more general for several months past," adding that now these complaints had given "place to downright indignation. Why are not the stamps forthcoming, we ask? Why have they not been furnished long ago?"[65] Four days later, on November 23, the editor reiterated the complaints of the Charlestonians: "The grievances of the community of Charleston in the matter of postage, are growing too pressing to be endured longer. Week after week, month after month, the City Post office has been grabbing up our supply of small change, until silver has at last disappeared altogether from circulation."[66] Stamps finally appeared in Charleston in early December, but by the summer of 1862, the *Mercury* again launched an attack because of the lack of stamps.[67] This was continued at irregular intervals throughout the war. Other newspapers were equally vehement in their denunciation and complaints.

Small change became one of the scarcest items in the Confederacy. Specie practically disappeared from the pockets of the civilian population, and the people became dependent upon the depreciating Confederate money. Late in the war, many farmers refused to sell their produce if it meant taking in exchange this paper money.[68] The shortage of small change appeared early and became a universal scarcity before the war ended. Because of this condition, merchants were forced to resort to the most unusual expedients in order to carry on business. Among the first rules adopted by most concerns was "No change for bills except at heavy discounts."[69] Some stores gave certificates worth the amount owed the customer in change. These were applied to later purchases at that same store. These "due bills," as they were called, were widely used. The following is an example of those used in Fredericksburg:

No. 7
Cunningham's Cash Dry Goods Store
Due to Bearer
25¢

William H. Cunningham & Co.
August 29, 1861[70]

Another method of "making change" was to cut a bank note in half, halves becoming redeemable.[71] Some merchants gave various articles of merchandise instead of change. Nails and stamps, when available, were often used in place of money. Betty Herndon Maury declared that silver passed out of circulation early in the war. She bought a spool of thread from a Fredericksburg merchant for thirty-seven and one-half cents; she gave him fifty cents and, since he had no change, he gave her "two five cent stamps and a row of pins."[72] Many business concerns issued "shin-plasters," grocers, butchers, and bartenders being among those most frequently resorting to this kind of money. Few Confederates had gold in their possession, although some of the wealthier citizens managed to keep a little until the end of the war. So precious was such a possession, however, that those having it usually sewed it into their clothing. Mrs. Roger A. Pryor and Mrs. James Chesnut, Jr., sewed their gold into belts and kept it constantly with them.[73] It consistently rose in value during the war until, in the early spring of 1865, one dollar in gold was equivalent to sixty or seventy dollars in Confederate money.[74]

The shortage of ice caused considerable trouble. Newspapers had almost as much to say about this as they did about the thousand and one ways of using sorghum. Ice for the lower South had formerly been imported from the colder climes. While the winters were cold enough in some areas to cut ice and pack it away in icehouses, the domestic production by no means took care of the demand. Since it was needed in cooling drinks and foods, and especially in hospitals and for general medicinal purposes, precautions were taken to economize on its use and to get additional quantities. Newspapers carried on a campaign to encourage people to use it in moderation, and signs appeared in bars which read "gentlemen will please refrain from eating the ice left in their glasses, after drinking."[75] Newspapers urged people to produce their own by cutting it when ponds and rivers froze, and encouraged them to build icehouses. They asked cities, states, and even the Confederate government to finance the building of these storage places.[76] When the people living in Charlotte, North Carolina, complained of the cold weather that produced icicles nine inches long, the Wilmington *Journal* reminded them that this was "not an unmixed evil." They were encouraged to save this ice to be used the next summer.[77] The only substitute suggested for ice water was the chewing of mint leaves followed by the drinking of water. This was said "to impart a degree of coolness to the draught."[78] People missed their customary supply of ice. There was little available in private homes or hotels and none in water coolers on trains.[79] A Louisiana girl recorded in her diary: "Nine months of the year I reveled in ice, thought it impossible to drink water without it. Since last November, I have tasted it but once, and that by accident." This was written in September, so apparently she had done without ice through the previous summer.[80] Her case was typical.

Both the amateur and professional seamstress in the South were plagued constantly by the lack of many sewing necessities. Needles came to be among the rarest of treasures in the Confederacy. It was catastrophic, from the standpoint of the housewife, to lose a good darning needle. It was said that such a loss was "a calamity involving perhaps half a neighborhood."[81] As early as July, 1861, needles were selling for five cents each,[82] and although some came in on blockade-runners, they became more expensive. One Richmond lady paid $5 for a paper of rusty, imported needles.[83] These items were "treasured like jewels,"[84] and when broken were not cast away but were made to do as pins. Soldiers who found needles and thread on enemy captives immediately seized them, and if they did not put them into use themselves, exchanged them with some nearby housewife for food.[85] Few were manufactured in the South, although blacksmiths sometimes tried to make an article resembling a needle. But a man who had never previously constructed anything "more delicate than a plough share"[86] was not successful in making them. Knitting needles, too, were hard to obtain and the demand for them was great during the war. These, unlike those used for sewing, could be made from wood. Oak or hickory were most often used for this purpose. Blacksmiths, too, were more successful in making knitting needles, so that these were never as difficult to obtain as those for sewing.[87] Pins were equally as scarce. There was never a time when the Confederate woman failed to keep a sharp lookout for stray pins. Gentlemen, too, were known "to stoop down and pick up any found in the street."[88] Clara Minor Lynn counted hers every night and if one was missing she "searched the house diligently" until she found it. She kept her pins under lock and key when not in use, and when the war ended she had ten.[89] Thorns were sometimes used instead but, like all substitutes, were less satisfactory than the genuine article. One editor quipped that the southern woman ceased to use the expression "I don't care a pin" for anyone. The phrase had lost the meaning it had before the war. Thread, braid, and tape were also scarce. Old garments were unraveled and the thread salvaged, and some was made from raw cotton. Some silk worms were raised, but the returns in fiber were so slight as scarcely to merit mention.[90] There were a few thread factories, but they never succeeded in producing and distributing a sufficiency of their products. Braids for trimming were made from crochet thread, and apparently served the purpose very well.[91] Commercially made buttons were almost unobtainable in the Confederacy, but they were capable of substitution. Wooden ones were most common; the shape and beauty of these depended upon the artistic abilities of the maker. Sometimes these were intricately carved and highly polished; at other times they were covered with material. Gourds, horns, pasteboard, and persimmon seeds were sometimes converted into buttons.[92] Most people made their own from these materials but there were some factories in existence. Probably the largest was in Macon, Georgia, where the machinery was made by hand and was run by men who had never before been inside of a button factory. In May, 1863, it was turning out 30,000 to 40,000 buttons per day. These were made primarily from bone.[93] Buckles, hooks, eyes, and snaps disappeared. Buckles were made from wood, horns, and gourds, while other accessories were replaced with thorns, pins, or homemade buttons.

The personal world of Confederate women was drastically affected by shortages. For example, milady's boudoir contained few if any bottles of cologne or sweet-scented imported soap. These were luxuries rather than necessities, but they were sadly missed by those accustomed to using them. An agricultural journal suggested the use of sawdust as a cleansing cream for the face and hands, but it did not prove popular with women.[94] General Kirby Smith, stationed in Camden, Arkansas, wrote his wife requesting that she send to two of his hostesses, as a thank-you gift, some of the French soap and cologne that she had obtained via Mexico. He cautioned her, however, to be thrifty with such rare articles, for the Rio Grande was "in possession of the enemy and the blockade is closer," making future imports more improbable.[95]

So rare was cologne that a young lady who saw it on a friend's dresser enthusiastically but whimsically recorded the fact in her diary.[96] Combs were difficult to obtain and wooden or thorn ones came into general use.[97] Hairpins were as scarce as regular pins and needles. They were carefully straightened after each use and "oiled to prevent rust." Like pins, they were counted and cherished by their possessors. Some used large thorns as substitutes. The heads of thorns were dipped with sealing wax and thereby became fairly satisfactory. Because of the lack of hairpins and the scarcity of ribbons, young ladies were forced to use corn shucks with which to tie up their hair.[98] Difficulties in the care of "their crowning glory," were sufficient to produce frayed nerves among women. The shortage of hair switches used in attaining ornate coiffures greatly upset some women. Switches were lost, wore out, or they simply disintegrated during four years of war. One diarist recorded that a horse ate hers.[99] They were never imported in any great quantity, consequently women had to be content to use simple hair styles or invent a substitute. One used a pillow, covering it with her own hair;[100] another "put a pair of black satin boots on the top of her head and piled her hair over them." Still, this odd arrangement brought the owner compliments.[101] Even during the darkest days of the war, women thought of personal ornamentation. Some managed to keep their old family jewels with them during the war; others deposited theirs in various places of "safe-keeping." Little new jewelry was available or could be afforded by most of the women, but much costume jewelry was made during the war. Rings, bracelets, and pins were carved from bits of wood. Gutta-percha was popular in making jewelry. One ring, made from this substance, was set with a little button, on either side of which was a golden olive leaf cut from a coin.[102] Bone was used also, and bracelets made from the palmetto were exquisite.[103] Necklaces as well as bracelets were made from "melon seeds, linked together, . . . varnished and dried. Earrings, pins, and bracelets were made of . . . Army buttons, . . . [and] gleaming pearl-like flowers were formed of bleached and polished fish scales."[104]

Man's world was also affected by the total absence or scarcity of personal items. Razors were difficult to obtain, but since beards were the order of the day, this shortage was not severely felt. One girl, however, said she was forced to shave her father with scis-

sors.[105]   Hair oil, like all other oils, became scarce during the
war. Lard was used as a substitute, sometimes mixed with rose
petals to give it a delicate scent.[106]   The scarcity of combs affected men's grooming just as it did women's and the shortage
of soap made it difficult to keep clean. Many men missed their
various tobacco needs more than all else. There was a shortage
of chewing tobacco in some parts of the Confederacy. In its place
rosin was substituted.[107]   Imported pipes became difficult to obtain, but men made their own out of corncobs, clay, cane, dogwood, cherry, mahogany, hickory, and walnut.[108]   Some of these
pipes were ornate. One, carved by a Mississippian and preserved
in the Confederate Museum in Richmond, was of special interest.
The bowl was modeled in the likeness of General "Stonewall"
Jackson. Those who became proficient in carving pipes managed
to build up a business for themselves. Some sold their pipes on
the streets, others took orders.[109]   Few able-bodied men had much
time for recreation and diversion, and those who did found their
activity restricted. The scarcity of hooks and lines made it impossible for people to indulge in the sport of fishing. Whenever a
pin could be spared, or filched from a lady's possession, it might
be bent to form a hook. But it was practically impossible to catch
anything but minnows with such hooks.[110]   Ammunition and guns
for hunting purposes were scarce. Checkers and chessmen, as well
as poker chips, had a way of getting lost, but this did not deter
the men's playing. They substituted corn kernels or made new
pieces from bits of wood. Chessmen, particularly, were colorful,
being dyed with vegetable dyes and berries.[111]   Playing cards
were not so easily replaced and after four years of war, sets were
worn and broken.[112]

The scarcity of toothbrushes, tooth powder, and toothpicks was
a nuisance, when on the market toothbrushes cost $2 or more
each.[113]   When hogs were slaughtered, bristles were saved and
new toothbrushes were manufactured or old ones rethreaded.[114]
The old standby, a twig, was also used for cleaning teeth. Tooth
powder was made from ground charcoal, guaranteed to "make the
breath sweet and the gums firm and comfortable."[115]   Toothpicks
were carved from wood and bone.[116]

Those with artistic tastes found them difficult to express during
the war. The shortage of art supplies was an impediment to
drawing and painting. Oil paints could be obtained only through

the blockade. Canvas was early replaced by "burlaps, domestic or even tent cloth." John R. Key, grandson of Francis Scott Key, and the painter of sea pictures, depicted his scenes of Fort Sumter on burlap and domestic, while the artist, William Dandridge Washington, painted his great work, "The Burial of Latané," on tent cloth. "Tubes, brushes, and all tools . . . were procurable only through the blockade." Castor oil was used to prime the material upon which pictures were to be painted.[117] Engravers had to depend upon the wood at hand for their work. Several native trees were found to be suitable for engraving. Among these were white beech, white oak, birch, dogwood, persimmon, holly, mountain laurel, and yellow locust.[118] Music, as well as art, was hard to follow either as a hobby or profession. Not only was sheet music scarce, but instruments became broken or destroyed and they were hard to replace. Orchestras for entertainment purposes usually dwindled until a lone fiddler remained.[119] The high price of rosin prevented many violins from being used, and the professional violinist charged more than formerly.[120] Violins were made of cracker boxes, but these were a far cry from the Stradivarius.[121] Drums, helpful in infusing the patriotic fervor in soldiers and civilians, were manufactured in Charleston, South Carolina, but such an endeavor was unusual in the Confederacy.[122]

Nails, locks, screws, and lumber were always inadequate to meet the demand and were very expensive.[123] Nails, like pins, were carefully straightened and used many times. Those not needed "were carefully drawn and laid away for future use."[124] A captain of a blockade-runner declared that coffin screws were always in great demand, and he brought many into port.[125] Coffins, too, were scarce. The common pine box had to suffice for even the most celebrated military figure, since those of mahogany were difficult to obtain. A mortician, receiving a cargo of coffins through the blockade, would advertise the arrival. During the last winter of the war, one funeral director advertised the arrival of such a shipment, tactlessly adding that he "would be glad to supply his friends and public generally."[126]

While there were many shortages to worry and exasperate adults, the generation that spent a part of its childhood in the war was aware of shortages in its own little world. The scarcity of books affected schooling and reading habits. Juvenile books were very hard to obtain, and few were written and published in the South during the war because of the shortage of paper, ink, and man-power. The stock of children's books on hand when the war began was soon exhausted, and old ones, considered obsolete, were taken from attics and closets, dusted off, and made to do. The Louisiana legislature in February, 1865, appropriated $100,000 with which to buy "Elementary School Books" to be distributed among children between the ages of six and sixteen, but the act was not put into effect.[127]   Notices frequently appeared in Confederate newspapers notifying students who were to attend schools or colleges that they must supply their own texts.   When some intensely patriotic young gentlemen chose to show their patriotism by throwing their books at General Longstreet's corps as it marched through Greenville, South Carolina, their distressed mother wrote Mrs. James Chesnut, Jr., that no new books could be found in Greenville.[128]   Pencils, tablets, and slates were so scarce and precious that robbers broke into a Mississippi school and took these articles.[129]   The lack of this essential equipment left its mark on the child in after years, but children were not greatly distressed over the shortage of school equipment.   They felt the absence of birthday parties[130] and valentines far more keenly.[131]   But shortages of Christmas toys caused the severest heartbreak.   Some dolls were brought through the blockade, but the price was exorbitant and prohibitive to most children.   Emma LeConte told of one sold at a bazaar in Columbia, South Carolina, for $2000.   A gentleman spectator was aghast, for, as he said, "one could buy a live Negro baby for that."[132]   Because of the scarcity and high price of dolls and other toys, most gifts placed under the Christmas tree or in Christmas stockings were made at home.   The dolls were usually rag, with painted face or nut heads, for china heads could not be found.   Stuffed cotton rabbits, dogs, and cats were also made by the skillful hands of the patient mothers.   For boys there were toy soldiers and swords carved and painted at home; "jumping jacks," and toy animals were likewise homemade.   Wood was most frequently used for these toys, but pasteboard was also converted into playthings.   Pasteboard was made at home from old newspapers, cloth, and paste, combined in layers, the number of layers depending on the thickness desired, packed and smoothed by a hot iron.[133]   In most homes, the only candy enjoyed by the children was made from sorghum.   Striped stick candy was not available during the war.   There were children, "born of well-to-do parents, who at the close of the conflict did not know the taste of candy."[134] Peanuts, popcorn, molasses cakes, and home grown fruit were usually put in the coarse homemade stockings that were so trustingly hung by the chimney. Even Christmas tree decorations were of the homemade variety, but unusual and pretty trimmings were produced out of odds and ends of materials. Many people used the patriotic motif in their decorations. Some substituted the customary star at the top of the tree with the "Stars and Bars" and pictures of General Lee.[135] A Richmond family decorated their tree with tails and ears salvaged from the slaughter of hogs. The tails were decorated with ruffled paper, while the ears held the "light-wood" candles. Strings of popcorn were used to decorate the tree.[136] These substitute trimmings, toys, and food may have been poor but many in the Confederacy could not obtain or afford even these simple expedients. Many a mother's heart was broken by the sobbing of her child whom "Santa Claus" had forgotten.[137] In an effort to explain to the children, stories and poems were printed in papers and magazines. Among the most widely circulated of all was the poem by Mary McCrimmon called "Santa Claus":

> I'm sorry to write,
> Our ports are blockaded, and Santa, tonight,
> Will hardly get down here; for if he should start,
> The Yankees would get him unless he was 'smart,'
> They beat all the men in creation to run,
> And if they could get him, they'd think it fine fun
> To put him in prison, and steal the nice toys
> He started to bring to our girls and boys.
> But try not to mind it—tell over your jokes—
> Be gay and be cheerful, like other good folks;
> For if you remember to be good and kind,
> Old Santa next Christmas will bear it in mind.[138]

X

THE BALANCE SHEET

S HORTAGES OF SUPPLIES DURING THE CIVIL WAR WERE SO NU-
merous and so prevalent that scarcely anyone escaped
them. A North Carolina farmer, living in the Piedmont area,
might have plenty to eat and a comfortable house in which to live,
but he might have to do without shoes or to cut his farm acreage
because an impressment officer had taken his last horse. A Richmond lady, heiress of great fortune, name, and prestige, might
be able to purchase high-priced imported clothing or even stretch
her extravagant prewar wardrobe over four years, but she might
be unable to purchase quinine when she contracted malaria or to
have brilliant illumination in her home. A Texas businessman
might have plenty of meat straight from the nearby range, or he
might obtain costly imported merchandise by way of Mexico,
but at the same time he might have no salt for his meat and no
newspaper to tell him the events of the day. Everyone in some
way suffered from the shortages. Some effects were far-reaching,
others were trifling, but all played a part in the drama of the war.

Of all the effects of the shortage, none was so outstanding as
the increased industrialization of the South during the war. In
each of the eleven Confederate States, the trend toward increased
industrialization was evident. The movement was motived by the
desire to make the Confederacy a self-sufficient nation. Some
steps had been taken in this direction prior to war, and the need
for industrialization had long been recognized by such leaders as
William Gregg, Daniel Pratt, and James Dunwoody Brownson
DeBow. Yet when war came, the South was unprepared for so
great an endeavor. Newspapers, journals, civilian and military
leaders, all joined in one mighty chorus, urging the people to
manufacture their needs. Thus stimulated, the people established
all kinds of industrial enterprises, from the banks of the James

159

to those of the Rio Grande. The new industries varied somewhat in size. None of the new factories was as large as the older, established Tredegar Iron Works and Graniteville Mills. Many were one-man-backroom-shops or the one-woman-one-loom homespun factories. Most new industries were small and their output scant, and some were reminiscent of the days before the "Industrial Revolution." But the most important point of all was the fact that the South experienced a greatly accelerated industrialization.

When the war started, there were already some industrial plants in the South, and in nearly every village and city there were artisans and craftsmen who had long plied their trade. Upon these the war industrialization was based. Agencies were established in the larger towns and cities to organize and utilize this scattered force of skilled and unskilled labor. In New Orleans, in the fall of 1861, an association was formed, its object being

> to promote mechanical interests; to provide Southern mechanics and workmen; to establish an office where a register will be kept of all the members out of employment, so that employers will know where to find such as they want; and to establish a branch or branches of the association in every state of the Confederacy.[1]

Realizing the value of those who could manufacture scarce articles, newspapers undertook the task of educating an agrarian people to appreciate and accept those who worked in such pursuits. The *Southern Cultivator*, a major spokesman of agrarian interests, began the campaign in June, 1861, when it raised its voice to proclaim, "Let no one in whatever sphere he may have been reared, whether rich or poor, educated or illiterate . . . look down on manufacturing enterprises or mechanical pursuits as beneath his dignity."[2] When Thomas J. Hudson, a Mississippi agricultural leader, told a group of his fellow planters that the "inventor of every machine calculated to save labor is a public benefactor," he voiced the changing opinion toward labor and industry.[3]

Three primary considerations were borne in mind in locating a new industry. First, the industry should be established in a locality believed to be safe from the enemy. During the first year of the war, that meant any area of the back country south of Kentucky or northern Virginia. As the invading enemy moved deeper into the South, the "safe area" became more circumscribed. A second consideration was either water or rail transportation facilities, in order that the industry might supply a large area and secure the raw materials from a distance. The third point of consideration centered around power facilities. Large industries had to be located near water power or coal fields. Towns having one or more of these necessary requirements hastened to advertise themselves and to seek the establishment of new factories. The people of Chattanooga believed that it might become the "Pittsburgh of the South,"[4] and the people of far-away Fort Smith, Arkansas, on the border of the Indian Territory, assured the people of the Confederacy that few places "presented so many advantages for a manufacturing city." They based their arguments on the nearby rich coal fields.[5] Georgia was the most highly industrialized state in the Confederacy; North Carolina, Alabama, and Virginia followed in that order. Texas, though far removed from the main theatre of war, experienced a growth of industrial pursuits. Certain towns in the Confederacy came to be symbols of wartime industrial growth. Among these were Lynchburg and Danville, Virginia; Wilmington, Charlotte, Raleigh, Fayetteville, and Carthage, North Carolina; Laurens, Spartanburg, Chester, Greenville, and Columbia, South Carolina; Augusta, Macon, Atlanta, and Columbus, Georgia; Montgomery, Eufala, and Selma, Alabama; Columbus, Mississippi; Shreveport and New Orleans, Louisiana; Camden and Batesville, Arkansas; Houston, San Antonio, and Tyler, Texas. One or more industrial plants were established in all of these towns during the war. At first glance, it would seem that practically every needed item was being made in these and other plants. High on the list were cotton cards, for these were made either privately or under state auspices in every state. Other items manufactured in the Confederacy included soap, candles, wool and cotton materials, thread, matches, looms and spinning jennies, boxes, ink, envelopes, writing paper, shoes, shoe pegs, various simple machines, utensils, lace, wagons, baskets, barrels, buckets, knitting-needles, rope, furniture, cigars, glass, raincoats, ploughs, starch, hats, cutlery, buttons, and sewing machines. In addition to commercial manufacturing on a sizable scale, domestic manufacturing increased rapidly during the war.

Why, one might ask, did shortages continue when manufacturing was so rapidly expanded and diversified? The answer is as complex as the problem, but five major reasons may be given. First, most of the new industries were small and their output was never able to supply the demands made upon them. Second, the industries were established in extraordinary times, and it was impossible for them to obtain proper equipment, adequate raw materials, experienced workers, and managerial help. Many were founded in a burst of patriotic fervor and discovered that they could work only spasmodically, often with the poorest of machines and materials, and sometimes they were forced to close entirely. Third, many plants were established either in the direct path of the enemy or near their line of march. After mid-1863, few places were safe from war destruction. Once taken over or destroyed by the enemy, the plants were worthless to the civilian population. For example, a man in Mississippi wrote his mother in the fall of 1862 that she would not recognize Columbus, Mississippi, because it was "filled with so many new shops and factories —the hum of the wheels and the creaking of the machinery [were] mingling with drum and bugle."[6] A year later, the Federal forces had so maneuvered that only a small surrounding area benefited by these Columbus factories. The story might be repeated many times. A fourth reason for the shortages despite the industrialization was inadequate transportation. Manufactured goods might be piled high at the factories while two hundred miles away people suffered for lack of them. Fifth, many of the best equipped, largest plants were under contract to either the Confederate or some state government, and their products were never available to civilians. An example of this was furnished by Texas, whose clothing factories, iron foundries (even those making skillets and cooking utensils), hat factories, and shoe factories were under contract to the state government.[7]

Considerable diversification resulted from the shortages of agricultural products and the effort to supply them. The scarcity of food and fodder, coupled with the difficulty of marketing cotton, caused many to turn to planting food crops instead of cotton. The newspapers championed the movement to increase the planting of food crops. The Chattanooga *Daily Rebel* encouraged "every man, woman, and child, with a yard square of ground, [to] scratch it and put in corn." It observed that "every grain carefully entrusted to the fruitful earth is a mite of contribution to the Nation's liberty."[8] The people answered this plea by planting many and various food crops. Even window boxes were made to produce food in the crowded cities. Planters substituted corn for cotton. One of the most interesting outcomes of wartime agriculture was the wide distribution and acceptance of Florida citrus fruit. Southerners formerly imported such fruit from the West Indies, but the blockade made this practically impossible. In August, 1861, the Charleston *Mercury* advised "fruit dealers to make arrangements during the blockade and hereafter to obtain supplies of these fruits from Florida."[9] Less than a year later, the people of Savannah, Georgia, appealed to Florida for lemons, limes, and oranges, and on April 28, 1862, an editor reported an "ample stock on hand."[10] Pineapples were missed by many, and some attempts were made to raise them. Some were grown in Hinds County, Mississippi, these being described as "rich-flavored."[11] Although much remained to be done, agriculture did become more diverse, for the people had to become self-sustaining to exist.

The shortages of food and supplies brought marked inflation in prices. The economic law of supply and demand ruled the economic lives of the people with an iron hand. Scarce items shot up in price, and became unobtainable to many. Aided by speculators and hoarders, many articles became scarce on the market, and those people with money enough to do so bid up the price to get what they wanted. Influenced by the instability of Confederate currency, prices skyrocketed until they were out of reason. It has been estimated that scarce articles rose from "ten to twenty times their pre-war prices."[12] This estimate seems to be a conservative one. As early as October, 1861, a North Carolina farmer wrote his son that "nearly every man, woman, and child you . . . [meet has] a long face, . . . since goods have advanced 100 per. ct. each one grins a ghastly smile."[13] The cost of all commodities advanced, nothing seemed to remain within reason. Spoiled food, left too long in storage, commanded outrageous prices.[14] J. B. Jones, dismayed at seeing people throw away their money, told of a man who paid $7.50 for a pair of secondhand boots that had large holes in them.[15] This inflationary trend was partially influenced by shortages, but in turn it aggravated the shortage problem. Many were forced to do without sufficient food and clothing when needed items were on the market; they could not afford to pay the prices.

Shortages brought real hardship and suffering to a great many people of the Confederacy. Those who had to live on salaries experienced a difficult time, for the increase in salaries did not keep pace with increase in prices.[16] But the very poor element in the Confederacy suffered even more than salaried people. Julia LeGrand saw people starving in the streets of New Orleans;[17] and J. B. Jones wrote that "A portion of the people look like vaga-bonds . . . [some are] in dingy and dilapidated clothes; some seem gaunt and pale with hunger."[18] By the spring of 1862, some slave-owners were trying to "hire out their Negroes to have them fed and clothed," but few met with success.[19] Even the "rich were driven to great straits to live," for shortages prevented them from getting many things needed or desired.[20] While some few people may have lived in the style to which they had been accustomed, there were thousands who actually suffered during the war.

Various programs were inaugurated to help those who were unable to obtain the essentials of life. These programs ran the gamut from simple charity to cooperative enterprises. Many towns and cities consolidated their organized charitable endeavors and accomplished much for the relief of the needy. Richmond had a soup kitchen where soup, which "could not be made by an in-dividual for less than $5,"[21] was sold for twenty-five cents a quart to the poor. Several cities had "free markets," where the poor could be fed at no cost to them. Among the more famous and successful of these markets was the one in New Orleans. Before the capture of the city, it functioned satisfactorily, supported by contributions from the surrounding rural area, but it is doubtful whether it could have continued on such a scale throughout the war. It was nothing unusual for this market to distribute supplies to a thousand people a day. On September 7, 1861, 1,292 fami-lies received such supplies.[22] Some charity cases were not happy with the food and drink supplied to them. Julia LeGrand found some poor people who "became angry" when they were given black instead of green tea.[23] States, as well as cities, tried to help the poor, especially those whose men-folk were serving in the army or navy. Industrial and business enterprises interested themselves in the poor. The Roswell, Georgia, Manufacturing Company distributed cotton yarn free of charge to the poor in the surrounding and nearby counties. In an effort to have fair distribution, the company sent the yarn to the county officials for distribution.[24] Individuals, too, helped support some of their neighbors who were in want. The poor came "down from the mountains or out of the piney woods, . . . drawing hand carts to get corn" donated to the needy.[25]

"Mutual Aid Societies" sprang into being throughout the Confederacy. These were cooperative enterprises or joint-stock companies through which the people tried to obtain the essentials of life at as low cost as possible. They conducted a constant search for food and clothing that often proved advantageous to the members.[26] The Charleston *Mercury* estimated that the prices paid by the Mutual Aid Societies ran from "20 to 25% below the usual prices."[27]

Little was done in the Confederacy in the realm of price-fixing, although various military commanders saw fit to try it within their sphere of command. Martial law was practically always accompanied by such measures, but the Confederate government, as a rule, shied away from such drastic steps on constitutional grounds. Some city councils attempted to couple a price-fixing program with one of rationing. The Richmond City Council undertook to distribute salt as fairly as possible and at a fixed price. Some suggested that fuel, meat, and bread "be furnished in the same manner."[28] A few factories, desiring equal distribution of scarce articles, tried their own system of rationing. Some limited the amount to each family, but this was not very successful for no records were kept, and it was difficult to carry out a rigid program. The Macon Factory, makers of cloth, allowed only "one piece of cloth to a family, the head of which . . . [had] to register . . . so that no advantage . . . [could] be gained."[29]

Shortages of food and supplies contributed in the Confederacy to the increase of crime, especially stealing and violence. Robbery too was on the increase during the war. In the fall of 1862 a farmer, constantly plagued with theft of chickens and hogs, declared that stealing was "the order of the day."[30] A year later conditions were no better, and the same farmer wrote his son: "Historians in after years will write of the Dark Ages, when Abraham the 1st reigned at the North and Jeff Davis at the South, and murder and theft was the order of the day—It may truly be called The Reign of Terror."[31] Mrs. Roger A. Pryor declared that to keep food of any kind in besieged Petersburg was impossible. "Cows, pigs, bacon, flour, everything was stolen, and even setting hens were taken from the nests."[32] J. B. Jones recorded that one evening in December, 1864, a servant "stepped into the yard just in time to save some clothes drying on the line. A thief was in the act of stealing them."[33] The next month Jones' woodhouse was broken into, and two of his nine sticks of wood were taken. This amounted to a $10 loss, for wood was selling at $5 a stick at the time.[34] One thief stole twenty-one hats from the checkroom in an Augusta hotel during a ball,[35] and a few months later a woman in the same city wrote her daughter that "men and women are robbed in the streets daily, also in the cars. Clothes are stolen out of the tubs and off the ironing table."[36] Quinine and other scarce medicines were frequently stolen and sold for fabulous prices. In August, 1861, a New Orleans man was caught with fifty-six ounces of quinine that he had stolen from a druggist.[37] Absolute necessities, such as food, clothing, fuel, and medicine were the usual objects of theft. General lawlessness and mob action were widespread during the war. The most famous disturbance was the "Bread Riot" of April 2, 1863, in Richmond. Many commodities, such as dry goods, brooms, meat, glassware, and even jewelry, were seized by the rioters. The mob, consisting mainly of the wives of the working class, marched through the main downtown section of Richmond, breaking into stores and carrying away whatever they could find. President Davis urged the crowd to cease its depredations but the "City Battalion" had to be called out before it would disperse. The group disbanded when ordered by the military to disperse or be fired upon; some were arrested; the next day several stores were again broken into.[38] The city streets were guarded for several days after this riot. Similar disturbances occurred in other Southern towns. In Mobile, Alabama, in the fall of 1863, women armed with knives and hatchets marched down Dauphine Street "breaking open the stores . . . and taking for their use such articles of food or clothing as they were in need of."[39] In the spring of 1864, there was a similar riot in Savannah, Georgia. This group demanded "bread or blood" and troops were called out to disperse them.[40] Trouble-makers pressed and jammed into stores whenever they received word that some scarce items had arrived. Swarms of women rushed into the shops at early hours trying to get a little of whatever was available.[41]

Because of the widespread shortage of commodities, business life was disrupted. The lack of merchandise caused many stores to close entirely. Many smaller towns were without any business places, and even cities looked like ghost towns. Betty Herndon Maury wrote that "most of the stores" in Fredericksburg, Virginia, were closed;[42] while many hundred miles away in Galveston, Texas, only a few shops remained open and these had small stocks. "All the large business houses on the Strand . . . [were] closed."[43] Between these distant points, many business houses found it necessary to discontinue service. In New Orleans, in the spring of 1862, there was almost complete cessation of business,[44] while in Memphis, in the same spring, stores were "at least half-closed; . . . no cotton, no sugar, no molasses anywhere to be seen."[45] In mid-December, 1862, Mobile registered none of the usual Christmas rush, for her "principal business houses" were closed.[46] Even in those towns where there was some merchandise, few stores stayed open all day. Shortage of fuel as well as shortage of merchandise caused them to keep indefinite hours. "When a merchant could find anything to sell, he opened his doors, disposed of it quickly, and [then] closed while in quest of another stock."[47]

Because of the lack of merchandise and the increased demand for practically every available article, sales people found that they need not go out of their way to be polite to the customers. Some were actually rude. It was said that the

> yard-stick gentlemen in Richmond . . . [had] arrived at a destitution of manners. . . . Should a lady perchance desire a skein of silk, she . . . [crept] meekly into a store, and . . . dared not express her surprize at being requested to pay something in the neighborhood of $100 for it. The chivalrous 'exempts' . . . [stood] behind the counter in whatever attitude they may . . . [have fancied] and . . . [smiled] with languid derision upon those presumptious customers who . . . [dared] aspire to the purchasing of their stock.[48]

There were salesmen who could laugh, but they did so only when the requests for nonexistent merchandise were so unreasonable as to be ludicrous.[49] There were frequent complaints from housewives that merchants always saved the scarce articles and prize merchandise for their best customers.[50] The best that could be credited to any of the merchants was that they remained unmoved and stoic to even the most impassioned pleas of the housewives.[51]

Because of the depreciating value of the Confederate money, and the scarcity of specie, the primitive system of barter came to be a popular method of exchange late in the war. After early 1864 it was said that bartering had become the "best mode of getting supplies, and those who . . . [had] things to barter fare well."[52] From 1864 until the end of the war, newspapers carried hundreds of notices of people willing to exchange one commodity for another. The following advertisement, which appeared in the Savannah *Republican,* was typical:

> I will barter salt from my salt factory for produce on the following terms: Salt, 50 pounds per bushel; 4 bushels of salt for 5 bushels of corn and peas; 1 bushel of salt for 5 pounds of lard or bacon; 2 bushels of salt for 7 pounds of sugar; 10 bushels of salt for a barrel of 'super' flour; 2 bushels of salt for 1 pr. of shoes.[53]

The acceptance of foodstuffs in return for tuition and board in colleges and schools became general. Forsaking altogether monetary payments, farmers would load whatever they had to offer on a wagon or cart and take it around the countryside trying to exchange it for what they had not.[54] Many people who were farsighted and financially able bought quantities of scarce commodities early in the war and held them for exchange later. However, many who were not speculators found themselves in a position to barter. Private Theodore Honour urged his wife to trade her six pounds of coffee for "bacon or supplies" she wanted. He added, "If the country people will not sell, they are generally willing to barter, and coffee is an item they all want. Sugar is up to such an extravagant price that . . . we can't afford to drink it, so . . . trade the coffee for eatibles."[55] One woman, once a lady of means, found it necessary to sell her $600 New Orleans-made bonnet. Instead of money, she took five turkeys in payment.[56] Barter became so general that he who had produce was in a better bargaining situation during the last year of the war than he who had millions in Confederate money and bonds.

One thing southern people learned, as a result of the scarcity of commodities, was economy. Those who had scarcely known the meaning of the word economy before the war were suddenly face to face with its full meaning. Necessity made it imperative. Women in all parts of the Confederacy were kept busy saving rags, paper, lead, and hundreds of other items and at the same time

stretching a little food to feed big families. It was said that between making, stretching, renovating, and remodeling, the Confederacy became a "nation of Crusoes."[57] Some complained, but
they were few. One young Georgia girl received a letter in which
her friend said: "This life of shifts and expedients of mere 'getting
along' has waked me up in a way that I needed."[58] Most women
would have preferred a more abundant store of worldly goods
than was available during the war, but they accepted the shortages graciously. One declared that it was well that she was
kept busy devising temporary expedients, for she "had no time
to brood."[59] Many laughed and were amused by the substitutes
devised for some nonexistent article. They learned that complaint
accomplished nothing, hard work accomplished much.

Shortages affected various parts of the Confederacy in different
ways. No one scene was typical, for every locality had its scarcities, its abundances, its expedients. Neither did the shortages
affect all people in the same way. Geography, economic and social
position, and lack or presence of ingenuity combined to make
each family a varying group. One area and its inhabitants might
be a community of moderately satisfied people on one day; it
might be a wasteland laid bare by an invading army the next.
Richmond feared famine early in the spring of 1862, but small,
quiet Lenoir, tucked away in the mountains of North Carolina,
seemed to have a sufficiency of the necessities throughout the
war. In Lenoir, Mrs. Ella A. R. Harper, wife of George W. F.
Harper, kept five volumes of diary covering the years of 1862 to
1865. Not one time did she mention a shortage of any kind,
and on April 4, 1865, less than a week before General Lee surrendered at Appomattox, she was preparing a box of food, clothing, and homemade candles to send to her husband who was in the
service.[60] By this time, most people of the Confederacy were
living a hand-to-mouth existence. The state that suffered least
from shortages was Texas. The people there were accustomed to
a simple life because of their frontier status. Great quantities of
goods came into Texas by way of the Rio Grande and Mexico,
until this artery was practically closed in December, 1863, when
Federal forces took the river. A committee, composed of repre-
sentatives from the states in the Trans-Mississippi area, reported
to the War Department in Richmond that Texas had, in April
1863, "bacon and beef enough to feed the Army and her people

for at least two years."[61] Texas, too, greatly increased its manufacturing interests during the war. Furthermore, it experienced
little war destruction in comparison with other states. The state
that suffered most was Virginia. From the first Battle of Manas-
sas to the final surrender at Appomattox, from the seacoast to the
Shenandoah Valley, Virginia was the major battlefield of the
War. It was a rich field for impressment agents, and fed more
than its share of the soldiers. Some areas escaped, but they were
few and small. Virginia's burdens were more than the state could
bear.

Another effect of shortages must be mentioned. They cut across
economic and social barriers and exerted a leveling influence
among the people. "The wealthiest were made poor"[62] by the
war and were forced to find expedients for scarce items as were
the poorest. "The practical class, both old and young, . . . [became]
more appreciated in the Confederacy."[63] "The neighborhood . . .
craftsmen found themselves springing into important personages."[64]
One woman wrote in later years:

> Many . . . suppose that only the poorer common people resorted
> to the makeshifts, . . . such was not the case. An elegant woman,
> a member of the distinguished families of Lee, Custis, and Ran-
> dolph of Virginia, the daughter of a wealthy Louisiana planter
> said to me, 'There were not only days when we were hungry for
> a crust of dry corn bread, but the means with which to make it.'[65]

The shortages affected the lives of most people economically,
socially, politically, culturally, and religiously. People were hungry, cold, ill-housed, and poorly clothed, because of the lack of
food, fuel, shelter, and clothing needs. Their social life was
disrupted; formal parties were few, and refreshments usually
nonexistent or simple. Shortages played a part in politics, too.
Speeches and debates on the subject reverberated through legislative halls. Petitions, requests, and complaints from constituents
kept lawmakers busy, for homefolks looked to their political rep-
resentatives for surcease of suffering resulting from lack of necessities. Expression of cultural interests was limited by shortages.
People who desired to paint, or to engage in music were prevented
from doing so because of the scarcity of materials. It was equally
difficult to obtain books and artistic items or to find satisfaction
for one's aesthetic desires. When Confederate congregations
assembled for worship they often found their respective churches

stripped bare of cushions and comforts. An anonymous correspondent, writing for the *Southern Illustrated News* in 1863, con-
cisely summed up the situation:

> Abuse me who will! I am ready and willing, glad and proud to
> wear old clothes from year's end to year's end; give parties of
> guba peas and ginger nuts. Go to church and sit and kneel upon
> bare boards; receive all my visitors in the Hades of a boarding-
> house, where the part of Ceberus is played by spiteful widows and
> accidental old maids, all ears, eyes, and knitting pins; to sit down
> to breakfast before a cup of Confederate rye coffee, and a news-
> paper printed on paper the hue of the 'Yellow Pest'; if worst comes
> to worst to pin my belt with thorns instead of pins; and bind up
> my bonny brown hair with ribbons of cornshucks.[66]

Shortages of essential commodities played an important part
in bringing about the collapse of the Confederacy.[67] In 1862
the problem of supplying the armed forces became increasingly
difficult, and after 1863 it became insuperable. So depleted was the
stock of food, clothing, medicine, and beasts of burden in those
areas near the battlefronts that the War Department could not
adequately feed and clothe the army. Neither could it fight
disease, properly care for the sick, nor transport men and food
with the necessary speed. Because of the almost total breakdown
of transportation throughout the Confederacy, it was impossible
to haul essential commodities from the few areas having a sufficiency in the last months of the war. The soldiers felt the privations in their day-to-day existence, and were less efficient because
of them. But they also felt the effects of the shortages on the
homefront. Their families wrote letters in which they depicted
the plight "back home." As conditions grew worse soldiers took
leave without permission, and some deserted and went home
to check on the situation and to aid their families. This leave-
taking and desertion weakened the fighting force and contributed
to the defeat of the Confederacy.[68]

Most people at home tried to maintain a spirit of optimism and
hope, but this became increasingly difficult as the war went from
bad to worse. After 1863 a spirit of war weariness settled over
the civilian population. This was especially noticeable among
those who found everyday existence difficult. The constant and
unrelenting battle for the essentials of life made many people
look to the day when the war would be over and life would re-

turn to normal. To them military victory became a secondary goal; sufficient food, clothing, housing, and other essentials were of primary importance. This spirit of weariness gradually passed into one of lethargy in the last months of the conflict, and mere existence then became the major problem of the folks at home.

War formally ended with the surrender of General Robert E. Lee on April 9, 1865. Shortly thereafter General Joseph Eggleston Johnston and General Edmund Kirby Smith surrendered their forces. The soldiers were free to return home, and as they drifted back during the late spring and early summer, what they saw depressed them beyond anything they had imagined. Buildings had been demolished and homes lay in ruins. Railroad tracks were wrapped around trees and roads were in disrepair. Once progressive farms and plantations lay bare and quiet, for the slaves had gone, the farm animals had been taken or slain, and the few inhabitants were dejected. Those who had been anxious for the war to cease so that normalcy might return found that prewar conditions could never return. It would be years before the South could restore the damage done by war. Shortages of certain commodities continued to make life difficult during the next few years. It was impossible to make crops when tools, beasts of burden, and labor were so scarce. There was an acute shortage of food in those areas most recently devastated by war. Clothing continued to be a problem, for it was years before normal stocks reappeared in the South, and even longer before many could afford new clothes. Houses had to be repaired or rebuilt before the population could be adequately housed. It took years to restore transportation facilities and agricultural equipment, and to replace beasts of burden. During the struggle for restoration which immediately followed the war, apathy seized many. To these it seemed useless to battle against such odds, for during the war they had managed to exist on so little that they now asked whether or not the heartbreaking struggle was worth while. Many answered in the negative and assumed an attitude of hopelessness and indifference; some even migrated to other countries. This condition of mind stemmed from the war and affected a large number of people for years to come.

Wartime shortages had a positive as well as a negative effect on the thinking of the people. Diametrically opposed to those who became impassive about the problem of rehabilitation were those who had learned a lesson from the war. The economic dependence of the South on outside sources was now understood by many who had heretofore only casually listened to such leaders as DeBow and Gregg. The South had to develop its resources with the ingenuity shown during the war. In time of want, a little was made to go a long way, and many items thought useless were found to possess precious properties. There were many possibilities for development in the South. The latent stirrings of industrialism were kept in check, however, for a decade or more until the necessary capital could be obtained. The ensuing chaotic political situation provided poor soil for these seeds of industrial inventiveness to spring to life. Nevertheless economic conditions in the South between 1861 and 1865, pathetic as they were, added fuel to an impetus that resulted in an industrial revolution in the "New" South.

FOOTNOTES

CHAPTER I

[1]Mrs. Felix G. de Fontaine, "Old Confederate Days," *Confederate Veteran*, IV (1896), 302.

[2]"Southern Patronage to Southern Imports and Domestic Industry," *Southern Planter*, XXXI (1861), 58-63.

[3]C. W. Howard, "Things Worthy of Attention," *Southern Cultivator*, XIX (1861), 201-3, 233-35; Howard, "The Future of the Confederate States," *ibid.*, p. 137.

[4]Richmond *Enquirer*, September 11, 1861.

[5]Charleston *Mercury*, June 15, 1861.

[6]*Floridian and Journal* (Tallahassee, Florida), June 29, 1861.

[7]Richmond *Enquirer*, May 10, 1861.

[8]*Daily Picayune* (New Orleans), May 17, 1861.

[9]William Howard Russell, *Pictures of Southern Life, Social, Political and Military*, p. 71.

[10]Howard, *Southern Cultivator*, XIX (1861), 137.

[11]Russell, *Pictures of Southern Life*, p. 71.

[12]John Beauchamp Jones, *A Rebel War-Clerk's Diary*, I, 33.

[13]Betty Herndon Maury Diary, Manuscript Division, Library of Congress, Washington, D. C.

[14]Jones, *A Rebel War-Clerk's Diary*, I, 25, 27.

[15]S. Sparkman to Mrs. John L. Bailey, John L. Bailey Papers, Southern Historical Collection, University of North Carolina, Chapel Hill, North Carolina.

[16]Parthenia Antoinette Hague, *A Blockaded Family: Life in Southern Alabama During the Civil War*, p. 5.

[17]Susan Dabney Smedes, *Memorials of a Southern Planter*, p. 193; Catherine Cooper Hopley, *Life in the South: From the Commencement of the War*, II, 116, 276.

[18]*Southern Confederacy* (Atlanta), September 20, 1861.

[19]Mrs. W. E. Turner, "Some Womanly Recollections of the War Between the States," MS, North Carolina Room, University of North Carolina, Chapel Hill, North Carolina.

[20]Mrs. M. P. Handy, "Confederate Makeshifts," *Harper's Monthly Magazine*, LII (1876), 576.

[21]Mrs. Charles R. Hyde, "The Women of the Confederacy," *Confederate Veteran*, XXXII (1924), 23.

[22]David Dodge, "Domestic Economy in the Confederacy," *Atlantic Monthly*, LVIII (1886), 229-30.

[23]Sarah Morgan Dawson, *A Confederate Girl's Diary*, p. 233.

[24]Hague, *A Blockaded Family*, p. 110.

CHAPTER II

[1]Thomas Cooper DeLeon, *Four Years in Rebel Capitals: An Inside View of the Life of the Southern Confederacy, From Birth to Death; From Original Notes Collected in the Years 1861 to 1865*, p. 273.

[2]Francis B. C. Bradlee, *Blockade Running During the Civil War: and the Effect of Land and Water Transportation on the Confederacy*, pp. 9-10.

[3]Hopley, *Life in the South*, I, 300.

[4]James D. Richardson (ed.), *A Compilation of the Messages and Papers of the Confederacy*, I, 187.

[5]James Dunwoody Brownson DeBow, "Editorial," *DeBow's Review and Industrial Resources, Statistics, Etc.*, XXXI (1861), 329-30.

[6]Bradlee, *Blockade Running*, p. 165.

[7]James Russell Soley, *The Blockade and the Cruisers*, pp. 45, 48.

[8]Bradlee, *Blockade Running*, p. 165.

[9]Mary Boykin Chesnut, *A Diary From Dixie*, p. 140.

[10]Dodge, *Atlantic Monthly*, LVIII (1886), 229.

[11]A. C. Gordon, "Hard Times in the Confederacy," *The Century Magazine*, XXXVI (1888), 762.

[12]DeLeon, *"Belles, Beaux, and Brains of the Sixties,"* p. 66.

[13]*Ibid.*, p. 273.

[14]DeLeon, *Four Years in Rebel Capitals*, p. 273.

[15]DeLeon, *Belles, Beaux and Brains of the Sixties*, p. 398.

[16]Soley, *The Blockade and the Cruisers*, p. 36.

[17]Lonn, *Foreigners in the Confederacy*, p. 314.

[18]*New York Herald*, March 13, 1863.

[19]General Edmund Kirby Smith to Mrs. Edmund Kirby Smith, December 19, 1863, Kirby Smith Papers, Southern Historical Collection, University of North Carolina, Chapel Hill, North Carolina.

[20]Captain A. Roberts, *Never Caught: Personal Adventures Connected With Twelve Trips in Blockade Running During the American Civil War*, pp. 3-5.

[21]DeLeon, *Four Years in Rebel Capitals*, p. 280.

[22]*Ibid.*, p. 281.

[23]Bradlee, *Blockade Running*, pp. 162-63.

[24]Thomas E. Taylor, *Running the Blockade: A Personal Narrative of Adventures, Risks, and Escapes During the American Civil War*, p. 38.

[25]Jones, *A Rebel War-Clerk's Diary*, I, 350.

[26]DeLeon, *Four Years in Rebel Capitals*, p. 284.

[27]Bradlee, *Blockade Running*, pp. 31-32.

[28]*Statutes at Large of the Confederate States of America*, First Congress, Second Session, February 6, 1864, pp. 179-81.

[29]Bradlee, *Blockade Running*, p. 32; Jones, *A Rebel War-Clerk's Diary*, II, 374.

[30]DeLeon, *Belles, Beaux, and Brains of the Sixties*, p. 412.

[31]Frank Moore (ed.), *The Rebellion Record: A Diary of American Events with Documents, Narratives, Illustrative Incidents, Poetry, Etc.*, III, 27.

[32]*Ibid.*

[33]"Running the Blockade," *Confederate Veteran*, XVII (1909), 410.

[34]Mrs. D. Giraud Wright, *A Southern Girl in '61: The War-Time Memoir of a Confederate Senator's Daughter*, p. 111.

[35]DeLeon, *Belles, Beaux and Brains of the Sixties*, p. 415.

[36]Charles William Ramsdell, "The Confederate Government and the Railroads," *American Historical Review*, XXII (1917), 795.

[37]*Ibid.*, p. 798.

[38]*Ibid.;* Richmond *Enquirer*, June 13, 1862.

[39]Ramsdell, *American Historical Review*, XXII (1917), 809.

[40]*The War of Rebellion: A Compilation of the Official Records of the Union and Confederate Armies*, Series IV, II, 505. Hereinafter cited as *Official Records*.

[41]*Ibid.*, Series IV, I, 1048.

[42]*Journal of the Congress of the Confederate States*, III, 426.

[43]*Official Records*, Series IV, II, 529.

[44]Richmond *Enquirer*, January 13, 1862.

[45]DeLeon, *Four Years in Rebel Capitals*, p. 132.

[46]Jones, *A Rebel War-Clerk's Diary*, I, 92; Moore, *Rebellion Record*, IV, 9.

[47]H. S. Fulkerson, *A Civilian's Recollections of the War Between the States*, p. 126; *Official Records*, Series IV, II, 616.

[48]DeLeon, *Four Years in Rebel Capitals*, p. 281.

[49]Dodge, *Atlantic Monthly*, LVIII (1886), 230; Bradlee, *Blockade Running*, pp. 46-47; Edward A. Pollard, *The Lost Cause: A New Southern History of the War of the Confederates*, p. 427.

[50]Vicksburg *Sun*, November 16, 1861.

[51]Wilmington *Journal*, March 15, 1862.

[52]Emma Florence LeConte Diary, December 13, 1864, Southern Historical Collection, University of North Carolina, Chapel Hill, North Carolina.

[53]Alfred Hoyt Bill, *Beleaguered City: Richmond 1861-1865*, p. 264.

[54]Arkansas *State Gazette*, December 27, 1862.

[55]*Southern Confederacy*, October 21, 1861.

[56]*Ibid.*, November 23, 1861.

[57]Richmond *Examiner*, June 15, 1861.

[58]*Carolina Watchman*, September 29, 1862.

[59]Petersburg *Daily Express*, October 21, 1861.

[60]Mrs. Virginia Clay-Clopton, *A Belle of the Fifties*, pp. 194-95.

[61]Jones, *A Rebel War-Clerk's Diary*, I, 196.

[62]This program is discussed in greater detail in Chapter III.

[63]*Official Records*, Series IV, II, 809-10.

[64]Jones, *A Rebel War-Clerk's Diary*, II, 183.

[65]DeLeon, *Four Years in Rebel Capitals*, p. 237.

[66]Sallie A. Putnam, *Richmond During the War: Four Years of Personal Observations*, p. 105; Jones, *A Rebel War-Clerk's Diary*, I, 164.

[67]Wilmington *Journal*, July 31, 1862.

[68]DeLeon, *Four Years in Rebel Capitals*, p. 236.

[69]Theodore A. Honour to Mrs. Theodore A. Honour, April 6, 1863, Theodore A. Honour Papers, Manuscript Division, South Caroliniana Library, University of South Carolina, Columbia, South Carolina.

[70]*Carolina Watchman*, September 14, 1863; John D. Ashmore to A. G. Magrath, February 15, 1865, A. G. Magrath Papers, Southern Historical Collection, University of North Carolina, Chapel Hill, North Carolina.

[71]Jones, *A Rebel War-Clerk's Diary*, I, 250-53.

[72]Joseph Jacobs, "Some Drug Conditions During the War Between the States," *Southern Historical Society Papers*, XXXIII (1905), 170.

[73]Wilmington *Journal*, March 27, 1862.

[74]Arkansas *State Gazette*, December 27, 1862.

[75]Richmond *Whig*, July 25, 1862.

[76]Putnam, *Richmond During the War*, p. 79.

[77]*Ibid.*, p. 78.

[78]Hopley, *Life in the South*, I, 299.

[79]D. M. Scott, "Selma and Dallas County, Alabama," *Confederate Veteran*, XXIV (1916), 278.

[80]Clay-Clopton, *A Belle of the Fifties*, p. 186.

[81]Frances Fearn, *Diary of a Refugee*, pp. 22-23.

[82]Henry Hunter Raymond to his mother, August [n. d.], 1863, Henry Hunter Raymond Papers, Manuscript Division, South Caroliniana Library, University of South Carolina, Columbia, South Carolina.

[83]*Ibid.*, September 3, 1863, September 9, 1863, September 29, 1863, October 5, 1863, November 8, 1863, January 29, 1864.

[84]*Ibid.*, September 21, 1863.

[85]*Ibid.*, October 28, 1863.

[86]Petersburg *Daily Express*, November 7, 1863.

[87]Hopley, *Life in the South*, I, 301.

[88]Putnam, *Richmond During the War*, p. 79.

[89]Wilmington *Journal*, January 28, 1864.

[90]Richmond *Enquirer*, October 30, 1863.

[91]Ella A. R. Harper Diary, Southern Historical Collection, University of North Carolina, Chapel Hill, North Carolina.

[92]Moore, *Rebellion Record*, VI, 24, 212.

[93]*Acts of the General Assembly of Arkansas*, March 21, 1862.

[94]Fontaine, *Confederate Veteran*, IV (1896), 301.

[95]George Cary Eggleston, *A Rebel's Recollections*, p. 68; Fannie A. Beers, *Memories: A Record of Personal Experiences and Adventures During Four Years of War*, p. 54.

[96]Mrs. P. A. McDavid, "What Women Did During the War," *Confederate Veteran*, XIV (1914), 69; Scott, *Confederate Veteran*, XXIV (1916), 217.

[97]McDavid, *Confederate Veteran*, XIV (1914), 69; Beers, *Memories*, p. 50.

[98]*Journal of the Congress of the Confederate States*, I, 726.

[99]Mrs. Judith Brockenbrough McGuire, *Diary of a Southern Refugee During the War*, p. 103.

[100]Matthew Page Andrews (ed.), *Women of the South in War Times*, p. 232.

[101]Elizabeth Allston Pringle, *Chronicles of Chicora Wood*, p. 198-99.

[102]Mrs. Laura Butler, "A Tribute," *Confederate Veteran*, XXIV (1916), 425.

[103]Hopley, *Life in the South*, I, 323.

[104]McGuire, *Diary*, p. 118; Butler, *Confederate Veteran*, XXIV (1916), 425; Mrs. Fannie A. Selph, "Army Relief Work By the Women of the Confederacy," *Confederate Veteran*, XXV (1915), 559.

[105]Mrs. Roger A. Pryor, *My Day*, p. 168; Smedes, *Memorials*, p. 219.

[106]Colonel Knox Livingston, "Florida Girl Gave Her Shoes to a Soldier," *Confederate Veteran*, XV (1907), 458.

[107]Selph, *Confederate Veteran*, XXV (1914), 559; Pryor, *My Day*, p. 168; Smedes, *Memorials*, p. 195 (the author's father, Thomas Dabney, gave away nineteen blankets at one time); Phoebe Yates Pember, *A Southern Woman's Story*, p. 62. Mrs. Pember, who was in charge of a hospital, wrote that "Piles of sheets, the cotton carded and spun in one room at home where the family lived, ate, and slept in backwoods Georgia . . . [and] bales of blankets so called by courtesy, but only drawing room carpets, the pride of the heart of thrifty housewives, perhaps their only extravagance in better days, but now cut up for field use [were sent to her hospital]. Dozens of pillow slips . . . of fine bleached cotton of better days, suggesting personal clothing sacrifice to the sick [and] . . . Boxes of woolen dressing gowns created from every dressing gown or flannel shirt in the country" also arrived at the hospital.

[108]Charleston *Courier*, May 31, 1862.

[109]Hopley, *Life in the South*, II, 293.

[110]*Ibid.*, I, 323.

[111]Jones, *A Rebel War-Clerk's Diary*, II, 7, 130, 282, 352.

[112]The subject of impressment is discussed in detail in Chapter III.

[113]Letter Books of the Secretary of War of the Confederate States of America, National Archives, Washington, D. C.

[114]*Official Records*, Series IV, III, 932.

[115]*Official Records*, Series IV, III, 404-5.

[116]Jones, *A Rebel War-Clerk's Diary*, I, 182, 194, 315; Richmond *Examiner*, October 30, 1863; April 27, 1864; Richmond *Enquirer*, June 15, 1864; Wilmington *Journal*, January 28, 1863; Moore, *Rebellion Record*, VII, 82.

[117]Wilmington *Journal*, November 21, 1863.

[118]Jones, *A Rebel War-Clerk's Diary*, I, 123-24; II, 105; Charleston *Mercury*, October 9, 1863.

[119]Richmond *Enquirer*, April 27, 1864.

[120]*Ibid.*, May 13, 1862.

[121]Richmond *Enquirer*, April 29, 1864.

[122]Joseph E. Brown to Josiah Gorgas, March 29, 1862, Josiah Gorgas Papers, Records of the Ordnance Department, National Archives, Washington, D. C.

[123]*Official Records*, Series IV, II, 594-95.

[124]Jones, *A Rebel War-Clerk's Diary*, II, 105, 186, 267-68; Pollard, *The Lost Cause*, p. 487; Richmond *Whig*, January 30, 1863.

[125]Richmond *Examiner*, October 30, 1863.

[126]Frances Caldwell Higgins, "Life on a Southern Plantation During the War Between the States," *Confederate Veteran*, XXI (1913), 161.

[127]Magnolia Plantation Record [Louisiana], Southern Historical Collection, University of North Carolina, Chapel Hill, North Carolina.

[128]J. W. Fears to the Editor, *Southern Cultivator* XXII (1864), 10.

[129]Moore, *Rebellion Record*, VII, 43.

[130]P. L. Ledford, *Reminiscences of the Civil War*, p. 20.

[131]Alexander Hunter, "The Women of Mosby's Confederacy," *Confederate Veteran*, XV (1907), 259.

[132]Fontaine, *Confederate Veteran*, IV (1896), 302-3.

[133]B. H. Greathouse, "Women in Northwest Arkansas," *Confederate Veteran*, XX (1920), 168.

[134]Bell Irvin Wiley, *The Plain People of the Confederacy*, p. 39.

[135]Dodge, *Atlantic Monthly*, LVIII (1886), 229.

[136]Charleston *Mercury*, September 17, 1863.

[137]*Ibid.*, April 22, 1864.

[138]A. T. Volwiler, "Letters From a Civil War Officer," *Mississippi Valley Historical Review*, XIX (1927-28), 584.

[139]Jones, *A Rebel War-Clerk's Diary*, II, 116.

[140]*Ibid.*, p. 119.

[141]Richmond *Enquirer*, April 22, 1862.

[142]Betty Herndon Maury Diary, March 16, 1862.

[143]Andrew Simonds to Governor A. G. Magrath, March 13, 1865, A. G. Magrath Papers.

[144]DeLeon, *Four Years in Rebel Capitals*, pp. 171-72, 284.

[145]Richmond *Whig*, June 28, 1862.

[146]*Southern Confederacy*, December 14, 1861.

[147]James Evans to James S. Evans, May 22, 1863, James Evans Papers, Southern Historical Collection, University of North Carolina, Chapel Hill, North Carolina.

[148]*Daily Picayune*, June 6, 1861; Richmond *Whig*, June 14, 1861.

[149]Richmond *Whig*, May 6, 1862.

[150]*Ibid.*, April 15, 1864.

[151]Jones, *A Rebel War-Clerk's Diary*, I, 278.

[152]Wilmington *Journal*, March 31, 1864.

[153]"Editorial," *Southern Cultivator*, XX (1862), 112.

[154]*Southern Confederacy*, June 14, 1862.

[155]Wilmington *Journal*, October 2, 4, 1862.
[156]Wilmington *Journal*, November 27, 1862.
[157]Charleston *Mercury*, December 12, 16, and 20, 1861.
[158]Jones, *A Rebel War-Clerk's Diary*, I, 272.
[159]Wilmington *Journal*, April 9, 1863.
[160]Jones, *A Rebel War-Clerk's Diary*, I, 324.

CHAPTER III

[1]Richardson, *Messages and Papers*, I, 123.
[2]*Ibid.*, I, 136.
[3]Richardson, *Messages and Papers*, I, 333-35; *Official Records*, Series IV, II, 475-77.
[4]*Official Records*, Series IV, II, 376.
[5]*Ibid.*, Series IV, II, 476-77.
[6]Richardson, *Messages and Papers*, I, 139.
[7]*Ibid.*, I, 333-35.
[8]*Official Records*, Series IV, II, 809-10.
[9]Richardson, *Messages and Papers*, I, 374.
[10]*Ibid.*, I, 136.
[11]*Ibid.*, I, 297.
[12]Ramsdell, *Behind the Lines in the Southern Confederacy*, p. 81.
[13]Jones, *A Rebel War-Clerk's Diary*, II, 101.
[14]James M. Matthews (ed.), *Statutes at Large of the Confederate States of America*, First Session, February 18, 1861, p. 28.
[15]*Ibid.*, First Session, March 15, 1861, p. 69.
[16]*Ibid.*, First Congress, First Session, April 7, 1862, p. 11.
[17]*Ibid.*, Third Session, April 29, 1863, p. 130.
[18]*Ibid.*, Second Congress, First Session, May 23, 1864, pp. 254-55.
[19]*Ibid.*, First Congress, Third Session, April 21, 1863, p. 50.
[20]*Ibid.*, First Congress, Third Session, February 6, 1864, pp. 178-81.
[21]*Ibid.*, Second Congress, First Session, June 14, 1864, p. 80.
[22]*Ibid.*, First Congress, Third Session, March 26, 1863, pp. 102-4.
[23]Ramsdell, *Laws and Joint Resolutions of the Last Session of the Confederate Congress Together with the Secret Acts of Previous Congress*, March 18, 1865, pp. 151-53.
[24]*Official Records*, Series IV, II, pp. 521-24; Matthews, *Statutes . . . Confederate States of America*, First Congress, Third Session, April 24, 1863, pp. 115-26.
[25]Larkin Smith, *Instructions to the Assessors of Tax in Kind*, pp. 2-3. Included in this levy were wheat, corn, oats, rye, buckwheat, rice, Irish potatoes, cured hay, cured fodder, sugar, molasses, cotton, wool, tobacco, peas, ground peas, and bacon.
[26]*Ibid.*, p. 4.
[27]*North Carolina Standard*, September 1, 1863.
[28]*Ibid.*, August 28, September 1, 8, 1863.
[29]Matthews, *Statutes . . . Confederate States of America*, First Congress, Second Session, October 8, 1862, p. 69.

[30]*Ibid.*, October 9, 1862.

[31]Mrs. Cornelia McDonald, *A Diary with Reminiscences of the War and Refugee Life in the Shenandoah Valley*, pp. 224-25.

[32]*Rules and Directions for Proceedings in the Confederate States*, p. 3; J. M. Matthews, *Statutes . . . Confederate States of America*, Second Session, May 21, 1861, pp. 136-49.

[33]Rufus R. Rhodes, *Report of the Commissioner of Patents of the Confederate States of America*, 1861-1862, 1863, 1864.

[34]*South Carolina Daily Guardian*, March 17, 1862.

[35]Matthews, *Statutes . . . Confederate States of America*, First Congress, Third Session, April 4, 1863, pp. 166-67.

[36]Ramsdell, *Behind the Lines*, p. 39.

[37]Matthews, *Statutes . . . Confederate States of America*, Second Congress, First Session, June 14, 1864, p. 271.

[38]*Journal of the Congress of the Confederate States of America*, III, 457, 514, 592.

[39]*Daily Southern Guardian*, February 26, 1862.

[40]Jones, *A Rebel War-Clerk's Diary*, I, 207-8.

[41]*Ibid.*, II, 95, 103.

[42]*Ibid.*, II, 89.

[43]Pollard, *The Lost Cause*, p. 487.

[44]*Official Records*, Series IV, III, 106-7.

[45]*Ibid.*, pp. 115-16.

[46]*Ibid.*, pp. 548, 835.

[47]*Ibid.*, p. 1074.

[48]Hunter, "The Women of Mosby's Confederacy," *Confederate Veteran*, XV (1907), 258.

[49]*Official Records*, Series IV, III, 686.

[50]*Ibid.*, p. 1160.

[51]Frank Owsley, *State-Rights in the Confederacy, passim.*

[52]*Carolina Watchman*, November 30, 1863.

[53]*Official Records*, Series IV, II, 85-86.

[54]*Ibid.*, pp. 180-90.

[55]*Ibid.*, pp. 214, 680.

[56]*Ibid.*, pp. 180-90.

[57]*Ibid.*, pp. 1072-73.

[58]*Ibid.*, III, 1063-64.

[59]Moore, *Rebellion Record*, VI, 524-25.

[60]Stephen Beauregard Weeks, "The University of North Carolina in the Civil War," *Southern Historical Society Papers*, XXIV (1896), 36; *Official Records*, Series IV, II, 413.

[61]*Official Records*, Series IV, II, pp. 404-5, 988.

[62]*Daily Southern Guardian*, March 6, 1862.

[63]*Official Records*, Series IV, III, 118-19.

[64]*Ibid.*, II, 487-89.

[65]*Ibid.*, pp. 501-11.

[66]*Ibid.*, p. 196.

[67]Moore, *Rebellion Record*, III, 349. The eleventh state was Tennessee.

[68]*Acts of the General Assembly of Alabama*, November 29, 1861, p. 74.

[69]*Acts and Resolutions Adopted by the General Assembly of Florida*, December 13, 1861, pp. 12-13.

[70]*Laws of the State of Mississippi*, December 16, 1861, pp. 53-56.

[71]*The Statutes at Large of South Carolina*, December 17, 1863, pp. 164-67.

[72]*Acts of the General Assembly of the State of Georgia*, December 13, 1862, p. 13; *Public Acts of the General Assembly of the State of Tennessee*, February 11, 1862, pp. 57-60; *Acts of the Legislature of the State of Louisiana*, January 3, 1863, pp. 35-36; *The Laws of Texas*, March 5, 1863, pp. 13, 29-30.

[73]*Acts of the General Assembly of the State of Virginia*, October 31, 1863, pp. 21-23.

[74]*Public and Private Laws of the State of North Carolina*, February 12, 1862, pp. 33-34.

[75]*Acts Passed by the General Assembly of Arkansas*, March 22, 1862.

[76]*Laws of Mississippi*, December 2, 1863, pp. 113-22.

[77]*Ibid.*, August 13, 1864, pp. 27-28.

[78]*Acts of Louisiana*, June 30, 1863, pp. 26-27; *Laws of Mississippi*, January 3, 1863, pp. 95-96.

[79]*Acts of Virginia*, October 6, 1862, p. 20; *Acts of Florida*, December 4, 1863, pp. 44-45; *Alabama Acts*, April 27, 1863, pp. 19-20, August 29, 1863, p. 19.

[80]*Acts of Georgia*, April 11, 1863, pp. 141-42.

[81]*Laws of North Carolina*, December 17, 1863, p. 20.

[82]*Ibid.*, May 26, 1864, pp. 8-9.

[83]*Acts of Virginia*, October 31, 1863, p. 25.

[84]*Acts of Arkansas*, March 19, 1862; *Laws of North Carolina*, December 17, 1863, p. 20.

[85]*Acts of Louisiana*, June 20, 1863, pp. 26-27.

[86]*Statutes of South Carolina*, December 18, 1862, pp. 97-98.

[87]*Acts of Arkansas*, March 19, 1862, pp. 97-98.

[88]*Acts of Louisiana*, June 20, 1863, pp. 26-27; *Acts of Alabama*, August 27, 1863, pp. 19-20.

[89]*Statutes of South Carolina*, April 10, 1863, pp. 98-99.

[90]*Acts of Florida*, December 4, 1863, pp. 44-45.

[91]*Laws of Texas*, December 15, 1863, pp. 16-20.

[92]*Acts of Virginia*, March 11, 1863, p. 19; *Acts of Georgia*, December 9, 1862, p. 28.

[93]*Acts of Virginia*, October 1, 1862, pp. 17-19; *Laws of Mississippi*, April 5, 1864, pp. 63-68; *Statutes of South Carolina*, April 10, 1863, pp. 98-99; *Acts of Georgia*, November 22, 1862, pp. 25-26 and December 12, 1863, p. 23; *Acts of Florida*, November 24, 1863, p. 51; *Acts of Alabama*, December 8, 1862, pp. 43-44.

[94]*Acts of Arkansas,* March 21, 1862.

[95]*Acts of Florida,* December 3, 1863, pp. 42-43.

[96]*Acts of Georgia,* December 11, 1862, pp. 5-7; *Statutes of South Carolina,* February 6, 1863, pp. 101-2, December 17, 1863, p. 171.

[97]*Acts of Georgia,* December 11, 1862, pp. 5-7; *Acts of Florida,* December 3, 1863, pp. 42-43; *Statutes of South Carolina,* April 10, 1863, pp. 101-2.

[98]*Acts of Florida,* November 28, 1861, pp. 8-9.

[99]*North Carolina Laws,* November 22, 1863, pp. 53-54.

[100]*Statutes of South Carolina,* April 10, 1863, p. 99; *Acts of Alabama,* December 8, 1862, pp. 44-46.

[101]*Acts of Florida,* November 27, 1863, p. 9.

[102]*Laws of North Carolina,* May 26, 1864, pp. 4-5.

[103]*Acts of Louisiana,* June 20, 1863, pp. 22-23, and February 1, 1865, p. 12; *Acts of Virginia,* March 9, 1864, pp. 33-35; *Laws of Mississippi,* December 9, 1863, pp. 143-45; *Acts of Georgia,* December 6, 1862, pp. 8-9, December 14, 1863, p. 8, and March 19, 1864, p. 123; *Acts of Florida,* December 8, 1862, p. 65, and December 7, 1864, pp. 26-27; *Acts of Arkansas,* October 1, 1864, p. 19; *Acts of Alabama,* December 4, 1861, p. 70, November 8, 1862, p. 49, November 25, 1862, pp. 49-50, and December 5, 1863, p. 111; *Laws of North Carolina,* February 25, 1862, pp. 61-62, January 26, 1863, p. 74.

[104]*Laws of Mississippi,* December 9, 1863, pp. 143-44; *Acts of Alabama,* December 4, 1861, p. 70.

[105]*Acts of Virginia,* March 9, 1864, pp. 33-35.

[106]*Acts of Georgia,* December 6, 1862, pp. 8-9, December 14, 1863, p. 8, and March 19, 1864, p. 123.

[107]*Laws of Texas,* March 6, 1863, p. 22.

[108]*Ibid.,* December 15, 1863, pp. 22-23.

[109]*Acts of Georgia,* December 14, 1861, pp. 66-67; *Acts of Florida,* November 28, 1861, pp. 8-9, December 17, 1861, p. 31, and December 10, 1862, pp. 36-37; *Acts of Alabama,* December 9, 1862, pp. 18-20; *Laws of North Carolina,* December 11, 1861, pp. 22-23, February 11, 1863, p. 20; *Statutes of South Carolina,* February 6, 1863, pp. 124-25; *Laws of Texas,* January 13, 1862, p. 65, and November 24, 1863, p. 3.

[110]*Acts of Georgia,* December 14, 1861, pp. 66-67.

[111]*Acts of Florida,* December 10, 1862, pp. 36-37.

[112]*Laws of North Carolina,* December 11, 1861, pp. 22-23.

[113]*Statutes of South Carolina,* February 6, 1863, pp. 123-25.

[114]*Laws of Texas,* January 13, 1863, p. 56, November 24, 1863, p. 3.

[115]*Acts of Alabama,* December 9, 1862, pp. 18-20.

[116]*Acts of Georgia,* November 23, 1862, pp. 101-3, March 19, 1864, p. 123; *Acts of Alabama,* November 19, 1862, pp. 47-48; *Laws of Mississippi,* April 4, 1864, pp. 53-54.

[117]*Acts of Georgia,* December 14, 1863, pp. 62-63; *Acts of Alabama,* November 25, 1863, p. 100; *Laws of Mississippi,* December 7, 1863, p. 156, and December 8, 1863, p. 157; *Laws of Texas,* May 27, 1864, pp.

16-17; *Acts of Virginia,* May 14, 1862, p. 14; *Acts of Arkansas,* October 1, 1864; *Acts of Florida,* December 3, 1863, pp. 33-35; *Laws of North Carolina,* February 7, 1863, pp. 75-76, February 12, 1863, pp. 79-80, December 12, 1863, p. 12, and December 18, 1863, pp. 30-31.

CHAPTER IV

[1]McDonald, *Diary,* p. 24.

[2]Mrs. Burton Harrison, *Recollections Grave and Gay,* p. 191.

[3]M. L. Avary, *A Virginia Girl in the Civil War,* p. 337.

[4]Courtney Robert Hall, "Confederate Medicine," *Medical Life,* XLII (1935), 480.

[5]George Alfred Townsend, *Campaigns of a Non-Combatant and His Ramount Abroad During the War,* p. 240; Hopley, *Life in the South,* II, 108; Clay-Clopton, *A Belle of the Fifties,* p. 222.

[6]Eliza Frances Andrews, *The War-Time Journal of a Georgia Girl,* p. 38.

[7]Mary A. H. Gay, *Life in Dixie During the War,* p. 248.

[8]Pollard, *The Lost Cause,* p. 482.

[9]Gordon, *The Century Magazine,* XXXVI (1888), 762.

[10]Jones, *A Rebel War-Clerk's Diary,* II, 156.

[11]*Official Records,* Series IV, III, 285.

[12]*Ibid.,* pp. 845-46.

[13]Harrison, *Recollections,* p. 86.

[14]William Dallam Armes, *Autobiography of Joseph LeConte,* p. 229.

[15]Emma Florence LeConte Diary, January 23, 1865.

[16]Harrison, *Recollections,* p. 191.

[17]Mrs. D. Giraud Wright, *A Southern Girl in '61,* p. 194.

[18]Mrs. Varina Howell Davis, *Jefferson Davis: Ex-President of the Confederate States of America: A Memoir,* II, 529.

[19]Chesnut, *Diary,* p. 284.

[20]Thomas Livingston Bayne, "Life in Richmond, 1863-1865," *Confederate Veteran,* XXX (1922), 100.

[21]Jones, *A Rebel War-Clerk's Diary,* II, 290.

[22]*Southern Illustrated News,* September 27, 1862.

[23]Confederate Recipe Book, Manuscript Division, Confederate Museum, Richmond, Virginia.

[24]Smedes, *Memorials,* p. 224.

[25]*Wilmington Journal,* April 24, 1862, quotes a resolution of farmers passed in Russell County, Alabama; *Southern Confederacy,* April 1, 1862; *Daily Express,* May 27, 1861, quoting the Oxford (Mississippi) *Mercury,* May 8, 1861.

[26]*Daily Southern Guardian,* February 28, 1862.

[27]*Southern Cultivator,* XX (1862), p. 80.

[28]*Wilmington Journal,* April 24, 1862.

[29]Jones, *A Rebel War-Clerk's Diary,* II, 9.

[30]*Ibid.,* p. 135.

[31]Chesnut, *Diary,* p. 294.

[32]Pringle, *Chronicles of Chicora Wood,* p. 294.

[33]*Daily Express,* October 21, 1861.

[34]Hopley, *Life in the South,* II, 293.

[35]Jones, *A Rebel War-Clerk's Diary,* I, 274.

[36]*Ibid.,* II, 293.

[37]Fulkerson, *Recollections,* p. 145.

[38]Richmond *Whig,* May 15, 1862.

[39]William S. Pettigrew to Charles Pettigrew, April 27, 1862, Pettigrew Papers, Southern Historical Collection, University of North Carolina, Chapel Hill, North Carolina; *see also* Arney Robinson Childs (ed.), *The Private Journal of Henry William Ravenel, 1859-1887,* p. 136. Mr. Ravenel was upset when he heard of the fall of New Orleans in the spring of 1862, because he was of the opinion that so many Texas cattle were brought through that city via the railroads. He said that "200,000 head of cattle were on their way to New Orleans from Texas, when it [New Orleans] fell."

[40]*Carolina Watchman,* November 10, 1862.

[41]Moore, *Rebellion Record,* VII, 67.

[42]Richmond *Enquirer,* November 2, 1863.

[43]Hunter, *Confederate Veteran,* IV (1896), 259.

[44]McDonald, *Diary,* p. 198.

[45]Jones, *A Rebel War-Clerk's Diary,* II, 185; Pryor, *My Day,* p. 208.

[46]Putnam, *Richmond During the War,* p. 113.

[47]Wilmington *Journal,* November 22, 1862.

[48]Charleston *Mercury,* October 16, 1862.

[49]*Confederate Receipt Book: A Compilation of Over One Hundred Receipts Adapted to the Times,* pp. 7-8. The recipe for artificial oyster is: "Take young green corn, grate it in a dish; To one pint of this add one egg, well-beaten, a small teacup of flour, two or three tablespoons of butter, some salt and pepper, mix them all together. A tablespoon of the batter will make the size of an oyster. Fry them light brown, and when done butter them."

[50]Fearn, *Diary,* pp. 18-19.

[51]*Official Records,* Series IV, II, 915-18.

[52]Harrison, *Recollections,* pp. 134-35.

[53]*Southern Confederacy,* October 7, 1862.

[54]Jones, *A Rebel War-Clerk's Diary,* II, 135.

[55]Montgomery *Daily Advertiser,* September 16, 1864.

[56]Jones, *A Rebel War-Clerk's Diary,* II, 175.

[57]George Washington Cable (ed.), "A Woman's Diary of the Siege of Vicksburg," *Century Magazine,* XXX (1885), 774.

[58]Putnam, *Richmond During the War,* p. 231.

[59]Pember, *A Southern Woman's Story,* p. 104. Mrs. Pember gives the following recipe for cooking a rat: "The rat must be skinned, cleaned, his head cut off and his body laid open upon a square board, the legs stretched to their full extent and secured upon it with small tacks, then baste with bacon fat and roast before a good fire quickly like canvasback ducks."

⁶⁰Mary Webster Loughborough, *My Cave Life in Vicksburg*, p. 116.

⁶¹Cable, *Century Magazine*, XXX (1885), 771.

⁶²Pryor, *My Day*, p. 204.

⁶³Loughborough, *My Cave Life in Vicksburg*, pp. 136-37.

⁶⁴Savannah *Republican*, July 30, 1863.

⁶⁵Lonn, *Salt as a Factor in the Confederacy*, p. 222. This work is an excellent, scholarly, and definitive study. Although mention of the salt shortage is frequent in newspapers, letters, diaries, and government records of the period, I have based most of this discussion of salt on Miss Lonn's study.

⁶⁶Petersburg *Daily Express*, June 18, 1861.

⁶⁷Howard, *Southern Cultivator*, XIX (1861), 201-3.

⁶⁸New Orleans *Picayune*, June 28, 1861, quoting the Galveston *Civilian*.

⁶⁹Reverend C. S. Vedder Diary, January 21, 1863, Manuscript Division, South Caroliniana Library, University of South Carolina, Columbia, South Carolina.

⁷⁰*Confederate Receipt Book*, p. 17. The following directions were given for sweetening butter: "Melt the butter in hot water, skim it off as clean as possible, and work it over again in a churn, add salt and fine sugar and press well."

⁷¹Confederate Recipe Book. "Mayonnaise without oil. Mix two teaspoons of mustard, 1 tablespoon of butter or bacon grease, salt to taste, pour gently on this 1 pt. of milk or water in which a piece of celery has been boiled to give it taste, put on fire, and when boiling, thicken with 1 tablespoon of flour or starch and yolk of 1 egg. When cold beat in a wine glass of vinegar and one of wine if possible."

⁷²Mrs. Kirby Smith to General Kirby Smith, June 30, 1862, Kirby Smith Papers.

⁷³William W. Renwick Papers, April 3, 1863, Manuscript Division, South Caroliniana Library, University of South Carolina, Columbia, South Carolina.

⁷⁴E. F. Andrews, *Journal*, pp. 26, 83.

⁷⁵Clara Minor Lynn Papers, Manuscript Division, Confederate Museum, Richmond, Virginia.

⁷⁶Dodge, *Atlantic Monthly*, LVIII (1886), 235.

⁷⁷Handy, *Harper's Monthly Magazine*, LII (1876), 577.

⁷⁸Dodge, *Atlantic Monthly*, LVIII (1886), 235.

⁷⁹Hague, *Blockaded Family*, p. 30.

⁸⁰J. Harold Easterby (ed.), *The South Carolina Rice Plantation as Revealed in the Papers of Robert F. W. Allston*, p. 188.

⁸¹Clara Minor Lynn Papers.

⁸²Confederate Recipe Book. "Sorghum jelly: Beat very light three eggs, and add to them 1 pt. of sorghum. Set on to boil, stirring slowly until it thickens to the consistency of hominy."

⁸³Handy, *Harper's Magazine*, LII (1876), 578-79.

⁸⁴Richmond *Enquirer*, July 25, 1864.

[85]Scott, *Confederate Veteran,* XXIV (1916), 217.

[86]N. H. R. Dawson to his fiancee, March 21, 1862, N. H. R. Dawson Papers, Southern Historical Collection, University of North Carolina, Chapel Hill, North Carolina. He wrote: "There is no maple sugar in town (Richmond). The soldiers eat it all up, in the mountains, and none of it comes to this market."

[87]"Nannie" to her grandfather, Edmund Ruffin, Edmund Ruffin Papers, Southern Historical Collection, University of North Carolina, Chapel Hill, North Carolina.

[88]Childs, *The Ravenel Journal,* p. 175.

[89]Pryor, *Reminiscences of a Long Life,* p. 319.

[90]Clara Minor Lynn Papers. The ginger snaps contained flour, sorghum and pepper.

[91]*Ibid.,* "Recipe for Plum Pudding, . . . dried apples, currants, suet, a little pepper for spice, and a mixture of corn meal and flour."

[92]Scott, *Confederate Veteran,* XXIV (1916), 220.

[93]L. L. Anderson, *North Carolina Women of the Confederacy,* p. 3.

[94]Francis Peyre Porcher, *Resources of the Southern Fields, and Forest, Medical, Economical, and Agricultural,* p. 228.

[95]Clara Minor Lynn Papers.

[96]*Confederate Receipt Book,* p. 7.

[97]Hague, *Blockaded Family,* p. 25.

[98]Higgins, *Confederate Veteran,* XXI, (1913), 162.

[99]Clay-Clopton, *A Belle of the Fifties,* p. 185.

[100]Mrs. Julia W. Bell, "My Confederate Grandmothers," *Confederate Veteran,* XXVIII (1920), 366-67.

[101]Pember, *A Southern Woman's Story,* p. 99.

[102]Richmond *Examiner,* March 29, 1865.

[103]Jones, *A Rebel War-Clerk's Diary,* pp. 100-1.

[104]Porcher, *Resources,* p. 620.

[105]*Confederate Receipt Book,* pp. 25-27.

[106]Cable, *Century Magazine,* XXX (1885), 769.

[107]Hague, *Blockaded Family,* p. 25.

[108]Houston *Tri-Weekly Telegraph,* September 8, 1862.

[109]James Evans to James S. Evans, June 23, 1862, James S. Evans Papers.

[110]Pryor, *My Day,* p. 204.

[111]Loughborough, *My Cave Life in Vicksburg,* p. 77. The main complaint against pea-meal was that it had to be mixed with cornmeal, and it cooked so much slower than the cornmeal that part of the bread would be burned while the other was half done.

[112]Richmond *Enquirer,* October 6, 1864; Wilmington *Journal,* October 4, 1864.

[113]Page 5.

[114]E. F. Andrews, *Journal,* p. 75.

[115]Hague, *Blockaded Family,* p. 102.

[116]Richmond *Enquirer,* June 4, 1862.

[117]Porcher, *Resources*, p. 69.

[118]*Confederate Receipt Book*, p. 7. "To one small bowl of crackers that have been soaked until no hard parts remain, add one teaspoon of tartaric acid, sweeten to taste, add some butter, and very little nutmeg."

[119]Wilmington *Journal*, November 10, 1864.

[120]Harrison, *Recollections*, p. 117.

[121]Rebecca Latimer Felton, *Country Life in the Days of My Youth*, p. 103.

[122]Porcher, *Resources*, p. 80.

[123]Clara Minor Lynn Papers.

[124]Hopley, *Life in the South*, II, 276.

[125]Jacobs, *Southern Historical Society Papers*, XXXIII (1905), 182.

[126]*Confederate Receipt Book*, p. 10.

[127]Wilmington *Journal*, July 23, 1864.

[128]Porcher, *Resources*, p. 635; Hague, *Blockaded Family*, pp. 57-58; Higgins, *Confederate Veteran*, XXI (1913), 162.

[129]Porcher, *Resources*, pp. 643-49.

[130]Hague, *Blockaded Family*, p. 17.

[131]Davis, *Jefferson Davis*, II, 529.

[132]Jones, *A Rebel War-Clerk's Diary*, II, 173, 258.

[133]Putnam, *Richmond During the War*, pp. 102-3.

[134]Dodge, *Atlantic Monthly*, LVIII (1886), 234.

[135]McGuire, *Diary*, p. 257.

[136]Hague, *Blockaded Family*, p. 101.

[137]DeLeon, *Belles, Beaux and Brains of the Sixties*, p. 268.

[138]*Southern Confederacy*, January 4, 1863.

[139]McGuire, *Diary*, pp. 81-82; Porcher, *Resources*, p. 273.

[140]McGuire, *Diary*, p. 82.

[141]Putnam, *Richmond During the War*, pp. 79-80.

[142]DeLeon, *Belles, Beaux, and Brains of the Sixties*, p. 201.

[143]Susan Gordon Waddell Diary, Southern Historical Collection, University of North Carolina, Chapel Hill, North Carolina.

[144]Wilmington *Journal*, December 17, 1863.

[145]Dodge, *Atlantic Monthly*, LVIII (1886), 234.

[146]Francis W. Dawson, *Our Women in the War*, p. 14.

[147]Laura Elizabeth Battle, *Forget-Me-Nots of the Civil War*, p. 157; Porcher, *Resources*, p. 681; *Southern Confederacy*, February 14, 1862.

[148]Hague, *Blockaded Family*, p. 102; *Daily Express*, November 18, 1861; Gay, *Life in Dixie*, p. 218; Porcher, *Resources*, p. 477.

[149]Porcher, *Resources*, p. 636; Jones, *A Rebel War-Clerk's Diary*, I, 165.

[150]Avary, *A Virginia Girl in the Civil War*, p. 248.

[151]Putnam, *Richmond During the War*, pp. 79-80; Pringle, *Chronicles of Chicora Wood*, p. 196.

[152]Porcher, *Resources*, p. 438.

[153]Montgomery *Daily Advertiser*, March 5, 1864.

[154]Loughborough, *My Cave Life in Vicksburg*, p. 103; F. C. Higgins, *Confederate Veteran*, XXI (1913), 168.

[155]Moore, *Rebellion Record*, II, 103, quoting the Raleigh *Standard.*

[156]Natchez Daily *Courier,* April 15, 1863.

[157]*Ibid.*

[158]*Southern Cultivator,* XX (1862), 115.

[159]Richmond *Examiner,* January 27, 1862.

[160]Jacobs, *Southern Historical Society Papers,* XXXIII (1905), 168.

[161]Charleston *Mercury,* February 16, 1863.

[162]Gordon, *The Century Magazine,* XXXVI (1888), 766.

[163]*Ibid.,* p. 200; *Arkansas State Gazette,* July 19, 1862.

[164]Richmond *Enquirer,* August 3, 1861.

[165]Mercer Otey, "Story of Our Great War," *Confederate Veteran,* IX (1901), 154.

[166]Otey, "Operations of the Signal Corps," *Confederate Veteran,* VIII (1900), 129.

[167]E. Philips to James J. Philips, March 27, 1864, James J. Philips Papers, Southern Historical Collection, University of North Carolina, Chapel Hill, North Carolina.

[168]Porcher, *Resources,* p. 425.

[169]McGuire, *Diary,* p. 324.

[170]W. D. Pender to Mrs. W. D. Pender, October 1, 1861, W. D. Pender Papers, Southern Historical Collection, University of North Carolina, Chapel Hill, North Carolina.

[171]Pryor, *My Day,* p. 264.

[172]*Confederate Receipt Book,* p. 17.

[173]Loughborough, *My Cave Life in Vicksburg,* p. 104.

[174]Clara Minor Lynn Papers.

[175]*Confederate Receipt Book,* p. 19. "Dissolve half an ounce of alum in a pint of warm water, and stirring it about in a puncheon of water from the river, all the impurities will soon settle to the bottom, and in a day or two it will become quite clear."

[176]Dodge, *Atlantic Monthly,* LVIII (1886), 240.

[177]Pringle, *Chronicles of Chicora Wood,* pp. 193-94.

[178]Avary, *A Virginia Girl in the Civil War,* p. 239.

[179]Clara Minor Lynn Papers.

[180]Clay-Clopton, *A Belle of the Fifties,* p. 179.

[181]*Daily Rebel,* March 3, 1863.

[182]DeLeon, *Belles, Beaux, and Brains of the Sixties,* p. 274. A menu in a slightly varied form was published in the Richmond *Examiner,* August 26, 1863. *See also* Moore, *Rebellion Records,* VII, 50-51.

[183]Chesnut, *Diary,* pp. 270, 260; DeLeon, *Belles, Beaux and Brains in the Sixties,* p. 396.

[184]Putnam, *Richmond During the War,* p. 315; Jones, *A Rebel War-Clerk's Diary,* II, 335.

[185]Chesnut, *Diary,* p. 376.

CHAPTER V

[1]Charleston *Mercury*, June 1, 1861.

[2]Beers, *Memories*, p. 116.

[3]Dodge, *Atlantic Monthly*, LVIII (1886), 234.

[4]Harrison, *Recollections*, pp. 108, 116.

[5]C. Clarke to Maxwell Clarke, December 7, 1863, Maxwell Troax Clarke Papers, Southern Historical Collection, University of North Carolina, Chapel Hill, North Carolina.

[6]Wilmington *Journal*, December 24, 1863.

[7]Chesnut, *Diary*, p. 224.

[8]Harrison, *Recollections*, p. 135.

[9]Fearn, *Diary*, pp. 40-41.

[10]"Nannie" to Edmund Ruffin, February 3, 1863, Edmund Ruffin Papers.

[11]Hopley, *Life in the South*, II, 105.

[12]Fontaine, *Confederate Veteran*, IV (1896), 301.

[13]Moore, *Rebellion Record*, VI, 42.

[14]Higgins, *Confederate Veteran*, XXI (1913), 163.

[15]*Daily Carolina Watchman*, January 25, 1864.

[16]Handy, *Harper's Monthly Magazine*, LII (1876), 578.

[17]Hague, *A Blockaded Family*, p. 37; Scott, *Confederate Veteran*, XXIV (1916), 218.

[18]Wilmington *Journal*, January 16, 1862, November 27, 1862.

[19]F. P. Porcher, *Resources*, pp. 284-96.

[20]Moore, *Rebellion Record*, III, 55.

[21]Clay-Clopton, *A Belle of the Fifties*, p. 223; Moore, *Rebellion Record*, IV, 48.

[22]Dodge, *Atlantic Monthly*, LVIII (1886), 232-33.

[23]Fontaine, *Confederate Veteran*, IV (1896), 301; Dodge, *Atlantic Monthly*, LVIII (1886), 232.

[24]Moore, *Rebellion Record*, IV, 10.

[25]Some of these may be seen in the Confederate Museum, Richmond, Virginia.

[26]Handy, *Harper's Monthly Magazine*, LII (1876), 579.

[27]Porcher, *Resources*, pp. 387-88.

[28]Dodge, *Atlantic Monthly*, LVIII (1886), 232.

[29]McGuire, *Diary*, pp. 251-52.

[30]Pryor, *My Day*, p. 229.

[31]Moore, *Rebellion Record*, VI, 48.

[32]Hague, *A Blockaded Family*, p. 52.

[33]John W. Mallet, "How the South Got Chemicals During the War," *Southern Historical Society Papers*, XXI (1903), 100-1.

[34]Higgins, *Confederate Veteran*, XXI (1913), 163.

[35]McDonald, *Diary*, p. 224.

[36]James Evans to his son, James S. Evans, November 18, 1863, James Evans Papers.

[37]Petersburg *Daily Express*, November 7, 1861.

[38]Porcher, *Resources*, p. 579.

[39]Jones, *A Rebel War-Clerk's Diary*, II, 354.

[40]Hopley, *Life in the South*, II, 76-77; Wright, *A Southern Girl*, p. 176; Easterby, *The South Carolina Rice Plantation*, p. 312.

[41]Wirt Armistead Cate, *Two Soldiers: The Campaign Diaries of Thomas J. Key, C. S. A. and Robert J. Campbell, U. S. A.*, p. 27.

[42]Scott, *Confederate Veteran*, XXIV (1916), 218; Gordon, *The Century Magazine*, XXXVI (1888), 767; Wilmington *Journal*, January 21, 1862; New Orleans *Picayune*, May 6, 1862.

[43]James Evans to James S. Evans, February 13, 1864, James Evans Papers.

[44]Margaret B. S. Robertson, "My Childhood Recollections of the War," *Southern Historical Society Papers*, VI (New Series, 1923), 219; Wiley, *The Plain People of the Confederacy*, p. 53.

[45]Jones, *A Rebel War-Clerk's Diary*, II, 132; S. M. Dawson, *Diary*, p. 37.

[46]Chesnut, *Diary*, p. 224; Harrison, *Recollections*, p. 135.

[47]Harrison, *Recollections*, p. 147.

[48]Alice West Allen, "Recollections of War in Virginia," *Confederate Veteran*, XXIII (1915), 269.

[49]Scott, *Confederate Veteran*, XXIV (1916), 218.

[50]Harrison, *Recollections*, pp. 141-42.

[51]*Daily Express*, May 6, 1861. This editorial, published less than a month after the war began, is among the more convincing of the hundreds published on this subject. After an introductory paragraph in which the editor urged women to start knitting and weaving, he adds: "There is nothing truer than the saying, "What has been done, can be done,' and we know that our women will provide for us in this emergency, as did our grandmothers in days of old for worthy sires, who wore their homemade socks, with honest pride. . . . Whatever the times demand must be cheerfully provided . . . let us recall everything and imitate everything which a Washington once approved of."

[52]Putnam, *Richmond During the War*, p. 251.

[53]Beers, *Memories*, p. 54.

[54]McGuire, *Diary*, p. 195.

[55]Fannie Evans to James S. Evans, December 3, 1862, James Evans Papers.

[56]Moore, *Rebellion Record*, VI, 42.

[57]*North Carolina Standard*, January 2, 1863.

[58]Dodge, *Atlantic Monthly*, LVIII (1886), 233.

[59]*North Carolina Standard*, February 3, 1863.

[60]Savannah *Republican*, February 2, 1863; Wilmington *Journal*, April 2, 1863, August 6, 1863.

[61]Wilmington *Journal*, February 11, 1864, quoted from the Eutaw (Ala.) *Whig*.

[62]James L. Alcorn to Mrs. James L. Alcorn, December 12, 1861, James L. Alcorn Papers, Southern Historical Collection, University of North Carolina, Chapel Hill, North Carolina.

63Wilmington *Journal,* December 11, 1862.

64Scott, *Confederate Veteran,* XXIV (1916), 218.

65Hague, *A Blockaded Family,* pp. 55-56.

66Richmond *Examiner,* December 7, 1861.

67*Southern Confederacy,* February 25, 1862.

68*Southern Cultivator,* XX (1862), 24.

69McDonald, *Diary,* p. 185.

70Hague, *A Blockaded Family,* p. 93; Richmond *Enquirer,* January 13, 1863.

71Harrison, *Recollections,* p. 135.

72Armes, *The Autobiography of Joseph Le Conte,* p. 230.

73Houston *Tri Weekly Telegraph,* January 23, 1863.

74W. H. Hardy, "The Homespun Dress," *Confederate Veteran,* IX (1901), 213-14.

75*Southern Illustrated News.* November 8, 1862. The editors' answer is very interesting. After asking for the scrap they add that it will "remind us in after years that there was one brave little heart somewhere in the good Old Dominion that pulsated with genuine patriotism, and with whom 'duty' was a higher word than 'fashion.' Don't mind the whispers and snickers of those who, while they profess great patriotism, had rather give aid and comfort to the enemy by the purchase of his silks and satins . . . than to encourage home industry. . . . Many a soldier as he reads your letter today in camp, will say, 'Well, boys, I'll bet a month's rations that little girl will make some lucky fellow a grand wife, and no mistake!"

76*Ibid.,* December 6, 1862, p. 8.

77*Ibid.,* December 20, 1862, p. 8.

78Harrison, *Recollections,* p. 152; McDonald, *Diary,* p. 235; Pringle, *Chronicles of Chicora Wood,* p. 196.

79DeLeon, *Belles, Beaux and Brains of the Sixties,* p. 396.

80Hague, *A Blockaded Family,* pp. 115, 116.

81M. P. Andrews, *The Women of the South in War-Times,* p. 419.

82Pringle, *Chronicles of Chicora Wood,* p. 182; Easterby, *The South Carolina Rice Plantation,* pp. 315, 316, 323.

83Moore, *Rebellion Record,* V, 10.

84Wilmington *Journal,* April 4, 1863.

85Porcher, *Resources,* p. 311.

86Hague, *A Blockaded Family,* pp. 91-92.

87Fontaine, *Confederate Veteran,* IV (1896), 302.

88Hague, *A Blockaded Family,* p. 57.

89Harrison, *Recollections,* p. 148.

90Mrs. Joseph Milligan to her daughter, "Octy," May 15, 1863, Milligan Papers, Southern Historical Collection, University of North Carolina, Chapel Hill, North Carolina.

91*Southern Illustrated News,* August 22, 1863.

92M. M. Jennings, "A Little Girl in the War," *Confederate Veteran,* XXX (1922), 375.

[93]Clara Minor Lynn Papers.

[94]Avary, *A Virginia Girl in the Civil War*, p. 359; Mrs. Mark Valentine, "A Girl in the Sixties in Richmond," *Confederate Veteran*, XX (1912), 280.

[95]E. F. Andrews, *Journal*, p. 117.

[96]Battle, *Forget-Me-Nots of the Civil War*, p. 156.

[97]Emma LeConte Diary.

[98]Gordon, *The Century Magazine*, XXXVI (1888), 768.

[99]Betty Herndon Maury Diary.

[100]J. B. Jones, *A Rebel War-Clerk's Diary*, II, 372.

[101]*Ibid.*, II, 16, 121; Mrs. J. B. McGuire, *Diary*, p. 16.

[102]Wilmington *Journal*, September 15, 1864.

[103]Emma Le Conte Diary.

[104]J. B. Jones, *A Rebel War-Clerk's Diary*, II, 90, 328-29.

[105]Harrison, *Recollections*, p. 136.

[106]Roberts, *Never Caught*, p. 23.

[107]Harrison, *Recollections*, p. 136.

[108]Pryor, *My Day*, pp. 229-30.

[109]Richmond *Examiner*, October 19, 1861.

[110]Mrs. Kirby Smith to General Kirby Smith, June 30, 1862, Kirby Smith Papers.

[111]Jones, *A Rebel War-Clerk's Diary*, II, 334.

[112]Handy, *Harper's Monthly Magazine*, LII (1876), 579.

[113]These may be seen in the Confederate Museum, Richmond, Virginia.

[114]Clay-Clopton, *A Belle of the Fifties*, p. 225.

[115]McGuire, *Diary*, pp. 196-97; Mrs. Bettie J. Lindsey, "Woman's Wit Versus Federal Vigilance," *Confederate Veteran*, XVI (1908), 401; Clay-Clopton, *A Belle of the Fifties*, p. 225.

[116]Dawson, *Our Women in the War*, p. 15.

[117]Memphis *Appeal*, October 22, 1861.

[118]*The Southern Illustrated News, passim;* Harrison, *Recollections*, pp. 124-25.

[119]Harrison, *Recollections*, p. 135.

[120]*Ibid.*

[121]Wiley, *The Plain People of the Confederacy*, p. 51.

[122]F. W. Dawson, *Our Women in the War*, p. 12.

[123]Clara Minor Lynn Papers. There was also a parody that became popular during the war:

> "I am dyeing! Mary! dyeing!
> Boils the kettle hot and fast.
> With bark of plum and walnut
> Gathered in the days long past."

[124]Hague, *A Blockaded Family*, pp. 41-42.

[125]*Southern Illustrated News*, September 27, 1862.

[126]Porcher, *Resources*, pp. 515-16.

[127]*Ibid.*, p. 273.

[128]*Southern Illustrated News*, August 15, 1863.

[129]Harrison, *Recollections*, p. 147.

CHAPTER VI

[1]Harrison, *Recollections*, p. 94; *see also* Harrison, "A Virginia Girl in the First Year of the War," *The Century Illustrated Monthly Magazine*, XXX (1885), 609-10.

[2]McGuire, *Diary*, p. 88.

[3]Fitzgerald Ross, *A Visit to the Cities and Camps of the Confederate States*, p. 102.

[4]Avary, *A Virginia Girl in the Civil War*, pp. 351-53.

[5]Clay-Clopton, *A Belle of the Fifties*, p. 180.

[6]Harrison, *The Century Illustrated Monthly Magazine*, XXX (1885), 609-10.

[7]DeLeon, *Four Years in Rebel Capitals*, p. 86.

[8]N. H. R. Dawson to his fiancee, March 24, 1862, N. H. R. Dawson Papers.

[9]Houston *Tri-Weekly Telegraph*, June 6, 1862.

[10]Richmond *Examiner*, March 24, 1865.

[11]Putnam, *Richmond During the War*, p. 252.

[12]DeLeon, *Four Years in Rebel Capitals*, p. 86.

[13]Bill, *Beleaguerd City*, p. 262; Beers, *Memories*, p. 45.

[14]McGuire, *Diary*, pp. 88-93.

[15]*Ibid.*, pp. 175, 205, 206.

[16]*Ibid.*, p. 168.

[17]Putnam, *Richmond During the War*, p. 320.

[18]E. F. Andrews, *Journal*, p. 133.

[19]McGuire, *Diary*, p. 173.

[20]Ross, *A Visit to the Cities and Camps of the Confederate States*, p. 24.

[21]Fearn, *Diary*, pp. 57-58.

[22]*Southern Confederacy*, September 11-30, 1861.

[23]F. W. Dawson, *Our Women in the War*, p. 16.

[24]McDonald, *Diary*, pp. 188-89.

[25]Russell, *Pictures of Southern Life*, pp. 74-75.

[26]Wilmington *Journal*, October 29, 1863.

[27]Houston *Tri-Weekly Telegraph*, June 23, 1862.

[28]Chesnut, *Diary*, p. 348.

[29]E. F. Andrews, *Journal*, p. 162.

[30]Wright, *A Southern Girl in '61*, pp. 201-2.

[31]*Ibid.*, p. 229.

[32]Ross, *A Visit to the Cities and Camps of the Confederate States*, p. 23.

[33]E. F. Andrews, *Journal*, p. 132; Charlotte R. Holmes (ed.), *The Burckmyer Letters, March 1863-June 1865*, p. 179; Fearn, *Diary*, pp. 17-18.

[34]C. J. Milling, "Ilium in Flames," *Confederate Veteran* XXXVI (1928), 182; Cable, *Century Magazine*, XXX (1885), 772; Beers, *Memories,* p. 45.

[35]Chesnut, *Diary*, p. 369; J. T. Trowbridge, *A Picture of the Desolated States and the Work of Reconstruction,* p. 559. Mayor Gibbs of Columbia, South Carolina, said that "two hundred women and children were in one house" a few days after the burning of Columbia.

[36]Harry Gilmor, *Four Years in the Saddle,* p. 123.

[37]Clara Minor Lynn Papers.

[38]Pryor, *My Day*, p. 201. Mrs. Pryor found the historian, Charles Campbell, living in a damp cellar in Petersburg.

[39]McGuire, *Diary*, p. 304; William Octave Hart, "A Boy's Recollection of the War," *Publications of the Mississippi Historical Society,* XII (1912), 150.

[40]Loughborough, *My Cave Life in Vicksburg,* pp. 17, 61-62, 72.

[41]McGuire, *Diary*, pp. 240, 307.

[42]Jones, *A Rebel War-Clerk's Diary,* I, 237.

[43]*Ibid.*, II, 127.

[44]Holmes, *The Burckmyer Letters,* p. 303.

[45]Wilmington *Journal*, January 10, 1863; Fontaine, *Confederate Veteran,* IV (1896), 302.

[46]Handy, *Harper's Monthly Magazine*, LII (1876), 578. Some Confederate matches may be seen in the Confederate Museum. They are guaranteed to be perfectly harmless.

[47]Iredell *Express*, February 19, 1863. The instructions were as follows: "Take strips of wood and dip them into melted sulphur, and let them dry, which will be done in a minute after dipping them. Then the point of these sulphured matches must be dipped into a composition made in the following manner, viz.; dissolve in hot water gum arabic four parts, chlorate of potassa one part and phosphorous one part. These are all to be added to hot water separately, and in the order herein prescribed; and as soon as the 1st ingredient is dissolved, then add a second, etc. until all are dissolved. This must be done in a water bath, and the mixture must be kept in a water bath while the process of dipping is going on. The matches are to be thoroughly dried before they are used. Dry in the shade for 24 hours. Cover the mixture closely."

[48]Higgins, *Confederate Veteran*, XXI (1913), 164.

[49]Richmond *Examiner,* October 19, 1862.

[50]Beers, *Memories*, p. 117; Porcher, *Resources*, p. 580; McDonald, *Diary*, p. 225; Otey, *Confederate Veteran,* IX (1901), 154.

[51]*Confederate Receipt Book*, p. 12. "Confederate Candle—Melt together a pound of beeswax and a quarter of a pound of rosin or of turpentine, fresh from the tree. Prepare a wick 20 or 30 yards long, made up of three threads of loosely spun cotton, saturate this well with the mixture, and draw it through your fingers, to press all closely together, and to keep the size even. Repeat the process until the candle attains the size of a large straw or quill, then wrap around a bottle, or into a

ball with a flat bottom. Six inches of this candle elevated above the rest will burn for fifteen or twenty minutes, and give a very pretty light, and forty yards have sufficed a small family a summer for all the usual purposes of the bedchamber."

[52]S. M. Dawson, *Diary*, p. 219.

[53]Jennings, *Confederate Veteran*, XXX (1922), 375.

[54]Robertson, *Southern Historical Society Papers*, VI (New Series, 1923), 217.

[55]Fontaine, *Confederate Veteran*, IV (1896), 303.

[56]Avary, *A Virginia Girl in the Civil War*, p. 51.

[57]Chesnut, *Diary*, p. 333; Porcher, *Resources*, p. 580; Montgomery *Daily Advertiser*, May 20, 1862.

[58]*Southern Confederacy*, November 2, 1862: "the tops of old home-made knit socks cut into strips of the proper width, make as good . . . [wicks] as the best that ever came from Yankeedom"; Wilmington *Journal*, December 22, 1864: "cotton flannel folded in 3 thickness', just wide enough to go into the tube" makes satisfactory wicks. Hopley, *Life in the South*, II, 119.

[59]S. M. Dawson, *Diary*, p. 273; Handy, *Harper's Monthly Magazine*, LII (1876), 577.

[60]Hague, *A Blockaded Family*, p. 105.

[61]Gordon, *The Century Magazine*, XXXVI (1888), 770.

[62]*Southern Confederacy*, November 7, 1862; *Confederate Receipt Book*, p. 22.

[63]Richmond *Examiner*, October 19, 1862, October 28, 1862.

[64]Richmond *Enquirer*, January 21, 31, and December 15, 1862; Richmond *Examiner*, October 28, 1862, January 3, 1865, February 7, 1865; Wilmington *Journal*, December 24, 1863; Memphis *Daily Appeal*, February 8, 1863; Charlottesville *Chronicle*, October 18, 1864; Savannah *Republican*, November 4, 1863; *Southern Confederacy*, September 14, 1862.

[65]Richmond *Examiner*, January 3, 1865.

[66]Richmond *Examiner*, January 21, 1865, February 7, 22, 1865.

[67]Emma Le Conte Diary, January 23, 1865; Handy, *Harper's Monthly Magazine*, LII (1876), 577.

[68]Holmes, *The Burckmyer Letters*, p. 446.

[69]Pember, *A Southern Woman's Story*, pp. 100-1.

[70]Wilmington *Journal*, October 1, 1863.

[71]Fearn, *Diary*, p. 19.

[72]Richmond *Examiner*, December 7, 1861; *Southern Confederacy*, October 29, 1862; Savannah *Republican*, March 25, 1862, July 18, 1863; Wilmington *Journal*, January 30, 1864; Richmond *Enquirer*, April 29, 1864.

[73]Emma Le Conte Diary, January 23, 1865.

[74]Pryor, *My Day*, p. 238.

[75]Richmond *Enquirer*, October 4, 1861.

[76]Jones, *A Rebel War-Clerk's Diary*, I, 196.

[77]Richmond *Enquirer*, January 14, 1864.

[78]*Confederate Receipt Book*, p. 19.

[79]Porcher, *Resources,* p. 277.

[80]Richmond *Whig and Advertiser,* March 29, 1864.

[81]Houston *Tri-Weekly Telegraph,* August 13, 1862.

[82]Gordon, *The Century Magazine,* XXX (1888), 770; Hague, *A Blockaded Family,* p. 61.

[83]Holmes, *The Burckmyer Letters,* pp. 101-3.

[84]E. F. Andrews, *Journal,* p. 42.

[85]Holmes, *The Burckmyer Letters,* p. 446; Hague, *A Blockaded Family,* pp. 116-17.

[86]S. M. Dawson, *Diary,* pp. 211, 377.

[87]McGuire, *Diary,* p. 169.

[88]Charleston *Mercury,* January 16, 1862.

[89]Clara Minor Lynn Papers.

[90]McGuire, *Diary,* p. 327.

[91]McDonald, *Diary,* p. 233.

[92]Harrison, *Recollections,* p. 117.

[93]Gay, *Life In Dixie During the War,* p. 214.

[94]Hague, *A Blockaded Family,* p. 48; Gordon, *The Century Magazine,* XXXVI (1888), 770.

[95]Clara Minor Lynn Papers.

[96]E. F. Andrews, *Journal,* p. 41.

[97]Examples of "wooden silver" may be seen in the Confederate Museum, Richmond, Virginia.

[98]Pember, *A Southern Woman's Story,* p. 37.

[99]Mrs. C. Clarke to Maxwell Clarke, Maxwell Clarke Papers.

[100]New Orleans *Picayune,* November 20, 1861.

[101]Porcher, *Resources,* p. 581.

[102]*Ibid.,* p. 127; Jacobs, *Southern Historical Society Papers,* XXXIII (1905), 181.

[103]*Official Records,* Series IV, III, 687.

[104]Scott, *Confederate Veteran,* XXIV (1916), 219.

[105]*Confederate Receipt Book,* p. 11.

[106]McGuire, *Diary,* p. 205.

[107]Richmond *Whig,* April 15, 1864.

[108]Hague, *A Blockaded Family,* pp. 102-3; Scott, *Confederate Veteran,* XXIV (1916), 219.

[109]Bertha Simpson Lucas, "Reminiscences of the Old South," MS., North Carolina Room, University of North Carolina, Chapel Hill, North Carolina.

[110]*Southern Confederacy,* June 17, 1862.

CHAPTER VII

[1]Transactions of the American Medical Association, XV (1864), 39-40. "Editorial," *Confederate States Medical and Surgical Journal,* I (1864), 106. This publication reported that Dr. Gardner of New

York, who made the motion to remove restrictions, was "hissed off the floor."

[2]Moore, *Rebellion Record*, II, 101.

[3]Jacobs, *Southern Historical Society Papers*, XXXIII (1905), 163.

[4]*Ibid.*, p. 171.

[5]*Daily Southern Guardian*, February 19, 1862; *True Democrat*, April 24, 1862; *Carolina Watchman*, May 12, 1862.

[6]Jacobs, *Southern Historical Society Papers*, XXXIII (1905), 172.

[7]Harrison, *Recollections*, p. 58.

[8]DeLeon, *Four Years in Rebel Capitals*, p. 286.

[9]Jacobs, *Southern Historical Society Papers*, XXXIII (1905), 171.

[10]Hall, *Medical Life*, XLII (1935), 456-58.

[11]Montgomery *Daily Advertiser*, January 15, 1863.

[12]Selph, *Confederate Veteran*, XXV (1915), 559.

[13]Hague, *A Blockaded Family*, p. 46; F. W. Dawson, *Our Women in the War*, p. 13.

[14]Clara Minor Lynn Papers.

[15]Hopley, *Life in the South*, II, 185.

[16]Charleston *Courier*, May 11, 1863.

[17]*Confederate States Medical and Surgical Journal*, I (1864), 13.

[18]Hopley, *Life in the South*, II, 275.

[19]*Official Records*, Series IV, II, 1041.

[20]C. R. Hall, *Medical Life*, XLII (1935), 456-58.

[21] "Indigenous Remedies of the South," *Confederate States Medical and Surgical Journal*, I (1864), 107; Jacobs, *Southern Historical Society Papers*, XXXIII (1905), 170; Wyndham B. Blanton, *Medicine in Virginia in the Nineteenth Century*, p. 283; Deering J. Roberts, "Confederate Medical Service," *The Photographic History of the Civil War*, VII, 244.

[22]Jacobs, *Southern Historical Society Papers*, XXXIII (1905), 170.

[23]Hall, *Medical Life*, XLII (1935), 492-93; Marion W. Woodrow (ed.), *Dr. James Woodrow As Seen by His Friends: Character Sketches by His Former Pupils, Colleagues and Associates*, p. 21.

[24]*Official Records*, Series IV, I, 1041.

[25]Hopley, *Life in the South*, II, 43.

[26]New Orleans *Picayune*, August 5, 1861.

[27]Avary, *A Virginia Girl in the Civil War*, p. 17; "Running the Blockade," *Southern Historical Society Papers*, XXIV (1896), 229.

[28]Fulkerson, *Recollections*, p. 127; Porcher, *Resources*, pp. 64-67, 374; Charleston *Mercury*, July 19, 1862; W. T. Grant, "Indigenous Medicinal Plants," *Confederate States Medical and Surgical Journal*, I (1864), 85; *Official Records*, Series IV, II, 1024.

[29]D. J. Roberts, *The Photographic History of the Civil War*, VII, 244.

[30]Wilmington *Journal*, October 1, 1863; Chattanooga *Daily Rebel*, November 21, 1864.

[31]Charleston *Courier*, August 11, 1862; Wilmington *Journal*, September 4, 1862; Porcher, *Resources*, p. 107.

[32]"Editorial," *Confederate States Medical and Surgical Journal,* I (1864), 119-20.

[33]Richmond *Enquirer,* September 23, 1861.

[34]Grant, *Confederate States Medical and Surgical Journal,* I (1864), 85.

[35]Mallett, *Southern Historical Society Papers,* XXI (1903), 102; Loughborough, *My Cave Life in Vicksburg,* p. 162.

[36]Porcher, *Resources,* pp. 25-28.

[37]*Official Records,* Series IV, II, 442.

[38]Charleston *Mercury,* April 3, 1863, May 29, 1863; Augusta *Chronicle and Sentinel,* September 10, 1863.

[39]Agnew Diary, January 18, 1865, January 19, 1865, February 27, 1865, March 21, 1865, Southern Historical Collection, University of North Carolina, Chapel Hill, North Carolina.

[40]Handy, *Harper's Monthly Magazine,* LII (1876), 578.

[41]Hall, *Medical Life,* XLII (1935), 458.

[42]Clara Minor Lynn Papers.

[43]"Table of Indigenous Remedies," *Confederate Medical and Surgical Journal,* I (1864), 107.

[44]Jacobs, *Southern Historical Society Papers,* XXXIII (1905), 168.

[45]Hall, *Medical Life,* XLII (1935), 481.

[46]*Confederate Receipt Book,* p. 13.

[47]Hall, *Medical Life,* XLII (1935), 481.

[48]Jacobs, *Southern Historical Society Papers,* XXXIII (1905), 168.

[49]*Confederate Receipt Book,* p. 14.

[50]S. R. Chambers, "On the Treatment of Camp Itch," *Confederate States Medical and Surgical Journal,* II (1865), 10.

[51]"Table of Indigenous Remedies," *Confederate States Medical and Surgical Journal,* I (1864), 107.

[52]"Castor Oil Bean," *Southern Cultivator,* XX (1862), 35.

[53]Jacobs, *Southern Historical Society Papers,* XXXIII (1905), 176.

[54]*Ibid.,* p. 167.

[55]*Ibid.*

[56]Porcher, *Resources,* p. 40.

[57]D. J. Roberts, *The Photographic History of the Civil War,* VII, 244.

[58]Grant, *Confederate States Medical and Surgical Journal,* I (1864), 85.

[59]Jacobs, *Southern Historical Society Papers,* XXXIII (1905), 167.

[60]*Carolina Watchman,* July 13, 1863.

[61]Grant, *Confederate States Medical and Surgical Journal,* I (1864), 85.

[62]*Confederate Receipt Book.*

[63]*Official Records,* Series IV, II, 48.

[64]Hall, *Medical Life,* XLII (1935), 451, 464.

[65]D. J. Roberts, *The Photographic History of the Civil War,* VII, 248.

[66]J. F. White, "Social Conditions in the South During the War Between the States," *Confederate Veteran,* XXX (1922), 181.

[67]Hall, *Medical Life,* XLII (1935), 464-65.

68Pember, *A Southern Woman's Story*, p. 128.

69Jacobs, *Southern Historical Society Papers*, XXXIII (1905), 166.

70Moore, *Rebellion Record*, IV, 10.

71D. J. Roberts, *The Photographic History of the Civil War*, VII, 248-50.

72Clara Minor Lynn Papers.

73Hunter, *Confederate Veteran*, XV (1907), 259.

74White, *Confederate Veteran*, XXX (1922), 181.

CHAPTER VIII

1Ramsdell, *American Historical Review*, XXII (1917), 804-5; F. B. C. Bradlee, *Blockade Running*, pp. 182-83.

2Ramsdell, *American Historical Review*, XXII (1917), 804-5.

3Bradlee, *Blockade Running*, pp. 182-83.

4*Official Records*, Series IV, II, 485.

5Jones, *A Rebel War-Clerk's Diary*, I, 302.

6*Official Records*, Series IV, II, 339.

7*Ibid.*, pp. 742-43.

8*Ibid.*, pp. 9-10, 478, 508, 514.

9*Southern Confederacy*, April 22, 1862.

10Porcher, *Resources*, p. 141.

11*Ibid.*, p. 229.

12Montgomery *Daily Advertiser*, January 15, 1863.

13*Official Records*, Series IV, II, 505-7.

14*Official Records*, Series VI, II, 500-5. The plan for the scrap drive was as follows: "Let those in the country bring it [scrap iron] to the nearest point of water or railroad transportation used by the Government, or to the nearest inland point visited by or easily accessible to the wagons of the Quartermaster's Department. . . . In cities, towns, and villages where Government wagons can be employed, let sufficient previous notice be published that on certain days those wagons, accompanied by a Government agent with means of weighing and money to pay, or blank forms of receipts for the iron, will call on each householder in certain wards or streets for such iron . . . and let the wagons have on them a conspicuous sign indicating their object, with a bell or horn or other signal to announce their coming." The railroad men believed such a drive would net a vast amount of scrap-iron.

15*Official Records*, Series IV, II, pp. 508-9.

16*Ibid.*, pp. 510.

17*Official Records*, Series IV, III, 226-27.

18Ramsdell, *Laws and Joint Resolutions*, First Congress, Second Session (Secret), May 1, 1863, pp. 167-69.

19Ramsdell, *American Historical Review*, XXII (1917), 804-5.

20*Official Records*, Series IV, II, 655; III, 694, 1085, 1091-93.

21*Ibid.*, III, 209.

22Ramsdell, *American Historical Review*, XXII, (1917), 806.

23Jones, *A Rebel War-Clerk's Diary,* II, 182.

24Ramsdell, *Laws and Joint Resolutions,* Second Congress, Second Session, February 18, 1865, pp. 45-46.

25DeLeon, *Four Years in Rebel Capitals,* p. 281.

26Bradlee, *Blockade Running,* p. 168.

27*Official Records,* Series IV, III, 258.

28*Laws of Virginia,* October 31, 1863, p. 14.

29*Acts of Georgia,* April 18, 1863, pp. 180-82.

30*Official Records,* Series IV, II, 417.

31*Ibid.,* p. 616.

32*Official Records,* Series IV, II, 552.

33Pember, *A Southern Woman's Story,* p. 154.

34"Diary of Miss Harriet Cary, Kept by Her From May 6, 1862, to July 24, 1862," *Tyler's Quarterly and Genealogical Magazine,* IX (1927), 106.

35Fulkerson, *Recollections,* p. 143; Chesnut, *Diary,* p. 336.

36Clara Minor Lynn Papers.

37Armes, *The Autobiography of Joseph LeConte,* p. 190.

38Beers, *Memories,* p. 20; Harrison, *Recollections,* p. 105.

39Chesnut, *Diary,* p. 173.

40Putnam, *Richmond During the War,* p. 106.

41Harrison, *Recollections,* p. 102. The couple was to have ridden in the presidential carriage, but the horses ran away and the couple had to change their plans. The conveyance described above was all that could be found.

42Chesnut, *Diary,* p. 272.

43Harrison, *Recollections,* p. 105.

44Beers, *Memories,* p. 20.

45Sarah Lawton to Sarah Jackson, June 16, 1864, Prince-Jackson Papers, Southern Historical Collection, University of North Carolina, Chapel Hill, North Carolina.

46Avary, *A Virginia Girl in the Civil War,* p. 227.

47Ross, *A Visit to the Cities and Camps of the Confederate States,* pp. 23-24.

48Easterby, *The South Carolina Rice Plantation,* p. 311.

49Wright, *A Southern Girl in '61,* p. 206.

50Fearn, *Diary,* p. 15.

51Houston *Tri-Weekly Telegraph,* June 6, 1862.

52E. F. Andrews, *Journal,* p. 23.

53Pember, *A Southern Woman's Story,* p. 151.

54Bradlee, *Blockade Running,* pp. 260-61.

55DeLeon, *Four Years in Rebel Capitals,* p. 77.

56Wilmington *Journal,* April 2, 1863.

57White, *Confederate Veteran,* XXX (1922), 142. White summarizes the conditions as follows: "The railroads were inadequate; the wagon roads were worse. The state of the transportation facilities interferred with the distribution of supplies. Delays were frequent. The agent of Alabama at Saltville wrote to his governor that he could not obtain cars in which to send salt to Alabama. Governor Vance complained that his salt trains were interferred with. Supplies badly needed in Richmond could not be transported from Georgia on account of the condition of the railroads. It seemed that while at times certain food supplies abounded in Georgia, in Virginia there was want." See also the Richmond *Enquirer,* September 25, 1861. As early as this, 150 cars of precious sugar were held at Grand Junction, Tennessee, "awaiting transportation eastward." At the same time 100,000 bushels of equally dear salt was held along the Virginia and Tennessee Railroad. Such complaints as this were common during the war.

[58]Magnolia Plantation Record [Louisiana], November 3, 8, 1861.

[59]DeLeon, *Four Years in Rebel Capitals,* p. 395.

[60]Richmond *Examiner,* June 13, 1862.

[61]Richmond *Examiner,* October 6, 1862.

[65]Letter Books of the Secretary of War (1862).

of the Secretary of War (1862); Fulkerson, *Recollections,* p. 126; Wiley, *The Plain People of the Confederacy,* p. 40; Richmond *Examiner,* April 27, 1864.

[63]*Southern Cultivator,* XXII (1864), 54.

[64]Greathouse, *Confederate Veteran,* XX (1912), 168.

[65]Letter Books of the Secretary of War (1862).

[66]Gay, *Life in Dixie During the War,* pp. 199-200.

[67]*Southern Confederacy,* December 10, 1862; *Southern Field and Fireside,* March 14, 1863, p. 86.

[68]*Official Records,* Series IV, III, 3-4.

[69]*Ibid.,* p. 34.

[70]Dodge, *Atlantic Monthly,* LVIII (1886), 233.

[71]Charleston *Mercury,* October 29, 1861.

[72]Dodge, *Atlantic Monthly,* LVIII (1886), 229.

[73]Montgomery *Daily Advertiser,* February 27, 1864.

[74]C. Clarke to Maxwell Clarke, July 20, 1862, Maxwell Clarke Papers.

[75]Hague, *A Blockaded Family,* p. 32.

[76]J. M. Hough to W. S. Pettigrew, March 22, 1862, Pettigrew Papers.

[77]Charleston *Mercury,* September 24, 1861.

[78]*Southern Confederacy,* January 11, 1863.

[79]*Ibid.,* January 29, 1862; Richmond *Whig,* October 15, 1862.

[80]Gay, *Life in Dixie During the War,* p. 117.

[81]William Gilmore Simms suggested the use of Bear-Grass.

[82]A fiber made from okra stalks was described as "an excellent substitute for hemp."

[83]New Orleans *Picayune,* May 1, 1862; Wilmington *Journal,* October 24, 1863; Charleston *Mercury,* December 3, 1861; *Southern Cultivator,* XIX (1861), 294.

[84]Jones, *A Rebel War-Clerk's Diary,* II, 197.

[85]Easterby, *The South Carolina Rice Plantation,* pp. 200-1.

[86]Putnam, *Richmond During the War,* p. 315.

[87]Scott, *Confederate Veteran*, XXIV (1916), 217.

[88]Scott, *Confederate Veteran*, XXIV (1916), 217; *see also* William W. Renwick Papers, September 27, 1864.

CHAPTER IX

[1]Richmond *Whig*, June 7, 1861.

[2]DeLeon, *Four Years in Rebel Capitals*, p. 290.

[3]Gordon, *The Century Magazine*, XXXVI (1888), 764.

[4]James D. McCabe, "Literature of the War," *Southern Historical Society Papers*, IV (1921), 200.

[5]*Southern Confederacy*, March 15, 1862.

[6]Richmond *Enquirer*, June 10, 1862.

[7]Jones, *A Rebel War-Clerk's Diary*, I, 161.

[8]*Southern Confederacy*, October 2, 1861.

[9]*Ibid.*, November 30, 1861.

[10]Charleston *Mercury*, May 19, June 20, 1862; Richmond *Whig*, May 12, 1862; Richmond *Enquirer*, May 12, 1862; Richmond *Examiner*, May 12, 1862; Richmond *Dispatch*, June 13, 1862.

[11]Charleston *Mercury*, January 25, 1862.

[12]*Ibid.*, October 12, 13, 1864, and January 19, 1865.

[13]Savannah *Republican*, May 17, 1862.

[14]Vicksburg *Daily Citizen*, July 2, 1863. The early edition of the *Citizen* did not carry this editorial.

[15]*Pictorial Democrat*, April 15, 1863.

[16]*Weekly Junior Register*, April 9, 1863.

[17]Charleston *Courier*, March 30, 1863.

[18]White, *Confederate Veteran*, XXX (1922), 183.

[19]Charleston *Mercury*, January 28, 1862.

[20]Richmond *Dispatch*, December 28, 1861.

[21]White, *Confederate Veteran*, XXX (1922), 183.

[22]Charleston *Courier*, June 4, 1863.

[23]Putnam, *Richmond During the War*, p. 195.

[24]*Southern Field and Fireside*, January 2, 1864.

[25]Eggleston, *Recollections*, p. 104; Selph, *Confederate Veteran*, XXV (1915), 560; Harrison, *Recollections*, p. 118.

[26]James W. Albright, "Books Made in Dixie," *Southern Historical Society Papers*, III (1896), 57-60.

[27]Jones, *A Rebel War-Clerk's Diary*, I, 341.

[28]Ross, *A Visit to the Cities and Camps of the Confederate States*, p. 173.

[29]Cable, *Century Magazine*, XXX (1885), 797.

[30]Kate Mason Rowland Diary, Confederate Museum, Richmond, Virginia; Harrison, *Recollections*, pp. 177-78.

[31]Gay, *Life in Dixie During the War*, p. 73.

[32]Harrison, *Recollections*, pp. 117-18.

[33]General W. D. Pender to his wife, March 26, 1863, W. D. Pender Papers.

[34]Jones, *A Rebel War-Clerk's Diary*, II, 10.

[35]Clara Dargan McLean, "Return of a Refugee," *Southern Historical Society Papers*, XIII (1885), 502.

[36]McGuire, *Diary*, p. 225.

[37]E. F. Andrews, *Journal*, p. 5.

[38]Chesnut, *Diary*, Introduction, p. xxi.

[39]Montgomery *Daily Advertiser*, June 9, 1863.

[40]*Daily Carolina Watchman*, September 23, 1864.

[41]Hopley, *Life in the South*, II, 103.

[42]Hopley, *Life in the South*, II, 104.

[43]N. H. R. Dawson to his fiancee, March 15, 1862, March 21, 1862, N. H. R. Dawson Papers.

[44]Isabel Maury to Mollie Maury, January 1, 1865, Maury Letter, Confederate Museum, Richmond, Virginia.

[45]*Confederate States Medical and Surgical Journal*, I (1864), 187.

[46]Dodge, *Atlantic Monthly*, LVIII (1886), 238.

[47]Jones, *A Rebel War-Clerk's Diary*, I, 341.

[48]Dodge, *Atlantic Monthly*, LVIII (1886), 238.

[49]Porcher, *Resources*, p. 302.

[50]Wilmington *Journal*, December 18, 1862.

[51]Hopley, *Life in the South*, II, 41.

[52]Clara Minor Lynn Papers.

[53]New Orleans *Picayune*, November 3, 1861.

[54]*Southern Confederacy*, May 28-31, June 3-13, 1862.

[55]*Daily Express*, September 12, 1861.

[56]*Confederate Receipt Book*, p. 19.

[57]Gordon, *The Century Magazine*, XXXVI (1888), 765.

[58]*Ibid.*

[59]Charleston *Mercury*, December 9, 1861; Savannah *Republican*, December 11, 1861.

[60]Richmond *Enquirer*, February 19, 1862.

[61]James Evans to his son, James Evans, Jr., June 1864, James Evans Papers.

[62]C. Clarke to Maxwell Clarke, August 10, 1862, Maxwell Clarke Papers.

[63]Richmond *Examiner*, September 26, 1861.

[64]Richmond *Whig*, November 15, 1864.

[65]Charleston *Mercury*, November 19, 1861.

[66]*Ibid.*, November 23, 1861.

[67]*Ibid.*, July 18, 1862.

[68]*North Carolina Standard*, February 12, 1864.

[69]New Orleans *Picayune*, October 18, 1861; Charleston *Mercury*, October 25, 1861.

[70]Betty Herndon Maury Diary, August 30, 1861.

[71]Charleston *Mercury*, November 23, 1861.

[72]Betty Herndon Maury Diary, April 6, 1862.

[73]Pryor, *My Day*, p. 198; Chesnut, *Diary*, p. 101.

[74]White, *Confederate Veteran*, XXX (1922), 143; Jones, *A Rebel War-Clerk's Diary*, II, 392.

[75]New Orleans *Picayune*, October 18, 1861; Charleston *Mercury*, October 25, 1861.

[76]Richmond *Examiner*, June 24, 1861, October 17, 1862; Charleston *Mercury*, March 19, 1862; *Daily Rebel*, November 30, 1862.

[77]Wilmington *Journal*, January 18, 1862.

[78]*Confederate Receipt Book*, p. 19.

[79]*Southern Confederacy*, June 3, 1862.

[80]S. M. Dawson, *Diary*, p. 224.

[81]Dodge, *Atlantic Monthly*, LVIII (1886), 233.

[82]*Daily Express*, July 30, 1861.

[83]Clara Minor Lynn Papers.

[84]Jennings, *Confederate Veteran*, XXX (1922), 375.

[85]Beers, *Memories*, pp. 294-95.

[86]Dodge, *Atlantic Monthly*, LVIII (1886), 234.

[87]Elizabeth Boone Chastain, "Plantation Life in the Sixties," *Confederate Veteran*, XXXIV (1926), 99.

[88]Jones, *A Rebel War-Clerk's Diary*, I, 294.

[89]Clara Minor Lynn Papers.

[90]Mrs. W. E. Turner, *Recollections*, p. 3.

[91]Hague, *A Blockaded Family*, p. 95.

[92]Examples of these substitute buttons can be seen in the Confederate Museum, Richmond, Virginia.

[93]*North Carolina Standard*, May 13, 1863.

[94]*Southern Cultivator*, XXI (1863), 119.

[95]Kirby Smith to Mrs. Kirby Smith, December 19, 1863, Kirby Smith Papers.

[96]Avary, *A Virginia Girl in the Civil War*, p. 53.

[97]Gordon, *The Century Magazine*, XXXVI (1888), 769. Some of these combs may be seen in the Confederate Museum.

[98]*Southern Illustrated News*, August 22, 1863, p. 61.

[99]Fontaine, *Confederate Veteran*, IV (1896), 301.

[100]Gordon, *The Century Magazine*, XXXVI (1888), 769.

[101]Chesnut, *Diary*, p. 285.

[102]Turner, *Recollections*, p. 5.

[103]These may be seen in the Confederate Museum.

[104]F. W. Dawson, *Our Women in the War*, p. 15.

[105]Fontaine, *Confederate Veteran*, IV (1896), 302.

[106]Hague, *A Blockaded Family*, pp. 118-19.

[107]*Southern Confederacy*, April 12, 1863.

[108]Montgomery *Daily Advertiser*, February 27, 1864; Charleston *Courier*, March 29, 1862, June 11, 1862. Examples of the homemade pipes may be seen in the Confederate Museum.

[109]Montgomery *Daily Advertiser*, February 27, 1864.

[110]Jones, *A Rebel War-Clerk's Diary*, II, 458.

[111]Pember, *A Southern Woman's Story*, p. 130; Elizabeth Fry Page, "Tampa During the War," *Confederate Veteran*, XXXV (1927), 125.

[112]Pember, *A Southern Woman's Story*, pp. 130-31.

[113]McGuire, *Diary*, p. 201; Kate Mason Rowland Diary, September 21, 1862.

[114]Hague, *A Blockaded Family*, p. 38; Clara Minor Lynn Papers.

[115]*Confederate Receipt Book*, p. 20.

[116]Examples of these are in the Confederate Museum.

[117]DeLeon, *Belles, Beaux, and Brains of the Sixties*, p. 283.

[118]Porcher, *Resources*, pp. 10-11.

[119]DeLeon, *Four Years in Rebel Capitals*, p. 352.

[120]Hopley, *Life in the South*, II, 87.

[121]Luther R. Mills, "The Capture and Imprisonment of Luther L. Mills," p. 12, M. S. North Carolina Room, University of North Carolina, Chapel Hill, North Carolina.

[122]Charleston *Mercury*, October 26, 1861.

[123]Pember, *A Southern Woman's Story*, p. 46.

[124]Dodge, *Atlantic Monthly*, LVIII (1886), 233.

[125]Roberts, *Never Caught*, pp. 24-25.

[126]Roberts, *Never Caught*, p. 237.

[127]*Acts of Louisiana*, February 3, 1865, p. 26.

[128]Chesnut, *Diary*, p. 312.

[129]Agnew Diary, March 24, 1863.

[130]James Evans to James S. Evans, January 7, 1862, James Evans Papers.

[131]Fannie Evans to James S. Evans, February 28, 1863, *ibid.*

[132]Emma LeConte Diary, January 18, 1865.

[133]Hague, *A Blockaded Family*, pp. 70-71.

[134]Handy, *Harper's Magazine*, LII (1876), 577.

[135]Isabel Maury to Mollie Maury, January 1, 1865, Maury Letter.

[136]Clara Minor Lynn Papers.

[137]Dolly Sumner Lunt Burge, *A Woman's Wartime Journal: An Account of the Passage Over a Georgia Plantation of Sherman's Army on the March to the Sea*, pp. 44-45.

[138]Mary McCrimmon, "Santa Claus," *Southern Illustrated News*, December 20, 1862.

CHAPTER X

[1]Charleston *Mercury*, October 24, 1861.

[2]"Editorial," *Southern Cultivator*, XIX (1861), 187.

[3]*Ibid.*, XX (1862), 104-5.

[4]*Daily Rebel*, September 30, 1862.

[5]Richmond *Enquirer*, October 9, 1861, quoting the Fort Smith *Texan*.

[6]T. B. Bailey to his mother, Mrs. John L. Bailey, October 19, 1862, John L. Bailey Papers.

[7]Houston *Tri-Weekly Telegraph*, February 12, 1864.

[8]*Daily Rebel*, February 28, 1863.

[9]Charleston *Mercury*, August 29, 1861.

[10]Savannah *Republican*, March 17, April 28, 1862.

[11]Natchez *Daily Courier*, March 4, 1863.

[12]Ramsdell, *Behind the Lines in the Southern Confederacy*, p. 42.

[13]James Evans to James S. Evans, October 2, 1861, James Evans Papers.

[14]*North Carolina Standard*, November 3, 1863. "In Petersburg 10,000 pounds of rotten bacon . . . was sold at 72½ cents per pound!—mouldy hard bread at 20¢ per pound, damaged rice at 13¢ per pound."

[15]Jones, *A Rebel War-Clerk's Diary*, II, 128.

[16]DeLeon, *Four Years in Rebel Capitals*, p. 236.

[17]Kate Mason Rowland and Mrs. Morris L. Croxall (eds.), *The Journal of Julia LeGrand*, p. 85.

[18]Jones, *A Rebel War-Clerk's Diary*, I, 200.

[19]Chesnut, *Diary*, p. 139.

[20]DeLeon, *Four Years in Rebel Capitals*, p. 233.

[21]Richmond *Whig*, December 2, 1864.

[22]New Orleans *Picayune*, September 7, 1861.

[23]Rowland and Croxall, *The Journal of Julia LeGrand*, pp. 37-38.

[24]Wilmington *Journal*, September 25, 1862.

[25]Clara Minor Lynn Papers.

[26]Charleston *Mercury*, September 10, 1863, and April 21, 1864.

[27]*Ibid.*, May 3, 1864.

[28]Jones, *A Rebel War-Clerk's Diary*, I, 183.

[29]*Southern Cultivator*, XXI (1863), 17.

[30]James Evans to James S. Evans, November 8, 1862, James Evans Papers.

[31]*Ibid.*, December 11, 1863.

[32]Pryor, *My Day*, p. 208.

[33]Jones, *A Rebel War-Clerk's Diary*, II, 345.

[34]*Ibid.*, II, 400.

[35]Augusta *Chronicle and Sentinel*, November 26, 1863.

[36]Childs *et al.* (eds.), *The Mason Smith Family Letters, 1860-1868*, p. 83.

[37]New Orleans *Picayune*, August 11, 1861.

[38]Kate Mason Rowland Diary, April 14, 1863; McGuire, *Diary*, p. 202; Richmond *Whig*, April 3, 1863; Richmond *Examiner*, April 3, 1863.

[39]Moore, *Rebellion Record*, VII, 48.

[40]*Ibid.*, VIII, 67.

[41]Charleston *Mercury*, October 26, 1863.

[42]Betty Herndon Maury Diary, April 6, 1862.

[43]Houston *Tri-Weekly Telegraph*, October 6, 1862.

[44]New Orleans *Picayune*, April 27, 1862.

[45]*Southern Confederacy*, May 21, 1862.

[46]*Ibid.*, December 24, 1862.

[47]Dodge, *Atlantic Monthly*, LVIII (1886), 241.

[48]*Southern Illustrated News*, August 8, 1863.

[49]S. M. Dawson, *Diary*, p. 213.

[50]Hopley, *Life in the South*, II, 116.

[51]Richmond *Examiner*, October 24, 1862.

[52]Childs, *The Ravenel Journal*, p. 194.

[53]Savannah *Republican*, July 9, 1864.

[54]Agnew Diary, March 13, 1865.

[55]Theodore Honour to Mrs. Theodore Honour, April 21, 1864, Theodore A. Honour Papers.

[56]Bayne, *Confederate Veteran*, XXX (1922), 100.

[57]Dodge, *Atlantic Monthly*, LVIII (1886), 229.

[58]"Kiskee" to Miss E. M. Barnett, January 17, 1865, Alexander-Hillhouse Papers, Southern Historical Collection, University of North Carolina, Chapel Hill, North Carolina.

[59]Hague, *A Blockaded Family*, p. 110.

[60]Ella A. R. Harper Diary, April 4, 1865.

[61]*Official Records*, Series I, Part 2, XXII, 1006-7.

[62]Kate Mason Rowland Diary, March 14, 1862.

[63]Hopley, *Life in the South*, II, 292.

[64]Dodge, *Atlantic Monthly*, LVIII (1886), 229.

[65]Turner, "Recollections," MS, p. 2.

[66]*Southern Illustrated News*, August 28, 1863, p. 61.

[67]Charles Harris Wesley, *The Collapse of the Confederacy*, pp. 1-46.

[68]Lonn, *Desertion During the Civil War*, pp. 12-14. The following letter is typical of the many pitiful letters from wives to husbands: "My dear Edward:—I have always been proud of you and since your connection with the Confederate army, I have been prouder of you than ever before. I would not have you do anything wrong for the world, but before God, Edward, unless you come home, we must die. Last night I was aroused by little Eddie's crying. I called and said, 'What is the matter Eddie?' and he said, 'O mamma! I am so hungry.' And Lucy, Edward, your darling Lucy: she never complains, but she is growing thinner and thinner every day. And before God, Edward, unless you come home, we must die. Your Mary."

BIBLIOGRAPHY

I. Primary

A. Manuscripts.

S. A. Agnew Diary. 6 Vols. Southern Historical Collection, University of North Carolina.

> This diary of The Reverend S. A. Agnew throws light on conditions in Lee County, Mississippi, during the Civil War. It touches on the general problem of shortages.

James Lusk Alcorn Papers. Southern Historical Collection, University of North Carolina.

> These papers deal almost entirely with political conditions during the Civil War and seldom mention economic problems.

Alexander-Hillhouse Papers. Southern Historical Collection, University of North Carolina.

> This collection covers the years 1759 to 1935, but the letters of the Civil War period only touch upon economic conditions.

Allston-Pringle-Hill Papers. Southern Historical Collection, University of North Carolina.

> Although this is a large collection covering ante-bellum and post-bellum years, the letters and papers for the war years are of little value in the study of shortages.

John L. Bailey Papers. Southern Historical Collection, University of North Carolina.

> These papers contain much interesting information about the economic conditions of the cotton belt of North Carolina during the war.

Boykin Papers. Southern Historical Collection, University of North Carolina.

> These deal mostly with military and camp life, but there are a few letters telling of conditions at home.

Maxwell Troax Clarke Papers (photostatic copies). Southern Historical Collection, University of North Carolina.

> This collection is of immense value for a study of economic conditions during the Civil War. The letters discuss many shortages in eastern Virginia.

Confederate Recipe Book. Manuscript Division, Confederate Museum, Richmond, Virginia.

> This recipe book was kept by a housewife during the war. Many interesting recipes, clipped from papers and magazines, are found here.

211

N. R. H. Dawson Papers. Southern Historical Collection, University of North Carolina.

These papers consist almost entirely of letters to and from N. R. H. Dawson. They are very valuable for a study such as this, and are especially illuminating on conditions in Alabama and Virginia.

William Dorsey Pender Papers. Southern Historical Collection, University of North Carolina.

This collection is of little value for the study of homefront shortages.

James Evans Papers. Southern Historical Collection, University of North Carolina.

These consist of letters and plantation records and give an interesting picture of conditions in North Carolina.

Josiah Gorgas Papers. Records of the Ordnance Department, National Archives, Washington, D. C.

These are few in number but they throw some light on the work of the Ordnance Department and on the problems created by the conflict of civilian and military forces.

General Thomas Jefferson Green Papers. Southern Historical Collection, University of North Carolina.

These papers deal almost entirely with military questions and were of little value in this study.

Wade Hampton Papers. Southern Historical Collection, University of North Carolina.

These only touch on home life during the war.

Ella A. R. Harper Diary. 5 vols. Southern Historical Collection, University of North Carolina.

This diary covers the years 1862-1865 and is informative about conditions in the North Carolina mountains.

Theodore A. Honour Papers. Manuscript Division, South Caroliniana Library, University of South Carolina.

An excellent collection dealing with military conditions around Charleston, 1859-1865. There is only an occasional mention of homefront shortages.

Emma Florence LeConte Diary. Southern Historical Collection, University of North Carolina.

This diary, covering the period from December 31, 1864, to August 6, 1865, is very interesting and valuable for any economic study of South Carolina. It was particularly useful for this study of shortages.

Letter Books of the Secretary of War of the Confederate States of America. National Archives, Washington, D. C.

These letter books give evidence of the civilian discontent resulting from various Confederate War Department policies.

Bertha Simpson Lucas. "Reminiscences of the Old South." North Carolina Room, University of North Carolina.

This brief paper is interesting and illuminating.

Clara Minor Lynn Papers. Manuscript Division, Confederate Museum, Richmond, Virginia.

This collection was the most valuable set of papers used for this study. It deals entirely with shortages and is very illuminating, containing material not available elsewhere.

A. G. Magrath Papers. Southern Historical Collection, University of North Carolina.

Although these papers stress military and governmental affairs, they throw light on the struggles of Governor Magrath to maintain transportation facilities and to furnish food to the people of South Carolina.

Betty Herndon Maury Diary. Manuscript Division, Library of Congress, Washington, D. C.

This brief diary is valuable for a study of women's problems during the first two years of the war.

Isabel Maury Letter. Manuscript Division, Confederate Museum, Richmond, Virginia.

This letter is especially interesting for its description of a wartime Christmas in Virginia.

William Porcher Miles Papers. Southern Historical Collection, University of North Carolina.

In this collection there are several descriptions of the effects of General Sherman's march through South Carolina, but there is little on the general subject of shortages.

Milligan Papers. Southern Historical Collection, University of North Carolina.

These are interesting and of some value in an economic study of the area around Augusta, Georgia.

Luther R. Mills. "The Capture and Imprisonment of Luther R. Mills." North Carolina Room, University of North Carolina.

In this paper there are infrequent but interesting comments about home problems during the war.

Nitre and Mining Papers. National Archives, Washington, D. C.

There are only a few of these papers and they give little information about the laboratories established by the Confederate government.

Pettigrew Family Papers. Southern Historical Collection, University of North Carolina.

This is a large and valuable collection for economic and political study of ante-bellum, war, and Reconstruction periods.

James J. Philips, II, Papers. Southern Historical Collection, University of North Carolina.
These letters are mostly of a business nature, but they throw some light on the home problems of Edgecomb County, North Carolina, during the war.

Plantation Record, Magnolia Plantation, Louisiana. Southern Historical Collection, University of North Carolina.
This depicts the problems and effects of the war on a large sugar plantation.

Jacqueline Prince-Thomas Jackson Papers. Southern Historical Collection, University of North Carolina.
This collection was of little value for this study.

Rast Family Papers. Manuscript Division, South Caroliniana Library, University of South Carolina.
These were of little value in this study. The collection is small and limited for the war years.

Henry Hunter Raymond Papers, Manuscript Division, South Caroliniana Library, University of South Carolina.
There is excellent material here concerning shortages, hoarding, and speculation during the war.

William W. Renwick Papers. Manuscript Division, South Caroliniana Library, University of South Carolina.
These business papers of a prominent Newberry County merchant give insight into shortage conditions during the Civil War period.

Kate Mason Rowland Diary. Manuscript Division, Confederate Museum, Richmond, Virginia.
This diary was interesting, illuminating, and extremely valuable for this study. It vividly describes Virginia homefront conditions.

Edmund Ruffin Papers. Southern Historical Collection, University of North Carolina.
These were interesting but of little value for this study.

Edmund Kirby Smith Papers. Southern Historical Collection, University of North Carolina.
These papers were among the most valuable used. They are especially illuminating on conditions in the Trans-Mississippi region.

Mrs. W. E. Turner. "Some Womanly Recollections of the War Between the States." North Carolina Room, University of North Carolina.
This paper was valuable and often used in this study of shortages.

Reverend C. S. Vedder Diary. Manuscript Division, South Caroliniana Library, University of South Carolina.
This diary covers the years 1861 to 1863 and gives some insight into the homefront conditions in and around Summerville, South Carolina.

Mrs. James Alexander (Susanna Gordon) Waddell Diary. 2 vols. Southern Historical Collection, University of North Carolina.
This diary covers the years 1863 to 1865 and contains excellent material on homefront problems.

B. *Published Diaries, Letters, Memoirs, Reminiscences.*

Allen, Alice West. "Recollections of War in Virginia," *Confederate Veteran*, XXIII (1915), 268-69.

Andrews, Eliza Frances. *The War-Time Journal of a Georgia Girl 1864-1865*. New York: D. Appleton and Company, 1908.

Armes, William Dallam (ed.). *The Autobiography of Joseph Le-Conte*. New York: D. Appleton and Company, 1903.

Avary, Myrta Lockett (ed.). *A Virginia Girl in the Civil War 1861-65*. New York: D. Appleton and Company, 1903.

Battle, Laura Elizabeth. *Forget-Me-Nots of the Civil War*. St. Louis: A. R. Fleming Printing Company, 1909.

Beers, Mrs. Fannie A. *Memories: A Record of Personal Experience and Adventure During the Four Years of War*. Philadelphia: J. B. Lippincott Company, 1888.

Borcke, Johann Heinrich Heros, von. *Memoires of the Confederate War for Independence*. 2 vols. New York: Peter Smith, 1938.

Burge, Dolly Summer Lunt. *A Woman's Wartime Journal: An Account of the Passage Over a Georgia Plantation of Sherman's Army on the March to the Sea*. New York: The Century Company, 1918.

Cable, George Washington (ed.). "A Woman's Diary of the Siege of Vicksburg," *The Century Illustrated Monthly Magazine*, XXX (1885), 767-75.

Campbell, John A. "A View of the Confederacy From the Inside," *The Century Illustrated Monthly Magazine*, XXXVIII (1889), 950-54.

Cate, Wirt Armistead (ed.). *Two Soldiers: The Campaign Diaries of Thomas J. Key, C.S.A. and Robert J. Campbell, U.S.A.* Chapel Hill: University of North Carolina Press, 1938.

Chesnut, Mary Boykin. *A Diary from Dixie*. New York: D. Appleton and Company, 1905.

Childs, Arney Robinson, *et al.* (eds.). *The Mason Smith Family Letters 1860-1868*. Columbia: University of South Carolina Press, 1950.

Childs, Arney Robinson (ed.). *The Private Journal of Henry William Ravenel 1859-1887.* Columbia: University of South Carolina Press, 1947.

Clay-Clopton, Mrs. Virginia. *A Belle of the Fifties.* New York: Doubleday, Page and Company, 1905.

Davis, Mrs. Jefferson (Varina Howell). *Jefferson Davis: A Memoir.* 2 vols. New York: Belford Company, 1890.

Dawson, Sarah Morgan. *A Confederate Girl's Diary.* Boston: Houghton, Mifflin Company, 1913.

DeBow, James Dunwoody Brownson. "Editorial," *DeBow's Review and Industrial Resources, Statistics, etc.,* VI, New Style, XXXI, Old Style, (1861), 329-30.

"Diary of Miss Harriet Cary, Kept by Her From May 6, 1862 to July 24, 1862," *Tyler's Quarterly and Genealogical Magazine,* IX (1927), 105-15 and XII (1930), 160-73.

Easterby, James Harold (ed.). *The South Carolina Rice Plantation as Revealed in the Papers of Robert F. W. Allston.* Chicago: University of Chicago Press, 1945.

Eggleston, George Cary. *A Rebel's Recollections.* New York: Hurd and Houghton, 1875.

Fearn, Frances. *Diary of a Refugee.* New York: Moffat, Yard and Company, 1910.

Felton, Rebecca Latimer. *Country Life in Georgia In the Days of My Youth.* Atlanta: Index Printing Company, 1919.

Fontaine, Mrs. Felix G. de. "Old Confederacy Days," *Confederate Veteran,* IV (1896), 301-3.

Fulkerson, Horace Smith. *A Civilian's Recollections of the War Between the States.* Baton Rouge: Otto Claitor, 1939.

Gay, Mary A. H. *Life In Dixie During the War.* Atlanta: The Foote and Davies Company, 1894.

Gilmor, Harry. *Four Years in the Saddle.* New York: Harper and Brothers, 1866.

"Girls and Cannon," *Appleton's Journal,* VII (1872), 65-68.

Hague, Parthenia Antoinette. *A Blockaded Family: Life in Southern Alabama During the Civil War.* Boston: Houghton-Mifflin Co., 1888.

Handy, Mrs. M. P. "Confederate Makeshifts," *Harper's Monthly Magazine,* LII (1876), 576-80.

Hardy, Captain W. H. "Homespun Dress," *Confederate Veteran,* I (1901), 213-14.

Harrison, Mrs. Burton (Constance Cary). *Recollections Grave and Gay.* New York: Charles Scribner's Sons, 1911.

Harrison, Mrs. Burton (Constance Cary). "A Virginia Girl in the First Year of the War," *The Century Illustrated Monthly Magazine,* XXX (1885), 606-14.

Hart, William Octave. "A Boy's Recollection of the War," *Publications of the Mississippi Historical Society*, XII (1912), 148-54.

Holmes, Charlotte R. (ed.). *The Burckmyer Letters, March 1863-June 1865*. Columbia: The State Company, 1926.

Howard, Charles Wallace. "The Future of the Confederate States," *Southern Cultivator*, XIX (1861), 137-40.

Howard, Charles Wallace. "Things Worthy of Attention," *Southern Cultivator*, XIX (1861), 201-3.

Hopley, Catherine Cooper. *Life in the South: From the Commencement of the War*. 2 vols. London: Chapman and Hall, 1863.

Jervey, Susan R. and Ravenel, Charlotte St. John. *Two Diaries from Middle St. John's, Berkeley, South Carolina*. Charleston: St. John's Hunting Club, 1921.

Jones, John Beauchamp. *A Rebel War-Clerk's Diary*. 2 vols. New York: Old Hickory Bookshop, 1935.

Ledford, Preston Lafayette. *Reminiscences of the Civil War*. Thomasville (North Carolina): News Printing House, 1909.

Lindsey, Mrs. Bettie J. "Woman's Wit Versus Federal Vigilance," *Confederate Veteran*, XVI (1908), 400-2.

Livingston, Colonel Knox. "Florida Girl Gave Her Shoes to a Soldier," *Confederate Veteran*, XV (1907), 548.

Loughborough, Mary Webster. *My Cave Life in Vicksburg*. New York: D. Appleton and Company, 1864.

MacLean, Mrs. Clara Dargan. "Return of a Refugee," *Southern Historical Society Papers*, XIII (1885), 502-15.

McDonald, Mrs. Cornelia. *A Diary with Reminiscences of the War and Refugee Life in the Shenandoah Valley*. Nashville: Cullom and Ghertner, 1934.

McGuire, Mrs. Judith Brockenbrough. *Diary of a Southern Refugee During the War*. New York: E. J. Hale and Son, 1867.

Miller, Mrs. Fannie Walker. "The Fall of Richmond," *Confederate Veteran*, XIII (1905), 305.

Otey, Mercer. "Operations of the Signal Corps," *Confederate Veteran*, VIII (1900), 129-30.

Otey, Mercer. "Story of Our Great War," *Confederate Veteran*, IX (1901), 153-55.

Pember, Phoebe Yates. *A Southern Woman's Story*. New York: G. W. Carlton and Company, 1879.

Philips, M. W. "Agriculture in Our Confederacy," *Southern Cultivator*, XIX (1861), 143-44.

Porcher, Francis Peyre. *Resources of the Southern Fields and Forests, Medical, Economical and Agricultural*. Charleston: Walker, Evans, and Cogswell, 1869.

Pringle, Elizabeth Waties Allston. *Chronicles of Chicora Wood.* New York: Charles Scribner's Sons, 1922.

Pryor, Mrs. Roger Atkinson. *My Day: Reminiscences of a Long Life.* New York: The Macmillan Company, 1904.

Pryor, Mrs. Roger Atkinson. *Reminiscences of Peace and War.* New York: The Macmillan Company, 1904.

Putnam, Sallie A. *Richmond During the War: Four Years of Personal Observations.* New York: G. W. Carlton and Company, 1867.

Roberts, Captain A. (pseud. of Augustus Charles Hobart-Hampden). *Never Caught: Personal Adventures Connected with Twelve Successful Trips in Blockade-Running During the American Civil War.* London: John Camden Hatten, Company, 1867.

Robertson, Margaret. "My Childhood Recollections of the War," *Southern Historical Society Papers,* VI (1923), 215-22.

Ross, Fitzgerald. *A Visit to the Cities and Camps of the Confederate States.* Edinburgh: William Blackwood and Sons, 1865.

Rowland, Kate Mason and Croxall, Mrs. Morris L. (eds.). *The Journal of Julia LeGrand, New Orleans, 1862-63.* Richmond: Everett Waddey Company, 1911.

"Running the Blockade," *Confederate Veteran,* XVII (1909), 410-11.

"Running the Blockade," *Southern Historical Society Papers,* XXIV (1896), 225-29.

Russell, William Howard. *My Diary North and South.* Boston: T. O. H. P. Burnham, 1863.

Russell, William Howard. *Pictures of Southern Life, Social, Political, Military.* New York: James G. Gregory, 1861.

Saint-Amand, Mary Scott. *A Balcony in Charleston.* Richmond: Garrett and Massie, 1941.

"Southern Manufactures," *Southern Cultivator,* XIX (1861), 187.

"Southern Patronage to Southern Imports and Domestic Industry," *Southern Planter,* XXXI (1861), 58-63.

Taylor, Thomas E. *Running the Blockade: A Personal Narrative of Adventures, Risks and Escapes During the American Civil War.* London: John Murray, 1896.

Townsend, George Alfred. *Campaigns of a Non-Combatant: Ramaunt Abroad During the War.* New York: Blalock and Company, 1866.

Valentine, Mrs. Mark. "A Girl in the Sixties in Richmond," *Confederate Veteran,* XX (1912), 279-81.

Volwiler, Albert Tangeman (ed.). "Letters Fom a Civil War Officer," *Mississippi Valley Historical Review,* XIX (1927-1928), 508-29.

Wilkinson, Captain John. *The Narratives of a Blockade Runner.* New York: Sheldon and Company, 1877.

Wright, Mrs. D. Giraud. *A Southern Girl in '61: The War-Time Memories of a Confederate Senator's Daughter.* New York: Doubleday, Page and Company, 1905.

Woodrow, Marion Woodwill (ed.). *Dr. James Woodrow As Seen by His Friends: Character Sketches by His Former Pupils, Colleagues and Associates.* Columbia: R. L. Bryan Company, 1909.

C. *Collected Sources, Journals, and Public Documents.*

1. General.

Freeman, Douglas Southall (ed.). *A Calendar of Confederate State Papers.* Richmond: The Confederate Museum, 1908.

Matthews, James M. (ed.). *The Statutes at Large of the Confederate States of America.* Richmond: R. M. Smith, Printer to Congress, 1862-1864.

Miller, Frances Trevelyan and Lanier, Robert S. (eds.). *The Photographic History of the Civil War.* 10 vols. New York: The Review of Reviews Co., 1911.

Moore, Frank (ed.). *The Rebellion Record: A Diary of American Events with Documents, Narratives, Illustrations, Incidents, Poetry, Etc.* 11 vols. New York: G. P. Putnam, 1862-1868.

Ramsdell, Charles William (ed.). *Laws and Joint Resolutions of the Last Session of the Confederate Congress Together with Secret Acts of Previous Congress.* Durham: Duke University Press, 1941.

Richardson, James Daniel (ed.). *A Compilation of the Messages and Papers of the Confederacy.* 2 vols. Nashville: United States Publishing Company, 1905.

Rhodes, Rufus R. *Report of Commissioner of Patents of Confederate States, 1861-1864.* Richmond: Tyler, Wise, Alleyne and Smith, 1861-1864.

Smith, Larkin. *Instructions to Assessors of Tax in Kind.* Richmond: (n. p.), 1864.

Journal of the Congress of the Confederate States, 1861-1865. 7 vols. Washington: Government Printing Office, 1904-1905.

The Medical and Surgical History of the War of Rebellion 1861-1865. 6 vols. Washington: Government Printing Office, 1870-1888.

Rules and Directions for Proceedings in the Confederate States Patent Office. Richmond: (n. p.), 1861.

Transactions of the American Medical Association. Chicago: 1850-1951.

The War of Rebellion: A Compilation of the Official Records of the Union and Confederate Armies. 130 vols. Washington: Government Printing Office, 1880-1902.

2. State.

Acts of the General Assembly of Alabama, 1861-1865.

Acts Passed by the General Assembly of Arkansas, 1861-1865.

Acts and Resolutions Adopted by the General Assembly of Florida, 1861-1865.

Acts of the General Assembly of the State of Georgia, 1861-1865.

Acts of the State of Louisiana, 1861-1863.

Acts of the State of Mississippi, 1861-1865.

Ordinances of the Convention of the State of North Carolina, 1864-1865.

Public Laws of the State of North Carolina, 1861-1865.

Private Laws of the State of North Carolina, 1864-1865.

Acts of the General Assembly of the State of South Carolina, 1861-1865.

Public Acts of the General Assembly of the State of Tennessee, 1861-1862.

General Laws of the State of Texas, 1861-1864.

Acts of the General Assembly of the State of Virginia, 1861-1865.

D. Newspapers.

Arkansas State Gazette, Little Rock, Arkansas, 1861-1863.

Arkansas True Democrat, Little Rock, Arkansas, 1861-1862.

Charleston Daily Courier, Charleston, South Carolina, 1861-1865.

Charleston Mercury, Charleston, South Carolina, 1861-1865.

Daily Carolina Watchman, Salisbury, North Carolina, 1861-1863.

Daily Chronicle and Sentinel, Augusta, Georgia, 1863-1865.

Daily Chronicle, Charlottesville, Virginia, 1864-1865.

Daily Citizen, Vicksburg, Mississippi, 1863.

Daily Express, Petersburg, Virginia, 1861-1862.

Daily Picayune, New Orleans, Louisiana, 1861-1862.

Daily Rebel, Chattanooga, Tennessee, Marietta and Griffin, Georgia, and Selma, Alabama, 1862-1865.

Daily Southern Guardian, Columbia, South Carolina, 1862-1863.

Floridian and Journal, Tallahassee, Florida, 1861-1862.

Houston Daily Telegraph, Houston, Texas, 1863-1864.

Iredell Express, Statesville, North Carolina, 1861-1862.

Memphis Daily Appeal, Memphis, Tennessee, 1861-1863.

Memphis Daily Argus, Memphis, Tennessee, 1862-1864.

Mobile Register, Mobile, Alabama, 1861-1863.

Montgomery Daily Advertiser, Montgomery, Alabama, 1862-1863.

Montgomery Daily Mail, Montgomery, Alabama, 1865.

Nashville Dispatch, Nashville, Tennessee, 1862-1863.

Natchez Daily Courier, Natchez, Mississippi, 1861-1863.

New York Herald, 1861-1863.

New York Times, 1864-1865.

North Carolina Presbyterian, Fayetteville, North Carolina, 1862.

North Carolina Standard, Raleigh, North Carolina, 1862.

Pictorial Democrat, Alexandria, Louisiana, 1863.

Richmond Dispatch, Richmond, Virginia, 1861-1864.

Richmond Enquirer, Richmond, Virginia, 1861-1865.

Richmond Examiner, Richmond, Virginia, 1861-1865.

Richmond Whig, Richmond, Virginia, 1861-1865.

Southern Confederacy, Atlanta, Georgia, 1861-1863.

Tri-Weekly Telegraph, Houston, Texas, 1862-1865.

Savannah Daily Republican, Savannah, Georgia, 1861-1865.

Selma Morning Reporter, Selma, Alabama, 1863-1864.

Vicksburg Sun, Vicksburg, Mississippi, 1861-1862.

Weekly Junior Register, Franklin, Louisiana, 1863.

Wilmington Journal, Wilmington, North Carolina, 1861-1865.

E. *Contemporary Magazines, Journals, and Published Recipe Book.*

Confederate Receipt Book, A Compilation of Over One Hundred Recipes Adapted to the Times. Richmond: (n. p.), 1863.

Confederate States Medical and Surgical Journal. 2 vols. (1864-1865), Richmond, Virginia.

DeBow's Review and Industrial Resources, Statistics, etc., V-VI (1861-1862), New Orleans, Louisiana.

Southern Cultivator, XIX-XXI (1861-1863), Augusta, Georgia.

Southern Field and Fireside, XI-XIV (1861-1864), Augusta, Georgia.

Southern Illustrated News, I-II (1862-1864), Richmond, Virginia.

Southern Planter Devoted to Agriculture, Horticulture and Household Arts, XXXI (1861), Richmond, Virginia.

II. SECONDARY

Albright, James W. "Books Made In Dixie," *Southern Historical Papers*, III (1896), 57-60.

Anderson, Lucy London. *North Carolina Women of the Confederacy*. Fayetteville: (n. p.), 1926.

Andrews, Matthew Page (ed.). *The Women of the South in War-Times.* Baltimore: The Norman Remington Company, 1920.

Bayne, Thomas Livingston. "Life in Richmond, 1863-1865," *Confederate Veteran,* XXX (1922), 100-1.

Bell, Mrs. Julia. "My Confederate Grandmothers," *Confederate Veteran,* XXVII (1920), 366-69.

Bill, Alfred Hoyt. *The Beleaguered City: Richmond 1861-1865.* New York: Alfred A. Knopf, 1946.

Blanton, Wyndham B. *Medicine in Virginia in the Nineteenth Century.* Richmond: Garrett and Massie, 1933.

Bradlee, Francis Boardman Crowinshield. *Blockade Running During the Civil War: And the Effect of Land and Water Transportation on the Confederacy.* Salem, Massachusetts: The Essex Institute, 1925.

Butler, Mrs. Laura. "A Tribute," *Confederate Veteran,* XXIV (1916), 425.

Butler, M. C. "Southern Genius," *Southern Historical Society Papers,* XVI (1888), 281-95.

Chastain, Elizabeth Boone. "Plantation Life in the Sixties," *Confederate Veteran,* XXXIV (1926), 99-100.

Dawson, Francis Warrington. *Our Women in the War.* Charleston: Walker, Evans and Cogswell, 1887.

DeLeon, Thomas Cooper. *Belles, Beaux and Brains of the 60's.* New York: G. W. Dillingham Company, 1909.

DeLeon, Thomas Cooper. *Four Years in Rebel Capitals: An Inside View of Life of the Southern Confederacy, From Birth to Death: From Original Notes, Collected in the Years 1861-1865.* Mobile: Gossip Printing Company, 1892.

Dodge, David (pseud. of O. W. Blacknall). "Domestic Economy in the Confederacy," *Atlantic Monthly,* LVIII (1886), 229-42.

Fisher, Clyde Olin. "Relief of Soldiers' Families in North Carolina During the Civil War," *South Atlantic Quarterly,* XVI (1917), 60-73.

Gordon, Armistead Churchill. "Hard-Times in the Confederacy," *The Century Magazine,* XXXVI (1888), 761-71.

Grant, W. T. "Indigenous Medicinal Plants," *Confederate States Medical and Surgical Journal,* I (1864), 84-86.

Greathouse, B. H. "Women of Northwest Arkansas," *Confederate Veteran,* XX (1912), 168-69.

Hall, Courtney Robert. "Confederate Medicine," *Medical Life,* XLII (1935), 445-504.

Higgins, Frances Caldwell. "Life on the Southern Plantation During the War Between the States," *Confederate Veteran,* XXI (1913), 161-66.

Hunter, Alexander. "The Women of Mosby's Confederacy," *Confederate Veteran*, XV (1907), 257-62.

Hyde, Mrs. Charles R. "The Women of the Confederacy," *Confederate Veteran*, XXXII (1924), 23.

Jacobs, Joseph. "Some of the Drug Conditions During the War Between the States, 1861-65," *Southern Historical Society Papers*, XXXIII (1905), 161-87.

Jennings, Miss M. M. "A Little Girl in the War," *Confederate Veteran*, XXX (1922), 374-76.

Lonn, Ella. *Desertion During the Civil War*. New York: The Century Company, 1928.

Lonn, Ella. *Foreigners in the Confederacy*. Chapel Hill: University of North Carolina Press, 1940.

Lonn, Ella. *Salt As A Factor in the Confederacy*. New York: Walter Neale, 1933.

Lyon, Mrs. M. R. "Our Women in the Sixties," *Confederate Veteran*, XXXV (1927), 35.

McCabe, James Dabney. "Literature of the War," *Southern Historical Society Papers*, XV (1921), 199-203.

McDavid, Mrs. P. A. "What Women Did During the War," *Confederate Veteran*, XIV (1906), 69-70.

Mallet, John W. "How the South Got Chemicals During The War," *Southern Historical Society Papers*, XXI (1903), 100-2.

Miller, Frances Trevelyan and Lanier, Robert. *The Photographic History of the Civil War*. 10 vols. New York: The Review of Reviews, 1911.

Owsley, Frank Lawrence. *State-Rights in the Confederacy*. Chicago: University of Chicago Press, 1925.

Page, Elizabeth Fry. "Tampa During the War," *Confederate Veteran*, XXXV (1927), 124-25.

Pollard, Edward Alfred. *The Lost Cause: A New Southern History of the War of the Confederates*. New York: E. B. Treat and Company, 1866.

Ramsdell, Charles William. *Behind the Lines in the Southern Confederacy*. Baton Rouge: Louisiana State University Press, 1944.

Ramsdell, Charles William. "General Robert E. Lee's Horse Supply," *American Historical Review*, XXXV (1930), 758-77.

Ramsdell, Charles William. "The Confederate Government and Railroads," *American Historical Review*, XXII (1917), 794-810.

Roberts, Deering J. "Confederate Medical Service," *The Photographic History of the Civil War*, VII, 327-50.

Scott, D. M. "Selma and Dallas County, Alabama," *Confederate Veteran*, XXIV (1916), 214-22.

Selph, Mrs. Fannie Eoline. "Army Relief Work By Women of the Confederacy," *Confederate Veteran*, XXV (1917), 558-60.

Simkins, Frances Butler and Patton, James Welch. *The Women of the Confederacy*. Richmond: Garrett and Massie, 1936.

Soley, James Russell. *The Blockade and the Cruisers*. New York: Charles Scribner's Sons, 1887.

Spencer, Cornelia Phillips. *The Last 90 Days of the War in North Carolina*. New York: Watchman Publishing Company, 1866.

Stewart, Richard D. "How Johnny Got His Gun," *Confederate Veteran*, XXXII (1924), 166-69.

Trowbridge, John Tyler. *A Picture of the Desolated States and the Work of Reconstruction*. Hartford: L. Stebbins, 1868.

Weeks, Stephen Beauregard. "The University of North Carolina in the Civil War," *Southern Historical Society Papers*, XXIV (1896), 1-40.

Welch, Mary J. "Makeshifts of the War Between the States," *Publications of the Mississippi Historical Society*, VII (1903), 101-13.

Wesley, Charles Harris. *The Collapse of the Confederacy*. Washington: Associated Publications, Inc., 1937.

White, Joseph F. "Social Conditions in the South During the War Between the States," *Confederate Veteran* XXX (1922), 142-45, 181-84.

Wiley, Bell Irwin. *The Plain People of the Confederacy*. Baton Rouge: Louisiana State University Press, 1944.

INDEX

Abbeville (South Carolina), soldiers eat provisions, 28

Ad-Vance, 44, 143

Agriculture, Bureau of, proposed, 6; diversification urged, 5-6, 33-34, 46; effect of war on, 162-63; shortages affecting, 136-37; state legislation on crop control, 50-51; state restrictions on exportations, 50, 51.

Aid to indigent families, rendered by localities, 164-65; rendered by states, 45-48, 164-65; War Department ruling on, 42

Alabama, acts of the General Assembly, 47, 49, 51-53; brandy, 73; clothing conditions, 86, 90; drought in, 29; governor seizes leather, 46; housing shortage in, 101, 103; industrialization in, 161; periodicals suspend publication, 142

Albright, James W., 143

Alcoholic beverages, Confederate government manufactures, 40; distillation opposed, 40-41, 44-46; shortage of, 74-75; smuggled, 13; state laws prohibiting distillation of, 47-50; substitutes for, 75-76

Alexandria (Virginia), 101

Allston, Elizabeth, 76

Allston, Mrs. Robert Francis Withers, 60, 133

Allston, Robert Francis Withers, 66, 91

American Medical Association, 115

American Revolution, substitutes copied, 8

Andrews, Eliza Frances, 103, 145

Appomattox County (Virginia), 57

Appomattox River, 29

Arkadelphia (Arkansas), 101

Arkansas, acts of the General Assembly, 22, 48, 49, 51; aid to soldiers, 23; clothing conditions in,

88; editor discusses speculation, 20; flood damage, 29; housing shortage in, 101

Art supplies, shortage of and substitutes for, 154-55

Ashes, substitute for salt, 63; for making soda, 71

Ashland (Virginia), 101

Atlanta, coffee used as sets in jewelry, 72; convention on paper shortage, 140; laboratory established, 119; merchant announces supply of seeds, 136; overcrowded, 101-2; publishing houses hit by shortages, 143

Augusta (Georgia), book shortage, 144; laboratory established, 119; overcrowded, 101; thefts, 166

Ayers, Professor J. J., 143

Babcock, Thomas S., 57

Baldwin, James B., 57

Bath Paper Mills, 31, 142

Bayou Plaquemine, 21

Beasts of burden, consumed as food substitutes, 63; impressment of, 26, 37, 131, 134-35; shortage of, 5, 16, 108, 130-31; speculation in, 52; substitutes for, 134; suffer from food shortage, 71

"Beauregard cake," 59

Beauregard, General, asks donations, 22; leader, 3

"Beauregard's March," 145

Benning, General Henry Lewis, 134

Bermuda, 12

Beverage shortage, 72-74

Bierfield, Isaac, 82

"Biscuit parties," 68

Blockade, effect of, 6, 11-15, 36; running of, 12-15, 44

Boarding houses, makeshift provisions for, 101; ration food, 76; shortage of, 101-2

Bonham, Governor M. L., 25

225

Borcke, Heros Von, 89
Bradlee, Francis B. C., 11
Bread, versus liquor, 46, 48, 50; shortage of, 67-69; substitutes for, 69
"Bread Riot," 166
Brown, Governor Joseph E., attempts to relieve shortages in Georgia, 45-46; orders confiscation of salt, 18; protests impressment, 26; wears homespun suit, 88
Brownsville (Texas), 12
Building supplies, 155
"Burial of Latane," 155
Burwell, William M., 128
Business, effect of shortages on, 166-67
Butter, shortage of, 28, 30, 64-65

Camden (Arkansas), 152
Campbell, Charles, 69
Cape Fear River, 84
Cary, Constance, 14, 55, 58, 80, 81, 95, 100, 117, 144
Cary, Hetty, 14, 80, 117, 132
Cattle, harmed by food shortage, 71; hides used for shoes, 81; impressment of, 37; shortage of, 61; speculation in prohibited, 52; states legislate on, 51; Texas cattle lost to Confederacy, 28
Charleston, devastated by fire, 30; drum factory in, 155; housing shortage, 105; meat shortage, 62; moss used for blankets, 110; outbreak of war, 3; port of entry, 12; protests shortage of postage stamps, 148; war begins, 3
Charleston Courier, 141
Charleston Mercury, 5, 79, 141, 149, 163, 165
Charlotte (North Carolina), 101, 150
Charlottesville (Virginia), 101
Chattanooga, 161
Chattanooga *Daily Rebel*, 162
Chesnut, Mrs. James Jr., 58, 60, 81, 103, 145, 150, 156
Chicot County (Arkansas), 29
Chisholm, Julian, 119
Christmas, food substitutes, 67; tree decorations, 157

Clark, William H., 23
Clay-Clopton, Mrs. Virginia, 100
Cleaning agents, patents for, 39; shortage of, 5, 21; speculation prohibited, 52; substitutes for, 73, 98
Cleaning establishments, scarcity of, 98
Clothing shortages, 79-99
Clover, for making bread, 69
Coffee, hoarded, 121; shortage of, 72; substitutes for, 72-73; used in jewelry, 72
Coffins, 4; shortages of and substitutes for, 155
Cole, Major A. H., 131
Columbia (South Carolina), 23, 40, 76, 101, 142, 156
Columbus (Mississippi), 101
Commissary of Subsistence, 42; *see also* Cummings
Committee on Judiciary, 40
Condiments, shortages of and substitutes for, 70-71
"Confederate," definition, 8
"Confederate Beer," 75
"Confederate candles," 106-7, 210
Confederate Congress, action on speculation, 18-19, 36-37, 40; criticized for policies, 33, 38; distilling program, 40-41; enacts "tax-in-kind," 36-38; encourages industry, 38-39; establishes patent office, 39; failure to solve transportation problem, 16, 128-30; handicapped by state-rights, 40, 42-43; impressment policy, 36-37; legislates on importation of luxuries, 14, 36; petitioned to remedy homefront conditions, 33; places homefront in secondary position, 35-43; praises generosity of the homefront, 23; tariff policy, 35-36
"Confederate ink," 147
Confederate Medical Department, advises on soap manufacture, 112; dissemination of medical knowledge, 118; examined, 23; establishes laboratories, 118-19
Confederate Museum, 154
"Confederate paper," 145

zens address Secretary of War, 41; clothing condition in, 88, 93; effect of "March to the Sea," 56; factories established, 113, 161; food situation in, 70; Governor Brown acts to relieve shortages, 18, 45; housing shortage in, 101, 104, 105; lacks dairy farms, 64; penitentiary makes cards, 87

Glue, shortage of and substitutes for, 148

Goodman, William, 127

Gorgas, Josiah, 26

Graniteville Mills, 160

Grant, General Ulysses Simpson, 108, 141

Green, General Duff, 87

Greensboro (North Carolina), 143

Greenville (South Carolina), 21, 101, 108, 156

Gregg, William 4, 159, 173

Halifax (Virginia), 23

Hammond, James Henry, 66

Harrison, Burton, 144

Harrison, Mrs. Burton, *see* Cary, Constance

Harper, Mrs. Ella A. R., 169

Hats, shortage of, 91-92, makeshifts for, 91-94

Havana, 12

Hill, Senator Benjamin H., 40

Hinds County (Mississippi), 163

Hoarding, as a cause of shortages, 31; President Davis hopes impressment will check, 34; prevalent practice, 20-21

Homespun, widespread use of, 88-90, 110, 207n

"Homespun Dress," poem, 89

Honour, Private Theodore, 19, 168

Hospitals, food shortage, 71; gifts sent to, 23, 193n; whiskey supplied to, 49

Hotels, food shortages, 76 furnishing problems, 110; makeshift accommodations, 101, 103-4; room shortage, 100-3

Household effects, cooking utensils, 105, 110-11; dishes, 110-11; fur-

nishings, 105, 109, 110, 113; heating, 105, 108; household articles donated to army, 24; laundry needs, 105, 112; lighting, 105-6; silverware, 110-11

Houses, destroyed by war, 27; substitutes for, 104-5

Housing shortage, 8, 28, 99-105

Houston Telegraph, 29, 141

Hudson, Thomas J., 160

Impressment policy, a cause of shortages, 25-26, 31; aimed at checking speculation, 40-41; attitudes toward, 25, 41, 46, 48, 53, 56; extended by Confederate Congress, 36-37; governors protest, 45, 46; President Davis supports, 34; press comment on, 26; state laws, 53

Industrialization, encouraged by state laws, 51-52; increase as result of war, 159-62; growth of small industries, 11; shortages affecting, 137-38; state of at beginning of war, 3-5; urged by Congress, 38-39; urged by President Davis, 34

Inflation, effect of war on, 163-64; Governor Vance on, 44; refusal to sell commodities for "just price," 37

Ink, shortage of and substitutes for, 146-47

Iron, duty imposed on, 35; shortage of, 135; seizure of, 26

Jackson, General "Stonewall," 154

Jackson (Mississippi), 101

James River, 83, 159

"Jeff Davis Waltz," 145

Jews, accused of speculation, 19

Johnston, General Joseph E., 58, 172

Johnston, Mrs. Joseph E., 58, 104

Johnston, W. R., 119

Jones, John Beauchamp, and the underwear shortage, 94; critical of impressment policy, 41; on conditions in general, 164; on crime, 166; on fuel supply, 143; on inflation, 163; on speculation, 18; on war destruction, 28; condemns blockade-running, 13; foresees trouble, 7; has trouble publishing book, 143; object of generosity, 24; plants garden, 59

Key, John R., 155

Labor, shortage of, 26-27, 31, 55, 136
Laredo (Texas), 102
Lawton, General Alexander Robert, 130
LeConte, Emma, 17, 58, 94, 156
LeConte, John, 119
LeConte, Joseph, 17, 58, 89, 119, 131
Lee, General Robert E., 29, 95, 157, 172
Lenoir (North Carolina), 22, 169
LeGrand, Julia, 164
Letcher, John, 22
Lexington (Virginia), 102
Lilies, used in making bread, 69
Lincoln, President Abraham, announces blockade, 6, 11
Little Rock (Arkansas), 101
Locusts, as substitute for meat, 62
Longstreet, General James, 156
Louisiana, acts of the Legislature, 47-51, 156 citizens urged to plant crops, 6; family buys contents of store, 21; flood, 29; housing conditions in, 101; refugees from, 102; children forced to fish for food, 62; salt mine, 64; source of sugar, 65
Luxuries, brought through blockade, 12-14; importation made illegal, 14; President Davis on importation of, 34
Lynchburg (Virginia), 65, 101

McCrimmon, Mary, 157
McDonald, Mrs. Cornelia, 39, 55, 102
McGuire, Mrs. Judith Brockenbrough, 83, 101, 145
Macon (Georgia), 143, 152
Magrath, Governor Andrew G., 28
Mallory, Stephen R., 58
Malsby, M. A., 144
Marietta (Georgia) Paper Mill, 27
Maryland, as source of supply, 95
Matamaras, 12

Maury, Betty Herndon, 7, 28, 93, 150, 167
Maury, Isabel, 146
Maury, Matthew Fontaine, 7
Meat, shortage of, 60-61; substitutes for, 61-63
Medical Equipment, 122-23
Medicine, auctions of, 116; brought through blockade, 14; laboratories established, 119; private manufacture, 117; shortages of, 115-23; sources of supply, 116, 118; substitutes for, 117-18, 121-22
Memphis (Tennessee), ladies challenge New York fashions, 96; newspapers reduce size, 141; shortages force stores to close, 167; women run blockade in, 14
Meridian (Mississippi), 35
Milk and cream, shortage of and substitutes for, 76
Milledgeville (Georgia), 103
Mississippi, acts of the Legislature, 46-53; clothing conditions in, 90; flood in, 29; housing shortage in, 101; newspapers cease publication, 141-42; railroad problem, 35; robbers break into school, 156
Mississippi Central Railroad, 127
Mississippi River, 28, 29, 58, 61, 65, 76, 77
Mobile (Alabama), as port of entry, 12; size of newspapers reduced, 141; overcrowded, 101; publishing houses handicapped by shortages, 143; food riot, 166
Montgomery (Alabama), 102-3
Montgomery and West Point Railroad, 127
"Moonshiners," 75
Moore, General Samuel Preston, 119, 121, 122
Music supplies, shortage of and substitutes for, 155
"Mutual Aid Societies," 165
Myers, General Abraham C., 130-31

Nashville (Tennessee), 19
Nassau, 12
Negroes, 26, 74, 91, 96

Newberry (South Carolina), 82

New Iberia (Louisiana), 64

New Orleans (Louisiana), association to promote mechanical interests, 164; blockade ineffective, 12; cessation of business, 167; falls to Federals, 65; fat drives, 112; free market, 164; newspapers reduced in size, 141; newspapers urge diversification of agriculture, 5-6; quinine theft, 166; stories on speculation, 20

North Carolina, acts of the General Assembly, 43-45, 47-51; as a source of supply, 25; blockade extended, 11; clothing condition, 83, 84, 86, 88; drought in, 29; editor on speculation, 18; effect of blockade, 95; effect of Federal invasion, 56; food conditions in, 69; housing shortage in, 101, 104, 105; industrialization in, 161; inflation in, 163; resident purchases contents of store, 21; shortage of stamps in, 149

Northrop, L. B., 25

Notions, buckles, 152; buttons, 152; combs, 153, 154; costume jewelry, 153; hairpins, 153; hooks and eyes, 152; knitting needles, 151; needles, 151; pins, 151; ribbons, 153; thread, 152

Overseers, 26

Paper, as substitutes for clothing, 80; duty on, 35; effect of shortage on civilians, 144-46; effect of shortage on government publications, 145; effect of shortage on newspapers and periodicals, 139-44; shortage of, 5, 139-46

Patents, 39

Pegram, General John, 132

Pemberton, General John C., 46

Pencils and pens, shortage of and substitutes for, 147-48

Pender, General W. D., 144

Personal accessories, fans, 95; handkerchiefs, 95; hoop skirts, 94-95; hosiery, 94-95; parasols, 95-96; suspenders, 95

Petersburg *Daily Express,* 18

Petersburg (Virginia), 29, 57, 63, 101, 165

Petitions, addressed to government agencies, 33

Pets, high cost of feeding, 71; substitutes for meat, 63

Pettus, Governor John J., 46

Philadelphia, 143-44

Physicians, shortage of, 123

Pictorial Democrat (Alexandria, Louisiana), 141

Pipes, shortage of, 154

"Poor Man's Soap," 112

Porcher, Dr. Francis Peyre, 109, 119, 121

Porcher's School, 76

"Portable Ink," 147

"Possum Beer," 75

Postage Stamps, complaints about, 148-49; shortage of, 148

Potomac River, 14, 151

Pratt, Daniel, 4, 159

Price-fixing, 40, 165

Prioleau, William H., 119

Pryor, Mrs. Roger A., 63, 83, 95, 150, 165

Pumpkin bread, 69

Quartermaster General, 38

Railroads, inadequacies, 15-16, 125-27, 133-34; meetings concerning, 126, 128; shortages affecting, 126-27, 135-36

Raincoats, 95

Raleigh, 83, 101

Rats, menu for cooking, 200n.; substitute for meat, 62-63

Ravenel, Henry William, 67, 200n

Ravenel, Mrs. Henry William, 67

"Rebel Bread," 59

Recipes, for beer, 74; for champagne, 75; for Confederate candles, 210n; for fruit preserves, 70; for matches, 219n; for mayonnaise, 201n; for substitute oysters, 62, 200n; for pie crust, 67; for pumpkin bread, 69; for purifying water, 204n; for rats, 63, 200n; for sweetening butter, 65, 201n; for sweet potato coffee, 73; for vinegar, 71; for whiskey, 74; published in newspapers and magazines, 58-59

The Record (Richmond), 104, 141

"Refugee havens," 56

"Refugitta," 96

Relief Fund, 47

Renwick, W. W., 65

Resources of Southern Fields and Forests, 119

Rhodes, Rufus R., 29

Richmond (Virginia), bread riot in, 167; cleaner shortage, 99; clothing shortage, 80, 90, 96; coal shortage, 108-9; conservation urged, 28; conveyance shortage, 132; depository for cloth, 51; editor arouses false optimism, 5; editor criticizes impressment, 26; fires, 30, 31; food shortage, 55-60, 63, 68, 70, 71, 169; horse shortage, 131; housing shortage, 16, 100, 101, 102; inflation, 68; medical laboratories in, 119; medicine shortage, 118; paper shortage, 140, 141, 143, 145-46; price-fixing in, 165; railroad presidents meet in, 126, 127, 128; rudeness in, 167; seed shortage, 60; speculation, 17, 19, 20; transportation problem, 134; "Victory gardens," 59-60; water shortage, 76

Richmond Dispatch, 141

Richmond Enquirer, 21, 28, 120, 140

Richmond Examiner, 18, 26, 75, 98, 140

Richmond Whig, 139

Ridgeway (North Carolina), 44

Rio Grande River, 13, 152, 160

Rockingham County (Virginia), 57

Ross, Fitzgerald, 104, 132

Roswell, Georgia, Manufacturing Company, 164

Ruffin, Edmund, 67, 81, 88

Russell, William Howard, 6, 103

Salem (North Carolina), 143

Saltville (Virginia), 64

"Santa Claus," poem. 157

Savannah (Georgia), alcoholic beverages in, 75; food shortages, 163; meat shortage, 63; port of entry, 12; postage shortage, 63; riot, 166

Savannah Republican, 168

School supplies, shortage of and substitutes for, 156

Scrap drive, 215n

"Secessia," 96

"Secession Bread," 68

Seddon, Secretary James A., 25, 41, 57, 126, 127, 128

Seeds, shortage of, 60, 70

Self sufficiency, as viewed by journals and newspapers, 4, 5; exponents of, 4, 159; lack of, 4-5

Selma (Alabama), 29, 35, 101

Semmes, Mrs. Raphael, 60

Shenandoah Valley, 29, 102

Sherman, General William T., 27, 56, 104

Shirts, makeshifts for, 91

Shoe polish, substitutes for, 84-85

Shoes, donated to soldiers, 24; embargo on, 52; patents for, 39; production increased, 34; shortage of, 5, 38, 80-83; smuggled through blockade, 44; speculation prohibited, 52; substitutes for, 83, 90

Shorter, Governor John Gill, 46

Shreveport (Louisiana), 101

Simms, William Gilmore, 75

Sims, Colonel F. W., 16, 130

Smith, General Edmund Kirby, 13, 65, 95, 132, 172

Smith, Mrs. Edmund Kirby, 65, 95

Snails, substitute for meat, 62

Snakes, substitute for meat, 62

Sources of supply, 3-4, 61, 65, 69, 95, 106, 145, 148, 152, 163, 169, 200n

South Carolina, acts of the General Assembly, 47, 49-52; as a source of supply, 25; clothing conditions, 82, 89, 91, 92; editor urges planting of food crop, 59; effect of General Sherman's invasion, 56; food conditions in, 64, 65, 72, 76; fuel supply, 108; gas shortage, 108; housewife's recipe book in, 59;

232

Vegetables, shortage of and substitutes for, 70
Vicksburg (Mississippi), book shortage, 144; caves in, 104; food shortage, 28, 57, 63, 77; newspapers, 141; water shortage, 76
Vicksburg *Daily Citizen*, 141
Vicksburg *Sun*, 17
Virginia, acts of the General Assembly, 47-49, 51, 130; blockaded, 11; clothing conditions, 81, 89, 90, 95, 96; conditions in the western area, 39; editor on the shoe shortage, 84; editor on speculation, 20; food situation in, 55-56, 65; household equipment, 11; housing, 101, 103, 104; industrialization, 161; salt production, 64

Wadley, William M., 16, 126
Wake Forest (North Carolina), 143
War destruction, cause of shortages, 27
Warrenton (North Carolina), 21
War weariness, 171-72
Washington (D. C.), 80

Washington, William Dandridge, 155
Water, diet of, 23; shortage of 76
Watts, Governor Thomas Hill, 135
Weather, as factor in shortages, 29
Weekly Junior Register (Franklin, Louisiana), 141
West Baton Rouge *Sugar Planter*, 142
Wigfall, Louise, 103
Wigfall, Senator Louis T., 103, 133
Wild Western Scenes, 143
Wilmington (North Carolina), as a port of entry, 12, 95, 96, 119; clothing shortage, 110; food shortage, 30, 59, 61, 62; wartime industrial growth, 161; yellow fever epidemic, 30
Wilmington Journal, 17, 19, 59, 96, 103, 110, 134, 147, 150
Winchester (Virginia), 102
Withers, Assistant Adjutant General John, 129
Woodrow, James, 119
Wool, substitutes for, 91

Yancey, William Lowndes, 100